Vigilantism and the State in Modern Latin America

ESSAYS ON EXTRALEGAL VIOLENCE

Edited by
MARTHA K. HUGGINS

PRAEGER

New York
Westport, Connecticut
London

Library of Congress Cataloging-in-Publication Data

Vigilantism and the state in modern Latin America : essays on extralegal violence / edited by Martha K. Huggins.

p. cm.

Includes bibliographical references and index.

ISBN 0-275-93476-4 (alk. paper)

1. Violence—Latin America. 2. Vigilance committees—Latin America. 3. Death squads—Latin America. I. Huggins, Martha Knisely, 1944– .

HN110.5.Z9V58 1991

364.4'045763'098—dc20 90-28185

British Library Cataloguing in Publication Data is available.

Library of Congress Catalog Card Number: 90-28185
ISBN: 0-275-93476-4

First published in 1991

Praeger Publishers, One Madison Avenue, New York, NY 10010
An imprint of Greenwood Publishing Group, Inc.

Printed in the United States of America

The paper used in this book complies with the Permanent Paper Standard issued by the National Information Standards Organization (Z39.48–1984).

10 9 8 7 6 5 4 3 2 1

CONTENTS

TABLES

PREFACE

This book was inspired by a December 1988 conference in Salvador, Bahia, Brazil, "Mortes Anunciadas: A (Des)Proteção da Vida na América Latina." It was attended by scholars from South and North America and focused on many topics that are covered in this volume.

The Brazilian conference demonstrates Latin Americans' deep commitment—both scholarly and political—to understanding and resolving the relationships among distributive justice, human rights, and crime. It also points to the problems that such scholars and human rights workers face when conducting research on these questions. Much information about crime, human rights abuses, and justice is not public or publicized. Students of human rights and distributive justice therefore must study what is covered up, censored, or distorted.

One source often used by Latin (and North) American social scientists and human rights workers is the newspaper. Latin Americans have devised ingenious ways of reading the daily journals to glean the hidden and the censored and to uncover the obfuscated. North American social scientists can learn much in this regard from their colleagues to the south.

Indeed, newspapers are frequently the only source of information about matters of justice. Latin American social scientists quickly learn that national, regional, and local government agencies are not receptive to probing research on crime and human rights. But Latin American scholars and human rights workers do not abandon the task because of difficulties obtaining information. Even when their lives are threatened by the "sensitivity" of their research topics, they do not pull back. Indeed, in many parts of South and Central America, researchers and journalists lose their lives for what North American scholars and journalists do routinely.

Much social science research in Latin America is politically dangerous. For example, the whole of Guatemala's social science establishment has had to be reconstituted because of threats, emigration, and assassination. The result of this repression is visible in this volume. One author, Alfonso Reyes Echandía, former President of the Supreme Court of Justice of Colombia, was assassinated in 1985 during a hostage incident when the Colombian military—in its refusal to talk with the M–19 guerrillas inside the Court—invaded the Supreme Court building. Over 100 people were killed; Reyes Echandía was one of them. Another contributor to this volume has had to flee his country or risk assassination for his work regarding vigilantism there, and the parents of another were murdered in counterinsurgency violence. Several authors have received death threats for their scholarship and human rights work. And one contributor considered not claiming authorship of an article in this collection, out of fear that, at the very least, future research would be imperiled.

This volume is, therefore, dedicated to the courageous South and Central American scholars and human rights workers who continue to study and fight for justice. These are the people who have died for justice, from injustice, and who pay daily for the absence of justice.

ACKNOWLEDGMENTS

Thanks are due many people for this collection. To the organizers of a 1988 conference in Salvador, Bahia, Brazil, on "Mortes Anunciadas: A (Des)Proteção da Vida na América Latina." Those responsible for this important conference on justice, law, and human rights in Latin America are Eliane Botelho Janqueira and Nilo Batista, both of Rio de Janeiro, and Raúl Zaffaroni of Buenos Aires. The Bahia conference inspired this book.

Equally central to this book is the ongoing research by the University of São Paulo's Núcleo de Estudos da Violência, and its director, Paulo Sérgio Pinheiro. Dr. Pinheiro was key in obtaining articles from Latin American scholars. He was invaluable in final manuscript preparation. And his belief in the book was a constant encouragement.

Others also worked to find articles for this collection. I especially thank Rosa del Olmo, director of the Institute of Penal Science and Criminology in Caracas, Diego García Sayan, general secretary of the Comisión Andina de Juristas in Lima, and Raúl Zaffaroni, professor of penal law at the Universidad Nacional de Buenos Aires. Without these generous and well-connected Latin Americans this book would not have been possible.

I wish also to thank Robert M. Levine, Department of History, University of Miami, and Scott G. McNall, Department of American Studies and Sociology, University of Kansas, for reading and critiquing the original book proposal. Their comments on this volume helped shape its progress. I also wish to thank Mary Glen, political science editor of Praeger Publishers, for her faith in this project. Thanks are also due to Beth Wilson, whose copy editing skills in three languages contributed to the quality of the finished manuscript.

Equally central to the success of this volume was my translator, William Shelton, who translated each article with care and precision. His dedication and enthusiasm went far beyond translation. From his translation, I worked to help it speak to audiences unfamiliar with Latin America and our subject matter. The revisions were then compared with the original Spanish or Portuguese version for sense and substance. If there are any distortions or errors in understanding, I take full responsibility.

This volume would not have been possible without financial support from the Union College Faculty Research Fund, and my own endowed chair, the Roger Thayer Stone Professorship in Sociology and Anthropology. My deepest thanks go also to Professor William Bristol for his instant historical facts of total accuracy. I could not have conducted background research for this book without student assistants: for bibliographic work, Dina Lee; for author solicitation, Hector Leon and Teresita Camacho; for some typing, Natalie Bennett. Four secretaries typed the bulk of manuscript revisions: Pat Galbraith, Carolyn Micklas, Marianne Moore, and Rita Michalec. Last minute editorial questions could not have been addressed without the help of Caio Cardoso in Brazil. I thank all of them for their hard and painstaking work.

In the end, this volume would not have been possible without the support and assistance of my husband, Malcolm R. Willison. He encouraged me, edited my own articles, and offered invaluable analytical insights. My mother, who died of cancer while this book was being prepared, inspired me by her courageous conversation with death.

Finally, this book is dedicated to Latin Americans—those who have died for justice, from injustice, and in the absence of justice.

Vigilantism and the State in Modern Latin America

INTRODUCTION: VIGILANTISM AND THE STATE—A LOOK SOUTH AND NORTH

Martha K. Huggins

Latin America's transition in the 1980s from military dictatorship to democracy has received much journalistic attention and some academic analysis.[1] The most dramatic evidence of this transition has been direct elections of government leaders in many countries—Argentina, Brazil, and Chile, for example—after years or even decades of military rule. These elections have led many to conclude that prospects for democratic government are bright throughout the region.

But many Latin American political analysts and scholars have urged caution. One Brazilian political scientist has argued that an emphasis on one visible sign of democracy has disguised the fact that much of Latin America is in the throes of political and social "disaggregation," the falling apart of state and society.[2] Moreover, as many of the authors in this volume point out, Latin American systems of justice still contain many structural supports for authoritarianism, even though these are masked by claims of democratic reform. In the end, the steps toward democracy that have been taken in Latin America hide a reality of economic, political, and social disintegration.

Particularly during the 1980s, Argentina, Brazil, Mexico, Venezuela, Bolivia, Peru, Ecuador, Nicaragua, El Salvador, and most other Latin American countries have suffered extreme economic dislocations—violent inflation and worthless currency (e.g., Argentina, Peru, and Brazil), falling primary product prices (e.g., Chile, Bolivia, Ecuador, Colombia, Central America, Venezuela, and Mexico), and, above all, declining national output per capita and enormous foreign debt (almost all of Latin America).

Disruptive battles between government forces and drug lords, guerrillas, and others are going on in states throughout Central and South America. In all these countries, formal government violence against opponents and suspected subversives is supplemented by the state's covert involvement with paramilitary and parapolice death squads, some of them, ironically, covertly connected with the drug trade.

Colombia, Peru, and Bolivia, in particular, have become the battleground for the U.S. "war on drugs." Police and army units, with U.S. assistance and training, have launched search-and-destroy missions, mostly against small peasant producers' crops, in the process eliminating most noncocaine-related agriculture. At the same time, an intense guerrilla–counterguerrilla war is being waged in Peru and Colombia, where there is also government repression against *narcotraficantes*. Thousands of civilians have been caught in the crossfire among government forces, the guerrillas, and drug barons.

In Panama, the U.S. drug war had its most dramatic confrontation of the decade, with the capture and arrest of U.S.-trained and longtime ally General Manuel Noriega. Whole sections of the capital—indeed, the economy as a whole—must be rebuilt. The U.S. putsch against Noriega resulted in the deaths of up to 4,000 civilians.[3]

U.S.-backed Contra violence in the 1980s against the Nicaraguan government, combined with the U.S. economic blockade and the CIA's not-so-covert economic and political operations, have left that Central American country in social, economic, and political shambles.

Across Latin America, death squads and paramilitary/parapolice groups, made up of off-duty police, military, and civilians, torture and murder as if the embodiment of law, order, and security. In some Latin American countries—Brazil, for example—the police and death squads are said to kill one "street child" a day with total impunity;[4] death squad murders of poor children are also on the rise in Colombia. In Guatemala and El Salvador, these assassination squads target primarily political opponents. In Colombia, they take action against the large narcotics traffickers, picking off civilians and government officials along the way.

As for these murders in other Latin American countries, during Guatemala's thirty-year civil war, over 100,000 citizens have been wiped out, with thousands more tortured and maimed. Since 1970 over 40,000 Salvadoran civilians have died at the hands of government security forces and affiliated death squads, usually after being tortured. Honduras experienced the rise of death squads, government terror, and citizen death during the 1980s.

Throughout Latin America, the police historically have been as likely to violate citizen rights as to protect them. Abuse of citizen rights by on-duty police often has not even violated a country's legal mandates. In fact, in many Latin American countries today, police extraconstitutionality has a legal foundation despite "democratic" reforms. In any case, the poor of Latin America, who are the frequent target of the violence of indiscriminate police sweeps and dragnets, have very little security and predictability in their lives.

But there are signs that some Latin Americans are standing up to the violence against them. In Brazil, citizen lynch mobs have sometimes attacked the police and police stations in order to get faster justice. Attackers then lynch suspected wrongdoers. In Argentina, citizens have taken violent action against the police themselves, for their corruption, dereliction of duty, and violence. In many economically troubled Latin American countries, citizens have invaded supermarkets for food.

Alongside the dramatic death squad and on-duty police violence, and sometimes even eclipsing it, is the daily violence of citizens against other citizens—muggings, assaults, and lynchings. In Brazil, lynchings initiated by citizens and murders by free-lance *justiceiros* (justice makers) are on the rise. Citizen lynchings seem also to be increasing in Argentina.

Thus, while some scholars and journalists view Latin America's transition from military rule to democracy with optimism, many of the contributors to this volume question whether such a transition is really occurring. They raise doubts about the reality of Latin America's new democratic trappings. All of the authors in this collection question whether the modernization of Latin American societies and their states has been associated with transformation to more democratic forms.

VIGILANTISM IN LATIN AMERICA

Recent violence in Latin America is not totally chaotic and unpredictable. Nor is it all interpersonal or exclusively in the hands of official political and government forces. The Latin American vigilantism discussed in this volume includes recent citizen violence against authority, against other citizens (lynchings), and citizen quasi-official violence against citizens (*justiceiro* violence); the covert state violence against citizens (death squads and paramilitary/parapolice violence); and on-duty official police violence against alleged criminals and subversives.

Discussing vigilantism in general, H. Jon Rosenbaum and Peter Sederberg define it as "conservative violence . . . designed to create, maintain, or recreate an established socio-political order."[5] According to historian Richard Maxwell Brown, vigilantism, as it was manifested historically in the United States "refers to organized, extralegal movements, the members of which take the law into their own hands."[6] These definitions provide guidelines for research on Latin American vigilantism, but they require some modification for that region.

For example, what is Latin America's "established" sociopolitical order? In some Latin American countries, close to a majority of all citizens have spent most of their adult lives under authoritarian rule. Are the citizen vigilantes in these systems using violence to re-create authoritarian control? Or are they using such violence to ensure a kind of personal security never realized directly through authoritarian government?

Brown's definition of vigilantism also may be misleading in that he speaks of it as organized movements. This was true for some citizen vigilantism in the United States. But very little Latin American vigilantism is organized in Brown's sense, although all Latin American vigilantism is organized in that it is intricately interwoven with normal social, political, and judicial institutions. And, of course, some Latin American vigilante groups are fairly well organized. But most are relatively spontaneous or clandestine, not showing the continuing public presence and standing, and the brazen assertion of legitimacy, of the older North American vigilante organizations.

Some Definitions of Types

We must now define more specifically those activities considered vigilantism in this collection.

Lynching involves citizens' action against another citizen presumed to have committed a crime or violated some social norm. Lynching may or may not result in the victim's death. At least in the Brazilian context, lynch violence can emerge relatively quickly and spontaneously, or it can progress in slower stages with more complex internal organization developing within the lynch mob (see Chapters 1 and 2 in this volume).

Justice makers, the *justiceiros* who have arisen above all in Brazil to assassinate presumed criminals and alleged—usually poor—troublemakers, are sometimes off-duty police and military, sometimes civilians. The *justiceiros* are often paid for their services, but they also do their work for nothing (see Chapters 1 and 4 in this volume).

In Latin America, *citizen attacks on authority* are another way that some people have redressed deficiencies in their justice systems. One such citizen uprising in Tres Arroyos, Argentina, reported in this volume, involved citizens taking to the streets in a violent signaling of their disapproval of police corruption, violence, and failure to do their duty. Citizens demanded more police protection and greater police accountability (see Chapter 3 in this volume).

Death squads are the most famous and dramatic form of Latin American vigilantism. These assassination squads are called "paramilitary/parapolice groups" in Colombia and Peru (see Chapters 6 and 7 in this volume). Whatever their label, death squads engage in what Manitzas calls criminal actions characterized by violations of human rights, a right-wing ideology supported by the acquiescence—if not involvement—of the state (see Chapter 6 in this volume). As Ibarra points out, death squad terror is not solely the work of "sick or heartless people" (Ch. 5)—although these people are necessary. In reality, such terror is a *political option*, coldly calculated and exercised, to achieve sociopolitical objectives (see Chapters 5–7 in this volume).

It is therefore, as Nairn points out, a mistake to see death squads as "discrete bands of gangsters who roam the Latin American countryside randomly picking off victims."[7] Death squads are not always isolated organizations. They are sometimes closely connected to one another. In any case, they always share indirect, and frequently direct, connections with the central government (see Chapters 5–7 in this volume). At times they are also connected with foreign states.[8] The victims of death squads are seldom selected totally at random. In all countries, they are the people considered "dangerous," whether as political and religious "subversives," guerrillas, or common "criminals." Death squad murders are coldly calculated to deliver a message to such "dangerous classes."

In parts of Latin America today, death squad activities are not so different from the *violence perpetrated by on-duty police*, except that the police have almost total immunity from prosecution for their violence against those not convicted of a crime. Such legally protected police violence is legitimated today by discourse on the "war on crime" or "war on drugs." This "war" has replaced, during Latin America's democratic transition, the national security ideology that justified repression during authoritarian rule (see Chapters 4, 5, 9, and 11 in this volume).

Much arbitrary on-duty police violence occurs during police street sweeps and dragnets; these cover large districts in central cities, particularly the poor, marginal zones. Such police operations, which often involve torture and other violations of citizen rights quite aside from random violence, result in many deaths. Hernández (see Chapter 10 in this volume) shows that in Venezuela these "extraordinary" police operations have increased during the democratic period; Oliveira and Tiscornia show that in Argentina, an increase in police abuses of citizen rights has accompanied the return to democracy.[9] Pinheiro (see Chapter 11 in this volume) demonstrates this same pattern for Brazil. Several authors in this volume (Fernandes, Pinheiro, Hernández), in fact, point to this refocusing of police violence with Latin America's transition to democracy.

The fact that many Latin American police institutions are embedded in formally democratic systems makes police violence seem legitimate (see Chapters 4, 7, 8, and 11 in this volume). In these newly democratizing states, police violence is made to appear as police self-defense against dangerous criminals (see Chapter 12 in this volume). Police immunity from prosecution is ensured in countries that retain authoritarian standards in their rules for police oversight and accountability. Such rules allow police wide latitude in law enforcement (see Chapters 1–3, 11 in this volume).

Many chapters in this volume (1, 3, 6–9) point out that ostensibly democratic legal and bureaucratic reforms often have not resulted in greater democratic practice in Latin America. By maintaining and promoting the facade of democracy through legal "reforms," and by encouraging indirect, seemingly informal mechanisms of social control, many Latin American states have been able to garner public support for blatently undemocratic legal structures and social control practices. Rejali (see Chapter 8 in this volume) discusses how the discourse on democracy and human rights affects official and academic thinking about violence in Latin America and elsewhere. This argument is applied to Colombia by Reyes (see Chapter 9 in this volume).

Commonalities and Differences

Most Latin American vigilantism, including lynching, murders by *justiceiros*, death squad and paramilitary/parapolice violence, and violence by on-duty police, involves action against common citizens, although some also is directed against public authorities. By contrast, all citizen uprisings are directed exclusively or primarily against public authorities and institutions.

In other cases, one set of vigilante acts (the uprisings, the lynchings, the free-lance justice makers) represents—sometimes indirectly—citizen demands for more personal security and/or accountable law and order. Another set represents actions by the state and its agents against groups of citizens perceived as threatening to security and "law and order" (the paramilitary/parapolice death squads and on-duty police violence).

But whatever the differences among types of vigilantism, most sociologically relevant are the similarities between these seemingly disparate acts of violence. In the first place, all of the vigilantism recounted in this volume goes beyond the formal (albeit often idealized and permeable) boundaries of system legality. Of course, in the case of on-duty police violence, such theoretically "extraordinary" police action is temporarily legitimated by social or political crisis.

Second, all of the vigilantism described in this volume is essentially conservative or reactionary: It represents demands for return to a real or idealized social past, whether or not that vision of the past actually serves the wider social good, or even the interests of the vigilantes themselves.

Motivations for Vigilantism

According to Rosenbaum and Sederberg, writing of vigilantism in general, past vigilantism has been motivated by a desire for control over crime, over social groups, and over the regime. They recognize that these objectives often overlap, and they point out that the perpetrators of vigilante violence can be private citizens or official state agents, or both. Such actors can participate in vigilantism overtly or covertly.

Crime control vigilantism is "directed against people believed to be committing acts proscribed by the formal legal system."[10] In this volume, much of the lynching and *justiceiro* justice focuses in its overt claims on crime control (see Chapters 1, 2, and 4). Some death squad violence also aims ostensibly at controlling ordinary civilian crime (see Chapter 11). On-duty police violence is directed formally at crime control (see Chapters 10–12). But much of this crime control vigilantism often hides a more subtle form of social group control.

Vigilantism for control of social groups is "establishment violence directed against groups that are competing for, or advocating a redistribution of values within the system."[11] Several articles in this collection (see Chapters 4, 10, and 11) suggest that powerful social group control objectives often lurk behind many lynchings by Brazilian citizens (see Chapters 1 and 2), as well as much *justiceiro* justice (see Chapter 4), quasi-official death squad violence in Peru (see Chapter 6), Colombia (see Chapter 7), and in Guatemala (see Chapter 5), and extralegal on-duty police violence (see Chapters 10–12).

Control of a regime may be the focus of vigilante action, which is "intended to alter the regime, in order to make the 'superstructure' into a more effective guardian of the 'base.' "[12] When public officials themselves engage in regime control vigilantism, there is a potential for coups d'état. Articles in this volume do not examine *official* involvement in regime control vigilantism, but there is an example of civilian involvement in the people's uprising at Tres Arroyos.

Theoretical taxonomies are useful for organizing and making sense out of complex materials. However, they are static and exclusive. In the real world, theoretical variables blend into one another, and there is change over time. For example, vigilantism can aim simultaneously at crime and social group control, as is the case for much of the vigilantism in this volume. Vigilante action also can shift from social group to regime control.

In an example of the latter, the U.S. State Department feared in 1967 that death squad activity in Guatemala could become a threat to the regime in power—a regime that was making liberal use of vigilante terror to achieve its political goals. Indeed, a State Department intelligence and research analyst pointed out in 1967 that Guatemalan President Julio César Méndez Montenegro had given his security forces "carte blanche in the field of internal security in exchange for [their] support for his administration."[13] By the late 1960s Méndez Montenegro's counterinsurgency machine had gotten out of control. In fact, the State Department argued that while "in some instances the [Guatemalan] government [could] still exercise a degree of control over the activities of the clandestine killer units, both civilian and military, . . . it would be foolhardy to count on it."[14] The State Department, in fact, warned that "continued use of . . . rough and ready counterinsurgency tactics could lead to popular agitation for the re-establishment of law and order, and eventually might create conditions propitious for a coup."[15]

The social group control death squads, formed to support Méndez Montenegro's war against guerrilla insurgency, were running the risk of inadvertently becoming instruments of regime control by undermining civil support for the Méndez Montenegro government through that government's failure (or inability) to control its own covert network of violence and terror.

Three Variables

The best way to understand the vigilante acts recounted in this volume is to see them on a continuum where variation depends on the degree of spontaneity, organization, and state involvement in each instance.

As for *spontaneity*, some of the vigilantism reported in this collection is quite spontaneous, with no prior planning and organization. Some of it is less so, characterized by preparation and prior organization.

Related to the variable of spontaneity is *organization*. Some vigilantism lacks much internal organization; there is little interaction and cohesion between vigilante participants, and little between various vigilante groups. With other types, there is a good deal of organization, both within the vigilante group itself, and between it and other such groups.

In some of the vigilantism reported in this volume, *state involvement* is largely indirect. Such vigilantism is fostered by what the state does not (or cannot) do, not so much by the state's direction of it. In many cases, however, the state is involved directly in vigilantism, either covertly or overtly, or both. The three variables of spontaneity, organization, and state involvement can be combined into a single continuum of vigilante groups' characteristics. The positioning of vigilante action on this continuum is tentative; much more research is required before the continuum can be completed.

Two Ends of a Continuum

The Informal Pole. Some kinds of lynching, especially some "anonymous crowd lynchings" (see Chapter 2), are very spontaneous, less internally organized, and have only indirect state involvement. These lynchings fall near the "informal" end of the vigilantism continuum.

The Formal Pole. At the other end of the vigilantism continuum is extralegal violence by on-duty police. As research reported in Chapters 10–12 suggests, such police violence is not spontaneous at all: Street sweeps and dragnets are planned and coordinated. The police who engage in such violence are frequently organized into elite units, often trained and equipped by the United States (see Chapter 13), and constitute formal elements within their country's criminal justice system. The state has direct connections to this police violence and terror. Such violence is often legitimated by existing or "extraordinary" legal mandates (see Chapters 10–12).

Intermediate Types. Between the continuum's two ends lie the Brazilian "communal" lynchings, *justiceiro* justice, the people's uprisings against authority, and the violence of quasi-official death squads and paramilitary/parapolice groups. It is difficult to fix exactly where these intermediate forms of vigilantism lie in relation to one another on the continuum; much more research on such violence needs to be carried out. But the research in this volume suggests an initial positioning of these various vigilante phenomena.

Closer to the more spontaneous, less organized, and less state-involved end of the vigilantism continuum lie the *justiceiros*. These "justice makers" clearly do not act totally spontaneously: They give thought to the kind of person they will murder, and sometimes are hired to carry out their assassinations (see Chapters 1 and 4). Furthermore, *justiceiros* are part of a socially organized interaction system: They are organizationally linked to the people and communities they "protect," as the research by Fernandes clearly illustrates. At the same time, Brazilian *justiceiros* seem to commit their murders mostly alone, although there are exceptions. As for their connections with the state, *justiceiros* are sometimes off-duty police and military. But, whether linked directly to the state or not, *justiceiros* gain legitimacy from the state's hands-off treatment of them. Such state inattention is legitimized by wide public support for *justiceiros* in Brazil.

The *citizen uprisings* in Argentina have been relatively spontaneous, although not totally so. They have grown out of prior forms of community and political organization, strengthened by social bonds among community participants. The citizen protest groups have lacked elaborate formal organization, although some organization has emerged within groups. Representatives of the state have not been formally involved in the uprisings, but in Argentina some democratizing of the state has made citizen challenges of it seem more possible and less politically costly (see Chapter 3).

Closer to the "formal" end of the vigilantism continuum lie the *"communal lynchings"* (see Chapter 2). They are somewhat spontaneous, although, like the Argentine uprisings and Brazilian justice makers, the "communal lynchings" have roots in existing citizen bonds and community ties (see Chapters 1 and 2). Some communal lynch groups develop elaborate forms of internal organization, often assigning to members different justice system roles—judge, jury, executioners. Formal state involvement in "communal lynchings" is usually fairly low, although such lynchings are informally encouraged by state officials who, on the one hand, do almost nothing to prevent or redress the crimes that lynch groups strike against and, on the other, do not punish citizens who resort to lynch "justice."

Death squads and parapolice/paramilitary groups fall closer to the vigilantism continuum's formal pole. There is some evidence in this volume (see Chapters 6 and 7) that in some Latin American countries, death squads or paramilitary/parapolice groups are organizationally related. There is also evidence that these assassination squads are linked to their national states, as Palacio, Manitzas, and Ibarra (Chapters 5–7) show, and also to foreign states.[16] In any case, death squads and paramilitary/parapolice groups could not exist without at least the implicit support of their national states. Such support is manifested in the state's unwillingess to act against them, and through deliberate state cover-ups of death squad violence (see Chapters 6 and 7).

Indeed, when all is said and done, the most important factor affecting the emergence, existence, and proliferation of Latin American vigilantism seems to be the national state and its international supporters. State penetration lowers the spontaneity, strengthens the organizational structure, and increases the continuation and continuity of such extralegal violence. It is, therefore, crucial to understand the relationship of states to vigilantism. Any analysis of this relationship for Latin America requires an understanding of the structure and dynamics of Third World states. For most of Latin America this means looking into the relationship of state authoritarianism to vigilantism.

THE LATIN AMERICAN PERIPHERAL STATE

Foreign penetration of Latin America occurred first through colonial domination, and then through the region's economic and political inclusion in the advanced capitalist world system. Independence for Latin America consisted mainly in a change of governing personnel: "Latin American states . . . remained linked to the world capitalist system as dependent economies."[17] Rather than twentieth-century industrialization freeing Latin America from colonial export relations, it deepened the region's reliance on foreign capital and loans, creating new economic and political crises in the process.

Latin American state structures are the product of economic and political asymmetry: "Even in independent nations . . . , the ruling classes owe their . . . wealth and power . . . to their positions in the chain [of dependency]."[18] The power of this elite "lumpenbourgeoisie" comes "as much [from] their place in the hierarchy of satellite–metropolis relations as . . . [from their] ownership of capital."[19] Consequently, there is "an unstable balance between the different dominating classes or factions, i.e., [there is] no effective and lasting integration of the 'bloc au pouvoir.' "[20] In practice, such elites are "in the government but [without] . . . political power."[21] In effect, "the influence and power of each [elite group] is . . . offset by that of the other."[22] Such states thus come to be dominated by "a native class of civil servants and soldiers."[23] This technomilitary elite mediates struggles within and between elite factions.

Repressive mediation of civil society becomes more and more necessary as Latin American states become increasingly "transnationalized," that is, as they are absorbed into the capitalist world system. Such transnationalization strengthens the accountability and even loyalty of national elites to foreign lenders, investors, and aid givers. As Cardoso points out for Brazil, transnationalization has meant that: "New spurts of industrial growth seemed to depend on coordinated policy initiatives which emphasized stabilization, the confidence of the international industrial and finance bourgeoisie, and the cooperation of more institutionalized segments of local export and manufacturing oligarchies."[24]

Not surprisingly, then, twentieth-century Latin American development has been a breeding ground for state authoritarianism.[25] Authoritarian states are characterized by "the imposition of a well-developed military bureaucratic superstructure of power over an underdeveloped infrastructure of participation."[26] Such states result from "the constant search for stability and long-term institutionalization."[27] Within this kind of development program, any political challenge must be crushed quickly: The state's transnationalized technocrats see popular mobilization as an obstacle to economic growth.

This emphasis on order for development has distanced Latin American governments from civil society. The state's subservience to foreign money, technology, markets, advice, and aid makes its well-being more dependent on foreign interests than on national priorities and the needs of civil society. Of course, political alienation in Latin American states also results because these states cannot retain the loyalty of people whom they feel they must repress.

PERIPHERAL STATES AND VIGILANTISM

Latin American vigilantism both mirrors and reproduces the structure and dynamics of Latin American states. It involves a variety of citizen and citizen–state groups, sometimes acting in concert, at other times struggling against one another, to bring "order" to the civil space. Each group may check the potential power of the others for a time. Indeed, no vigilante group has yet fully taken over the state's monopoly of legitimate force, although in some Latin American countries the death squads and paramilitary/parapolice groups have come close to taking power, as in parts of Colombia.

The relative autonomy of social action, and the divisiveness that characterizes much Latin American vigilantism, reflect the class structure and dynamics of Latin American states. Such states are battlegrounds for factional struggles: None of the propertied classes can control the state by itself. When order is imposed upon such intrastate factionalism, it is frequently by a military–technocratic elite. Just as this elite mediates conflict within the state, so citizen and citizen–state vigilante groups mediate conflicts within the civil area, usually alongside the police and the military. Thus Latin American vigilantism reflects the state's loss of some direct control over force by its giving over some of its monopoly on violence to private "justice" groups.

In the process, of course, a symbiotic relationship develops between Latin American national states and private vigilante groups: These private and quasi-private groups are both *of* and *not of* the state, just as many Latin American central states are both *of* and *not of* their national societies.

Vigilantism both indirectly and directly reflects Latin American states' ties to foreign governments and economic interests. Private justice is partly an indirect product of the peripheral state's dependence on foreign loans and capital. The fiscal crisis of many Latin American states makes it impossible for them fully to address their populations' security needs, even if the government wants to provide such security for poor and marginalized people. Thus, even reluctant Latin American states have been forced to transfer some of their formal monopoly over force to informal "law and order" groups under only indirect state control.

But some Latin American vigilantism more directly reflects the transnationalization of Latin American states (see Chapter 7). Indeed, quite aside from private U.S. support for vigilantism, there is evidence of direct U.S. government involvement with Latin American death squads and paramilitary/parapolice groups, not to speak of U.S. training of undemocratic Latin American police[28] (see Chapter 13).

Vigilantism results from and fosters authoritarian states and their inegalitarian ideologies and practices. The people who are systematically marginalized from their society's economic and political life, and who are violently repressed along the way, often turn such aggression against one another, sometimes even directing it against the state. As Fernandes argues for Brazil in Chapter 4 of this volume, under "The 'Democratic Transition' ":

> For those excluded from first-class citizenship, society appears to be sharply polarized between rulers and ruled, rich and poor, powerful and weak. . . . This

division is marked by an idealized morality—good . . . [and] . . . evil. . . . In such a morally divided public order, . . . punishment does not remain abstract or formal. . . . The search for quick, personal justice, combined with a belief that the law has failed, . . . acts as a breeding ground for *justiceiros*.

STATES AND VIGILANTISM: CONTINUITY OR DISCONTINUITY

Latin American vigilantism is intimately related to political and social life and to the state. But it is not necessarily related solely to survivals from a precapitalist colonial state. In any case, in the earlier periods, private justice by local political bosses seems to have resulted from a *lack* of central state development and control, and from the absolute control of such local bosses over their regions. In the absence of effective state structures of protection and punishment, local potentates and bosses, private militias, and even bandits took justice into their own hands. Indeed, extralegal repression by elite-related political forces is not new to Latin America: Historically it has formed the basis of much control over civil society. And, on the other hand, citizens, slaves, and oppressed Native Americans sometimes struck out against the violence directed at them by their peers and/or their bosses.

But if an absence of central government and state control and protection explains much past vigilante violence in Latin America, how are we to explain its reemergence—and increase—in industrialized societies with highly structured, capitalist states? After all, some of these states—recently authoritarian and undergoing "democratization"—already have highly developed capacities to control civil society through their internal security bureaucracies, police intelligence systems, and population-monitoring technologies. But the fiscal crises of such states prevent them from maintaining this repressive apparatus even with foreign assistance. Furthermore, national and international public opinion frequently condemns violent, overt state repression, making it necessary for elements in such states to relinquish some direct control over civil society to informal lynch mobs and death squads. Death squads, which are sometimes seen as evidence that a country's social control system is not yet modern, are in fact very modern. As already indicated, they are the dialectical outcome of extreme centralization and bureaucratization of internal repression and control.

COMPARATIVE VIGILANTISM

One way to further the analysis of Latin American vigilantism is to compare it with similar manifestations in the United States. Latin American vigilantism must be taken out of the realm of the exotic—to separate it from "deviant culture" explanations. Latin American vigilantism clearly is not solely the product of a deviant "culture of machismo."[29] Nor does it result primarily from peculiarly Latin American Ibero-Spanish Catholic-corporatist cultural foundations.[30] Latin American vigilantism is a direct outgrowth of contemporary state and social organization, which includes Latin American national states' relationship to, and dependence upon, international capital.

One way to expose the weaknesses in culturally specific explanations for vigilantism is to compare Latin American vigilantism with its historical manifestations in the United States, where vigilantism flourished under a cultural ethos and within politicolegal foundations different from those of Latin America today.

The United States has a long history of vigilantism. Such extralegal violence has included lynching, murder by hired gunmen, citizen uprisings against public authority, gang assassinations, and a wide variety of extralegal and extraconstitutional police violence against citizens. Any reasonably complete history of the United States makes it clear that Latin American vigilantism cannot be explained solely by that region's machismo, or its Iberian and Catholic legal traditions.

One of the foremost historians of vigilantism in the United States, Richard Maxwell Brown,[31] points out that U.S. vigilantism was indigenous: There was no long-standing vigilante tradition on the Continent or in the British Isles. Moreover, U.S. vigilantism grew out of quintessentially North American values: a doctrine of alertness to danger ("vigilance"); popular sovereignty; the rights of self-preservation and revolution. Such values are central to the North American cultural ethos, not deviant from or marginal to it.

But while such cultural values may have given ideological legitimation to North American vigilantism, they cannot wholly explain the specific situations in which it emerged. Perhaps more important are factors linked to the social and political organization of frontier life and to the dislocations brought by urbanization. Such factors may foster Latin American vigilantism today.

North American vigilantism occurred where government institutions were weak or nonexistent, or where the regular system was functioning, but not to the satisfaction of vigilance committee members. In the first instance, vigilantism filled a void. This occurred most often when new communities were being formed on the frontier, during the period of U. S. vigilantism known as "early vigilantism" (1767–1850). Vigilante violence during this period was aimed primarily at "horse thieves, counterfeiters, outlaws, bad men, and lower [class] people."[32] Brown points out:

On the frontier, the normal foundations of a stable, orderly society—churches, schools, cohesive community life—were either absent or present only in rough, makeshift forms. The regular, legal system of law enforcement often proved to be woefully inadequate for the needs of the settlers.[33]

It was the more powerful settlers of such American frontier communities who took up vigilantism. They attempted to re-create through violence the class structure of the communities they had left behind. According to Brown, this community reconstruction process ran most smoothly where residents had migrated together. The biggest problem came where " 'cumulative' communities of inhabitants [were] thrown together helter-skelter by the migration process."[34] This bred a clash of opposites—and greater vigilante violence. Martins's discussion of the causes of lynching in São Paulo today (see Chapter 1) suggests that community reconstruction in a "helter-skelter" migration process may account for some lynchings in Latin America's second-largest city.

Other realities of American frontier social organization nurtured vigilantism in the United States: "Throughout most of the nineteenth century (and not just on the frontier) [law enforcement] was restricted to the immediate vicinity of county seat, town, or township."[35] Many of the more isolated communities lacked the financial resources to support a justice system. This was further complicated by the lack of transportation between towns and regions, so that "a fugitive, having gained any sort of lead, was difficult to catch."[36] On top of these problems, many juries failed to convict alleged criminals. As Brown points out, instant vigilante justice was a frontier solution for such inadequacies of community social organization. Many articles in this volume point to state inaction and inattention to citizen security and justice as contributing to extralegal violence in Latin America.

But Brown argues that North American vigilantism also emerged parallel to regular law enforcement. This "neo-vigilantism" (post–1850) aimed at reducing the cost of official law enforcement and addressing problems dealt with too slowly, or not at all, by the formal law enforcement system. Neo-vigilantism in the United States was largely urban—"a response to the problems of an emerging, urban, industrial, racially and ethnically diverse America." The victims of neo-vigilantism were usually "Catholics, Jews, immigrants, Negroes, laboring men and labor leaders, political radicals, and proponents of civil liberties."[37]

The best example of late "parallel vigilantism" in the United States was the San Francisco Vigilance Committee of 1856. The ostensible objective of this committee was to to stamp out local corruption and crime. But, in fact, the committee was "concerned with local political and fiscal reform"; it wanted to shift control of government in San Francisco from the Irish–Catholic Democrats, who ran the city under Mayor David C. Broderick, to Protestant, eastern-seaboard-linked "upper and middle-class, old American, Protestant merchants."[38] Indeed, the bulk of membership in the San Francisco Vigilance Committee had come originally from the northeastern United States—the old-stock Yankees.[39]

Many of the San Francisco merchants who opposed David C. Broderick's Democratic regime wanted to protect their own fiscal profile and credit status. According to Decker, they were attempting to "halt the corrosive effects of economic recession" by protecting both their individual credit ratings and the general fiscal reputation of the city.[40] The San Francisco businessmen who joined the Vigilance Committee wanted to reestablish the image of San Francisco as fiscally healthy. Apparently a number of Eastern businessmen felt likewise. Brown points out that "in the eyes of Eastern businessmen, San Francisco's economic stability was being jeopardized by . . . soaring municipal debt, rising taxes, and approaching bankruptcy under the Broderick machine."[41] The local business community seemed to reason that the way to restore creditors' confidence in the city was to destroy Broderick's largely Irish–Catholic, working-class machine. Accomplishing this involved a "partnership" between San Francisco's official and parallel justice systems: "Law enforcement officials often connived with vigilantes."[42]

While it can be misleading to draw parallels too closely between U.S. and Latin American vigilantism, the San Francisco Vigilance Committee seems to have emerged in a socioeconomic and political climate somewhat akin to conditions in Latin America today. In San Francisco in the 1850s, as in much of Latin America today, political and economic planning was influenced, in part, by the interests and priorities of outside capital: "The merchants of San Francisco were dependent on Eastern connections for their credit."[43] Lenders could withhold or withdraw the financial support that businesses and local government needed to operate. The local groups that most benefited from this capital, and who therefore risked the most from losing it, took action to protect their own or their government's lender–borrower relationship. Similar conditions seem also to motivate some Latin American government officials to upgrade their police (see Chapter 13), to give covert support to death squads and paramilitary/parapolice groups (see Chapters 5–7), and to overlook citizen lynchings and justice-maker murders.

This brief review of vigilantism in the United States suggests that understanding Latin American vigilantism requires examining how state and social organizational structures and dynamics shape and promote vigilantism. For Latin America, this also means exploring the relationship of peripheral to dominant metropolitan states. This volume is designed to open the door to such issues and to offer a first attempt to bring all of Latin America into a comparative framework for studying vigilantism's relationship to the state.

NOTES

1. Tomas Amadeo Visconti, "Argentina e Brasil: Perspectivas de dos transiciónes democrática," *Revista mexicana de sociología*, 48, no. 3 (1986), 31–43; Teresa Castro Escudero, "Movimiento popular y democracia em Chile," *Revista mexicana de sociología*, 48, no. 3 (1986), 51–73; G. O'Donnell, *Transições do regime autoritario: Primeiras conclusões* (São Paulo: Vertice, 1988); Alfred Stepan, *Democratizing Brazil: Problems of Transition and Consolidation* (London and New York: Oxford University Press, 1989).

2. In discussion with Francisco Weffort, São Paulo, 11/6/89.

3. "60 Minutes," 9/30/90.

4. *New York Times*, 9/6/90.

5. H. Jon Rosenbaum and Peter Sederberg, *Vigilante Politics* (Philadelphia: University of Pennsylvania Press, 1976), p. 4.

6. Richard Maxwell Brown, *The Strain of Violence* (New York: Oxford University Press, 1975), pp. 95–96.

7. Allan Nairn, "An Exclusive Report on the U.S. Role in El Salvador's Official Terror," *The Progressive*, May 1984, pp. 20–29, see p. 25.

8. See Noam Chomsky, "Our Little Region over Here," *The National Reporter*, Fall 1987; Martha K. Huggins, *Political Policing: Eighty Years of United States Training of Latin American Police* (forthcoming); A. J. Langguth, *Hidden Terrors* (New York: Pantheon, 1978); J. Le Moyne, "Testifying to Torture," *The New York Times Magazine*, 6/5/88, pp. 45–66; J. Mathebula, "Vigilantes: An Arm of State Terrorism," *Sechaba*, December 1987, pp. 19–29; Nairn, "Exclusive Report," p. 25; Allan Nairn, "Senate Report Says CIA Created Ties to Salvadoran Death Squad Figures," *Philadelphia Inquirer*, September 1984; J. Petras and M. Morley, "Supporting Repression: U.S. Policy and the Demise of Human Rights in El Salvador, 1970–1981," *The Socialist Register, 1981* (London: The Merlin Press, 1981), pp. 47–71.

9. A. Oliveira and Sofia Tiscornia, "Extra-Legal Executions Among Popular Sectors in Argentina (1982–1989)" (Buenos Aires: CELS, Unpublished report, 1989).

10. Rosenbaum and Sederberg, *Vigilante Politics*, pp. 10–11.

11. Ibid., p. 12.

12. Ibid., p. 17.

13. Thomas L. Hughes, "Guatemala: A Country Running Wild," Intelligence Note, U.S. Department of State, Intelligence and Research Memorandum, 10/23/67, p. 1.

14. Ibid., p. 4.

15. Ibid., p. 1.

16. See note 8.

17. R. King, *The State in Modern Society: New Directions in Political Sociology* (Chatham, N.J.: Chatham House, 1986), p. 215.

18. Ibid.

19. A. G. Frank, *Lumpenbourgeoisie, Lumpendevelopment*. New York: Monthly Review Press, 1972).

20. H. Alavi, "The State in Post-Colonial Societies: Pakistan and Bangladesh," *New Left Review*, 74 (July-August 1972), 59–81.

21. King, *The State in Modern Society*, p. 215.

22. W. Hein and K. Stenzel, "The Capitalist State and Underdevelopment in Latin America—The Case of Venezuela," *Kapitalistate*, 2 (1973), 31–48, see 35.

23. Ibid.

24. F. H. Cardoso, "On the Characterization of Authoritarian Regimes in Latin America," in David Collier, ed., *The New Authoritarianism in Latin America* (Princeton, N.J.: Princeton University Press, 1979).

25. See David Collier, ed., *The New Authoritarianism in Latin America* (Princeton, N.J.: Princeton University Press, 1979).

26. E. Ahmad, "The New Fascist State: Notes on the Pathology of Power in the Third World," *Arab Studies Quarterly*, 3, no. 2 (1980), 170–180, see 177.

27. Maria Helena Alves, *State and Opposition in Military Brazil* (Austin: University of Texas Press, 1985), 259.

28. Huggins, *Political Policing*.

29. M. Wolfgang and F. Ferracuti, *The Subculture of Violence* (London: Tavistock, 1967).

30. H. J. Wiarda, "Toward a Framework for the Study of Political Change: The Corporative Model," *World Politics* 25, no. 2 (January 1973), 206–235.

31. Brown, *The Strain of Violence*, p. 96.

32. Ibid., p. 127.

33. Ibid., p. 96.

34. Ibid., p. 104.

35. Ibid., p. 112.

36. Ibid., pp. 112–13.

37. Ibid., p. 127.

38. Cited in Robert M. Senkiewicz, S.J., *Vigilantes in Gold Rush San Francisco* (Stanford, Calif.: Stanford University Press, 1985), p. 223.

39. Ibid.

40. Ibid., p. 229.

41. Brown, *The Strain of Violence*, pp. 137–38.

42. Ibid., p. 124.

43. Senkiewicz, *Vigilanties*, pp. 223–25.

I
MOB LYNCHING, POPULAR VIOLENCE, AND *JUSTICEIROS*

1

LYNCHINGS—LIFE BY A THREAD: STREET JUSTICE IN BRAZIL, 1979–1988

José de Souza Martins

Lynchings are sociologically very complex. They are not adequately explained by any generic and elementary discourse on urban violence, or by the vague and distorted term "people's justice."[1] I prefer to call lynching "street justice": It involves the "lower classes";[2] is practiced in a strongly symbolic manner; and occurs where political institutions are weak.

Lynchings powerfully reflect the Brazilian social crisis. They are an essential part of the disintegration of social and political order in Brazil, characterized also by institutional crises within the police and court system from the 1964 military takeover to the present. Lynchings are not the only evidence of social dissolution. Other indicators are brawls on trains and buses, and looting and pillaging. These suggest a moral declaration of the right to life and the need to challenge the conditions and rules of capitalist accumulation. The large number of city and rural land invasions also suggest such a challenge.

It is worth keeping in mind the significant number of lynchings in Brazil's rural areas, and at least two cases of lynchings of Indians in Amazonas and Maranhão. The latter are areas with very tense ethnic relations. By the same token, we must consider that many lynchings are carried out (or instigated) by middle-class groups. Many lynchings in the working-class suburbs[3] of São Paulo and in the Northeastern city of Salvador, while committed by lower-class people, are instigated by owners of small shops or stores. Nearly 10 percent of such lynch incidents began with conflicts in commercial establishments; 9.2 percent were committed by taxi drivers.

METHODS

This chapter incorporates data on lynchings and attempted lynchings during the ten-year period from 1979 to 1988, as well as four individual cases between 1970 and 1978. The data come from newspaper articles, principally from *O Estado de S. Paulo* and *Folha de S. Paulo*. They include 272 cases, as of December 31, 1988. Of these, 53.3 percent were actual lynchings (145 cases), 39.7 percent attempted lynchings (14 cases), 0.4 percent threatened lynchings (1 case), 5.1 percent (14 cases) where a lynching had probably occurred; and 1.5 percent involved the "lynching" of someone already dead (4 cases). In this text, only lynchings or attempted lynchings are analyzed. I shall refer to these two together as "lynch incidents." In all the lynch incidents in this study, 40 percent of the lynch victims were killed, 30 percent were injured, 6 percent escaped, and 29 percent were rescued.[4]

Occasionally, news items were added to the data from papers other than the *Estado* or *Folha*. The lynchings in Brazil's northern State of Rondônia (in the Amazon), which were not reported in the two São Paulo newspapers, were related to me by agents of Rondônia's Comissão Pastoral da Terra. One 1988 lynching in Osasco, São Paulo, was reported to a social scientist colleague. None of these lynchings were reported in the newspapers. Comparing my figures with those of a 1982 report on lynchings, covering the period from late 1979 to 1982,[5] I established that the number of lynch incidents would have been significantly greater if my research had surveyed other regions' newspapers. In other words, my data contain only a portion of all lynchings that occurred in Brazil between 1979 and 1982.

But such deficiencies in the newspaper coverage of lynching are not relevant to this study. I do not want to measure the intensity of that type of violence in Brazilian society. I want to understand the internal characteristics of lynching—its logic and what it teaches about the Brazilian institutional crisis in "moral justice." I am thinking particularly about those people on the "razor's edge" of incomplete transition, in that space where property, work, and authority relations are disintegrating. It is possible to define this time and space where lynch violence occurs as the urban and political threshold of an unfinished intersection—where temporary and permanent migrants are gathered, and populations are barred in time and space from entering the modern world. Such people are the unwanted refuse of traditional agriculture, the feared rejects of large-scale industry and the city.

LYNCHING IN BRAZIL

The Brazilian states with the greatest number of lynchings and lynch attempts were, in order, São Paulo (131 cases), Rio de Janeiro (47 cases),

Bahia (32 cases), and Pará (15 cases). Overall, lynch incidents were recorded in 17 states and the Brazilian Federal District, and in 132 municipalities, of which 10 were state capitals. The regional distribution of such lynch incidents was 67.3 percent in the Southeast, 16.9 percent in the Northeast, 8.5 percent in the North, 4.0 percent in the South, and 3.3 percent in the Center-West.

With the exception of the South, where there were very few lynch incidents, there is an inverse relation between lynchings and the other forms of violence that express a conflict between legitimacy and legality. For example, in the Brazilian North, Center-West, and Northeast, the struggle for land is intense and there are numerous cases of debt slavery or peonage. In those regions, a smaller proportion of lynch incidents has occurred, even though these are areas where rural lynchings and the lynchings of Indians have taken place. In the Southeast, where São Paulo is located, and where the struggle for land is proportionally lower (but not, therefore, any less significant), lynch incidents are more numerous. Southeast Brazil is the final and often temporary destination for victims of agrarian violence from other regions.

As for the periods during which lynch incidents were most commonly committed, there were fifty-six in 1987, thirty-two in 1984, and thirty in 1986 and 1988. These figures do not show a linear and progressive increase in lynchings. If we divide the ten years for which there are systematic data into two distinct periods (1979–1984 and 1985–1988), important differences come to light. During the last four years of the military regime (1981–1984), there were ninety-one lynch incidents. In the first 4 years (1985–1988) of the new political regime (the "New Republic"), there were 136 lynch incidents. This means that there were 50 percent more lynchings under the "New Republic," one and a half times the number of lynchings that occurred during the final period of Brazil's dictatorship. There has been a similar growth of rural violence in Brazil, which also became more intense during the first years of the "New Republic."

THE SOCIOLOGY OF LYNCHING

There is no easy explanation for this increase in lynch violence with the formal ending of military rule. Some speculations are possible. First, since the new political regime resulted from a pact between certain military sectors, the urban bourgeoisie, and the more or less liberal sectors of old local oligarchies—the latter consisting of large rural property holders—the "New Republic" resurrected the conceptions and practices of private justice from Brazil's more backward rural areas. In fact, Brazil's cities have been invaded by the country in many ways—not only by migrants and immigrants, but also by a more rural style of political practice. Consequently, the state—although long since transformed by a capitalist and apparently modern appearance—has resurrected and/or failed to prevent the rebirth of local potentates' personal power. Thus, in large Brazilian cities the straw bosses of fictitious *bairro*[6] organizations have come to exercise an increasingly important role in mediating political relations.

Lynchings are not unrelated to the emergence, in these same bairros, of *justiceiros* (hired guns).[7] The justiceiros execute innocent people, as well as those guilty of crimes, under the patronage of local merchants. The symbiosis between these justiceiros and the police, and the protection of such hired killers' illegal activities by government authorities, has been brought to light by Brazilian newspapers.

But the actions of justiceiros and lynch mobs should not, without a better understanding of both the continuities and the discontinuities between Brazil's dictatorship and its "New Republic," automatically be equated with the death squads that operated in the period of military dictatorship. For example, the smaller proportion of lynchings under the military dictatorship does not mean that there was less violence at that time against the people who today are lynch victims. However, there does seem to be an initial relation between the end of visible death squads and the increase in lynchings.

GEOGRAPHY OF LYNCHING

The local and regional classification of lynch incidents gives rise to an important fact: Those incidents which occur today in Brazil's state capitals and nearby suburbs tend to differ from the lynchings that occur in smaller towns of the interior. The lynch incidents that occur in each of these settings are different in terms of their predominant motivation, social class, and number of participants. In the capital cities and suburbs, lynchings are carried out predominantly by poor and working-class people, though there is also a partly hidden lower-middle-class presence. In cities in the interior, the lynchings and attempted lynchings are committed by middle-class people who are directly challenging and criticizing the courts and police. This is illustrated in the interior by some lynch mobs' invasion and torching of police stations and courthouses. In the capital city lynchings, such direct criticisms of, and challenges to, the legal system are not always as visible. In both types of lynching there is a conservative or reactionary motivation; both types deny self-defense to the victim; both eliminate trial by an impartial judge and the right of appeal. For a victim of lynching, the verdict is final.

Sociologists must distinguish the types of lynching. The classification proposed here focuses on the differing motives for lynchings in each setting. In the lynchings that occur in capital cities, the poor and working class demonstrate their will; they are their own judges—rendering decisions about the crimes to which they are subjected, demonstrating the importance to them of recovering a predictable system of formal justice. Brazilians are mistaken when they claim that capital city lynchings, particularly those in poor bairros, suggest a demand for enactment of the death penalty. Rather, lynchers proclaim their desire for justice; they do not want to continue to be the helpless victims of robbery, rape, and murder. It goes against the death penalty argument that many lynch incidents are often preceded by public displeasure about police failure to take action against criminals. Public unhappiness with the criminal justice system is shown by attacks on police stations and courts that result from the apparent failure of Brazil's criminal justice institutions to act on behalf of the public. The idea that the victimized poor and the working class of Brazil's capital cities use lynching to demonstrate their demand for the death penalty is an interpretation given to lynching by the urban middle class and by authoritarian sectors of Brazilian public opinion.

Lynchings in Brazil's interior towns are often carried out to preserve the middle class. These lynchings reflect the relatively closed nature of local elites. They are aimed at protecting local middle-class society from the outside. The reactionary intent of these interior city lynchings is suggested by an incident that occurred in a wealthy town of São Paulo state where, "principally on weekends and holidays, . . . groups of young men, the sons of traditional local middle class families, meet and aggressively respond to 'audacious strangers'—young men from other locales. Their violence is worse . . . if the visitor is seen in the company of one of the local girls."[8]

There is still another difference between the capital city lynchings and those in towns of the interior. In capital cities, one lynching is likely to be followed by another; the lynch incident seems to predispose the local population toward repeating the act. This is not so much the case with lynchings in interior towns. One explanation for this difference is that lynchings in the capital cities manifest and contribute to a broken link in the chain of social relations and respect. These lynchings sever the organizational connection sustaining institutional legitimacy. This contributes to a repetition of extralegal executions.

These differences between lynchings in Brazil's capital cities and in interior towns do not eliminate the similarities between lynchings in these two contexts. Lynching represents a punitive act that denies its victim the right to a judgment about the relative severity of an alleged crime. It also denies the lynch victim an opportunity to pay a penalty short of death. All alleged infractions become equal—whether petty

Table 1.1
Lynchers' Motives for Killing (in percentages)

The Lynched's Alleged Crime	Percentage of Lynchings
Crime against persons (rape, assault, murder)	43.1%
Crime against property alone (robbery, theft, etc.)	32.4
Crime against persons and property (e.g., murder during a robbery)	13.4
Violation of taken-for-granted norms of sociability and reciprocity	8.7
TOTAL	97.6%*

*Percentages do not total 100 due to rounding.

larceny or murder. Lynchers seem to be motivated by their empathy with the original crime victim; they see this person as an impotent object of irreparable harm.

LYNCH MOTIVES

Violence against persons is a principal motivation for lynchers' taking the law into their own hands (Table 1.1). However, the death penalty they impose should not be confused with the one meted out by a court; the latter is based on equivalence—the convict is exchanged for the damage done to another person or to society. Lynchings involve—in the case of alleged crimes against persons—the ad hoc judgment that the perpetrator of a crime was unable to control his desires, hatreds, or ambitions. Such a criminal presumably cannot recognize limits, is unable to live with others, and does not have the right to a state-imposed punishment. This criminal's humanity is taken away by his lynchers.

In the case of lynchings for crimes against property, possession of a stolen object is invested with moral significance. Frequently the victims of robbery and assault are impoverished laborers whose property was stolen while they were at work, or who are forced to pay protection money in order to be free from assault, in their own bairros, especially on payday. The robbery of a small shop owner—a baker or a barkeeper—may give impetus to "people's punishment,"[9] since these merchants are often seen by their neighbors as common working people. Lynch mobs also may form when the customers of local establishments are assaulted.

Lynchers see theft of a poor person's possible gain as a crime against a person, and ultimately against a family's survival. It is not a crime against possession but against being. It is in this sense that we can understand an attempted lynching in an Espírito Santo slum (*favela*), where a resident was taken to be lynched for delivering found money to the police. It turned out that the money was a ransom paid by a wealthy family for the return of its kidnapped child. The bairro inhabitants were prepared to lynch one of their own because they believed the ransom money should have been distributed among the neighborhood poor, instead of being given to the police. The slum dwellers' logic seemed to be that since the ransom money was related to a crime in the first place, and the kidnapping had not been committed by the slum dwellers themselves, the money belonged to the slum. And the wealthy family had already given it up, anyway. The lynchers seemed to question the ethics of the person who returned the money to the police: They saw him as lacking solidarity with the bairro.

We should see lynching as secondary violence. It is violence against some other act that is defined as criminal or violent. Lynching results from the judgment that there are limits to crime and, as contradictory as it may seem, to violence. Lynchers make the moral judgment that some kinds of crime are legitimate, although illegal (e.g., lynching), and others are simply illegitimate. It is the latter, "illegitimate crimes," for which someone is lynched. This lynchers' ethic—that some kinds of violence require counterviolence—is illustrated by a lynching in a poor São Paulo suburb in which a mother took lynch action against her own son. The enraged mother even participated in the lynchers' "victory celebration" held immediately after her son's death. She justified her violence by explaining that her son had mistreated her badly—the boy's negation of their sacred blood link had made him socially dead, even before the lynchers killed him.

At least twenty-two of the lynch incidents reported in this study involved cases where lynch victims were seen as having violated certain fundamental moral principles. The victim's original transgression had broken important social ties, without which, in the lynchers' view, society cannot function. Lynching is justified because the transgressor's original norm-breaking behavior made ongoing social life impossible. An example of how a breach of normative social expectations lies behind lynching is the case of a driver who accidentally ran over someone who was waiting in line for a bus. The driver was lynched because he failed to stop and help the victim. Another example is the previously mentioned attempted lynching in Espírito Santo State, where a slum dweller was attacked by his neighbors because he turned ransom money over to the police instead of distributing it among needy slum dwellers.

Lynching will remain poorly understood as long as its analysis is limited to the summary execution itself. In fact, significant information about lynching can be gleaned from the lynch process and the lynch location. The typical lynching begins with the discovery of an alleged criminal; the next step is pursuit, then stoning, followed by beating and kicking—at times with the victim tied to a post. Sometimes there is also physical mutilation and castration (in the case of sexual crimes) while the victim is still alive. A lynching often ends with burning of the body.

Lynching involves the collective participation of local men, women, and children. A prospective lynch participant can be punished for failing to take part. In a São Paulo bairro, a large group formed—armed with rocks, clubs, and other implements—to search for a man accused of raping several local women. One member of the mob decided not to participate and left for home. Part of the mob attacked the man, shouting, "Lynch him! Lynch him!" The man was rescued by the police.

In Brazil there are documented incidents of a lynch victim's capture and execution being solemnly and ritualistically carried out. In a São Paulo bairro a local resident who had perpetrated a number of crimes against his neighbors was judged by a "people's tribunal." One morning his neighbors, on their way to the bakery, were invited to decide his fate. After some deliberation, this informal "neighborhood court" brought the man to the bakery. There the accused listened to his accusers, was given the floor, and was asked if he wanted to say goodbye to his family. He was offered a last cigarette, then taken into the street and stoned and beaten to death.

There have been similar cases of ritualistic lynchings in metropolitan Rio de Janeiro. One case involved lynchers' leaving their victim's body on a rubbish heap for several days. The local residents who had participated in this lynching gathered daily in silence to view their human garbage; finally, someone made an anonymous call to the police. In another case, a mother begged her neighbors for money to bury her son who had been lynched. The neighbors refused to contribute; they denied this lynch victim a burial. Such a denial is notable in Brazilian culture, where death is believed to transform the deceased's prior status. For example, the *cangaceiros*[10]—social bandits of northeast Brazil—prayed for their victims' souls. They believed that the contradictions of body and soul could be resolved only in death; burial marked the ritual solution to those contradictions.

LYNCHING AS SYMBOLIC EXCLUSION

Lynching violates the symbolic meaning of death in Brazilian culture by denying the victim's body integrity. The dead enter the world of the departed through burial; it is through burial that they confront sin and achieve redemption. The manner in which a lynching takes place, and frequently the treatment of the body, are rites of disfiguration; they preclude death's becoming a passing. More than killing, lynching furthers the victim's damnation; the lynch victim loses his way on the road of the dead. Mutilation forever alienates him from the great moment of "disalienation" that, in the Brazilian belief system, is brought about by resurrection. The lynchings that are carried out by prisoners against child molesters, and the castration of living victims and the burning of their bodies, are declarations of the lynch victim's lack of humanity. They mark the victim's exclusion from the human species.

But this exclusion begins long before the lynching takes place and, frequently, long before the victim is known to the accusers. Some say that lynching is guided by prejudice (for example, against blacks); that it is a way of declaring who is of our social world and who is not, who is accepted and who is a stranger. Prejudice is, in fact, behind lynching. But more is involved than prejudice. Two nineteenth-century lynchings in São Paulo, shortly before the abolition of slavery, are illustrative. One of the victims was a freed black accused of raping a white woman. In this case, prejudice clearly played a part: Rape, particularly the rape of black women by white men, was common at the time without the white male rapist being lynched. Another case involved a white police officer who was attacked in his home by lynchers because he had sheltered and protected runaway slaves. In this incident the officer was lynched because he identified with the interests of people not considered human, thereby negating the interests of his own racial and political group. That police officer was lynched because he violated important taken-for-granted norms. In more recent cases, it is also possible to discover the prejudices that prompt lynch action, as well as the taken-for-granted assumptions that automatically make someone a candidate for lynching.

Even when there is no immediate candidate for lynching, there is still a sketch in the minds of prospective lynchers of the person who "deserves" to be lynched. Both the social image of the prospective lynch victim and the lynching itself occur within a well-defined social universe. This suggests that there are fixed cultural images about the kinds of crime and the categories of people susceptible to lynching. Those people who fall into such a category often find that life hangs by a thread.

What are the Brazilian cultural images that make a person or a crime vulnerable to lynch action? Unfortunately, news reports rarely mention the victim's color. The few cases that give color show a high number of lynch victims to be black and mestizo, but the number is insufficient to arrive at any firm conclusions. More commonly mentioned in newspaper reports is the victim's age. Of the total sample, 56.7 percent of the reports gave some idea of the victim's age. (See Table 1.2.)

The data on age show that the majority of lynch victims are young, suggesting lynch vulnerability for the young. By combining age and

Table 1.2
Lynch Victims by Age (in percentages)

Under 18	15.1%
Up to 20	32.9
Up to 30	78.7
Over 50	4.9

Note: Percentages overlap because of double counting due to vagaries in newspaper reporting.

occupation, we see that young and poor people have the greatest lynch vulnerability. These are the "idle youth." In general, when a lynch victim's occupation is listed, it tends to have "criminal characteristics." Almost half of the lynch victims whose occupations were listed (98 out of 225) were classified as "criminals," "thieves," or "gunmen." In one case, the victim was described as a "carpenter and thief." Among the lynched were several ex-convicts and many unemployed. There were 127 lynch victims with regular employment, although they were in occupations on the fringes of the urban job market, on the margins of what Brazilians themselves classify as work, or at least as respectable work.[11] A number of the other lynch victims were soldiers or civil policemen; one was a soldier's wife.

The lynched were predominantly male. Only 3.3 percent were female; of the thirteen women, usually because they were in an incriminating place (e.g., a brothel) with a man about to be lynched, five were killed and eight were rescued.

An innocent person can become a lynch victim. Of the lynch incidents in this sample, 4.8 percent of the victims were only suspects. Among these suspects, a significant number, although exact figures are difficult to determine, had a history of committing violence against their relatives, neighbors, or acquaintances. The data also show that when people find someone actually committing a crime, the possibility of lynching is intense, with everything—from pursuit to stoning—happening in a matter of minutes. When a lynch victim is rescued by the police and taken to jail, the object of the lynchers' wrath often includes the police and government property. In such cases, lynching takes on an additional social meaning: The lynch act represents a loss of respect for the institutions charged with sentencing and punishment.

The data show that some locations are more "lynch vulnerable" than others. The basic tendency is for lynch incidents to occur outdoors. The least likely lynch locations are, in order, inside vehicles, residences, hospitals, and commercial establishments. In fact, the prospective lynch victim is usually taken from such enclosed places to a street or plaza. In this study, the most usual site for the victim's execution was a street (55.9 percent), although only 29.7 percent of lynchings began on the street; others began in a vacant lot or field.

There seems to be a taken-for-granted assumption among some sectors of the Brazilian public that lynching is not a crime, in part because the collective action takes place in public. Crimes, on the other hand, are committed secretly; they are hidden. Lynching involves public participation and complicity—whether voluntary or not. It is significant that, in this study, the majority of lynch *attempts* occurred during the day (58.1 percent), with an average of 808 participants per attempt. The lynchings that were *actually carried out* took place predominantly at night (62.9 percent), generally with a considerably smaller average number of participants per incident (381). This difference is due to the greater difficulty of carrying out a lynching during the day, occasional police patrolling, and the lyncher's preference for night to hide from himself, as much as from others. Nevertheless, in spite of this tendency for "successful" lynchings to occur under safety of night, the lynchers still conducted them most often out in the open.

CONCLUSIONS

Lynching defines the "stranger" and "strangeness"; it gives definition to the refused and excluded. It is in this sense that lynchings are sociologically important. They expose the narrowing of possibilities for social participation, as well as public institutions' loss of legitimacy. Lynchings do this through the appearance of a legitimated alternative to the rules of law and "reason." In effect, the social contract is broken by a lynching.

Lynching represents a challenge to police legitimacy, the law, and the court system, and even to the official conception of crime and punishment. The socially and culturally interstitial nature of lynching allows participants—immediate ones and Brazilian society itself—to deny the political nature of this political act. In its anonymity, lynching seems to lose its political character. It becomes a common crime.

NOTES

1. *Justiça popular* in the original text, translated here as "people's justice" to avoid confusion about *popular*, meaning "of or pertaining to the common people" in Portuguese.

2. *Classes populares,* in the original text.

3. *Periferia* in the original. For want of a more satisfactory translation, "suburbs" has been used throughout this text. However, one should bear in mind that the *periferia* (literally "periphery" or "outskirts"), unlike North American suburbs, often contain slums in some aspects similar to the decaying inner cities found in the United States.

4. For 2.8 percent the information is inconsistent or there is no indication of what happened.

5. Cf. Maria-Victoria Benevides, "Linchamentos: Violência e justiça popular," in Roberto da Matta et al., *Violência brasilera* (São Paulo: Brasiliense, 1982), pp. 93–117.

6. *Bairro* is Portuguese for barrio.

7. *Justicieros* literally means "justice makers."

8. Flazio Cordiero, "Guerra entre jovens no interior," in *O Estado de S. Paulo*, Feb. 19, 1989, p. 28. See also José María Mayrink, "Briga no carnaval deixa rapaz em estado de coma," in *O Estado de S. Paulo*, Feb. 15, 1989, p. 11.

9. *Punição popular* in the original text.

10. *Congaceiro*, a traditional bandit figure.

11. Students, delivery boys, night watchmen, garbage collectors, handymen, bricklayers, bricklayer's helpers, general laborers, farm workers or squatters, ranch hands, cleaners, maids, circus employees, wandering photographers, waiters, manicurists, prostitutes, and madams.

2
POPULAR RESPONSES AND URBAN VIOLENCE: LYNCHING IN BRAZIL

Maria-Victoria Benevides and
Rosa-Maria Fischer Ferreira

"Catch him!" "Kill him!" "Lynch him!" The young man—a thin, dark mulatto no more than twenty years old—runs frantically down the street. Shoppers have taken off after him because he appeared "suspicious." As the young man is chased down the street, he drops the few things he has taken. The pursuers' shouts attract neighbors and passersby. At that moment, peaceful citizens are transformed into a "community of lynchers." They have become implacable "justice makers." The young man is pummeled, kicked, clubbed, stoned—even women and children take part. The man's pursuers tear off his clothes and tie one end of a rope to his neck; the other end is attached to a horse's tail. The horse gallops off, dragging the hapless victim along the ground. The young boy's body is torn to shreds; he is a victim of "people's justice."[1] The police who finally arrive to take away the body are not able to identify the mutilated lynch victim. The lynchers have a clear conscience about their battered victim: "Bandits must do more than merely die, they must [physically] suffer."

The punitive fury of lynching is far removed from any real desire for "justice." Lynch violence goes far beyond rehabilitative action, as illustrated by the countless lynchings in Brazil in which the victim's body is assaulted with extreme brutality even after death. Many lynch victims are castrated (particularly in cases of suspected rape) and mutilated; others are tortured beyond recognition, the skull often crushed by paving stones.

The above example of lynching illustrates what this chapter labels "anonymous lynch action." These lynchings are usually carried out on the streets of large Brazilian cities by people who are strangers to one another. In contrast with such "anonymous lynchings" are "communal lynchings," which involve participation by a large part of the population of a *bairro* or small city. The crime allegedly committed by the lynch victim generates very broad popular mobilization. Communal lynchings are highly ritualized; there is a degree of coordination, with leadership and a certain degree of planning.

In one communal lynching, in the small Brazilian city of Matão, a large number of residents pulled their young lynch victim from the court and strung him up in the public plaza. The lynchers are said not to have shown the slightest vestige of remorse or pity. For the townspeople—even those who did not take part in the lynching—"the young man's death represented no less than an act of justice." The naturalness with which residents witnessed the lynchers' violence was so disturbing that it frightened even the police commissioner.[2]

While it can be said that in Brazil lynchings occur more frequently among the lower classes,[3] where lynchers and the lynched live in the same misery and marginality, it must be recognized that lynching also takes place in middle-class neighborhoods, in prosperous cities of São Paulo State, and in otherwise tranquil rural communities. In fact, a large portion of Brazil's upper and middle classes defend lynching and the death squads. In 1980 research by the Brazilian Institute of Public Opinion (IBOPE) revealed that 44 percent of the respondents supported lynching, on the grounds that "if the courts don't act, the people must." At times, lynching is even justified by the authorities.

There is substantial evidence in Brazil of generalized support for lynching. One 1981 letter to the editor of a Rio de Janeiro newspaper complained:

> The criminal commits all of the crimes imaginable, including murder, and frequently no investigation is made (pleading lack of police manpower, means of transport, gasoline, etc.). Nevertheless, when people, tired of being treated so badly, take justice into their own hands through lynching, a patrol car almost always arrives to "save" the pervert. Why don't the police ever show up when a citizen is being attacked?[4]

This is not an isolated example of public support for lynching. In November 1979, TV Globo[5] received thousands of letters responding to a segment on the Sunday news show "Fantástico." Of the 4,194 letters, 810 (19 percent) explicitly supported lynching, and more than half defended such parallel justice as lynching and death squads.[6]

There is also support for lynching among police officials. A Rio de Janeiro police commissioner proclaimed that "Lynchings make the bandits see that they do not own the streets" and that lynching "doesn't mean creating justice with a hatred of criminals, but with love for their victims."[7] A police commissioner in Rio's Baixada Fluminense district declared, "To kill a worker is appalling, but if it is the police who kill a criminal, I look the other way."[8] São Paulo's former secretary of public security, Octávio Gonzaga Júnior, declared, "We have no choice. Whatever happens, we are going to fight violence with violence, because there is no other way."[9]

In Brazil lynching is not as commonplace as either police violence against prisoners or the systematic deaths of criminals in alleged shootouts with the police. But it is sociologically just as important as these phenomena. It must be seen as part and parcel of economic marginalization, another structurally rooted form of contemporary urban violence. The economically marginalized are exposed to the daily violence of unemployment, malnutrition, precarious housing, and inadequate health and transportation services. They have a disbelief in police effectiveness and court "justice," and are exposed to police violence. The victims of police violence utlimately incorporate such violence in their own justice making.

This chapter analyzes lynching in Brazil. Lynching is the most extreme expression of collective popular violence.[10] The research reported here is the first phase of a broader study of urban violence in Brazil focusing on citizens' rights and the types of violence experienced by the lower classes.[11]

The first step in this study is to establish the extent of lynching in Brazil, its immediate historical causes, and the forms of popular participation in it. This will help us understand lynching; it also will facilitate a reconstruction of the social contexts for lynching. The data will allow us to identify differences between lynchings carried out by a conscious community (communal lynching) and those committed by strangers to one another (anonymous lynch action). We do not distinguish in this analysis between lynchings where the victim actually dies and attempted lynchings. Both are taken together because they can be seen as forming a single behavioral phenomenon.

This chapter also seeks to analyze, in a preliminary way, relations between the popular classes and the police. We hope that this will make understandable the reasons that many poor Brazilians have little faith in official legal and political institutions, and bring to light the reasons for those classes' reliance on parallel systems of justice.

BACKGROUND

The most commonly accepted interpretation of lynching takes us to Charles Lynch, a Virginia plantation owner and leader of a band of "justice makers" who punished common criminals and British loyalists during the American Revolution. Historically, such informal organizations for the prevention and repression of crime have been described as lynch mobs. These groups, which set themselves up as substitutes for, or as complements to, legal proceedings are systems of parallel justice. Some historical examples of parallel justice are the medieval German *Fahmgerechte*, the "gibbet law" and Cowper's justice in England, the Sociedades de Santa Hermanidad of small medieval Spanish communities, Russian and Polish pogroms, and the Nazi persecution of Jews, Gypsies, homosexuals, leftists, and the handicapped. Another example of parallel justice is the lynching of blacks in South Africa, and in the United States by the Ku Klux Klan. In fact, in the United States between 1882 and 1951, there were 4,730 reported lynchings—90 percent of the victims were black. Since the 1950s the median number of lynchings in the United States has been one a year, and other murders for racial reasons also continue.[12]

In popular language, lynching means "to take justice into your own hands." In general, lynching has come to designate all collective violent action for summary punishment of those accused of a crime. The crime can be as simple as theft or as serious as murder. In certain regions of Brazil, lynching has been a reaction to political and racial movements or to a perceived stigma attached to race. Lynchings are characterized by revenge; they are punitive justice generally accompanied by torture. Lynching occurs outside the framework of a judicial trial and other legal norms. A curiosity about lynching is that even when it has clear leadership and planning, it is still considered explosive and spontaneous; it is often associated with a "mass pathology."

LYNCHING IN BRAZIL

In Brazil lynching is much less frequent than death squad carnage or "legal" killings by police patrols. Lynchings, in fact, do not seem to cause a great deal of public scandal. They are part of daily violence in Brazil, the major tragedy of which lies in its banality. Lynchings are sporadic: They attract authorities' attention, and that of the major press, only when a mob includes large numbers of people (e.g., the majority of a big-city suburb, a small city, or a country town), particularly when the population of lynchers is otherwise thought to be "peaceful, orderly, and religious." It is when such a population, armed with knives, clubs, and rocks, cries "Catch him," "Kill him," "Lynch him," that Brazilian authorities and the press become aroused.

The lack of systematic data on lynching in Brazil, or even explicit references to it in studies of violence and crime, is notable. In the 1980 *Special Report on Urban Violence* of the Brazilian Ministry of Justice, there are only two brief references to lynching. In the sociologists' report in that same volume, there is only one reference to it, associating lynching with community size.

The data for our study are lynch incidents reported in Brazilian newspapers and newsweeklies during the four-year period 1979–1982. Five Rio de Janeiro and São Paulo newspapers and three Brazilian newsweeklies were consulted.[13] According to these sources, there were eighty-two lynch incidents between 1979 and 1982: thirty-eight fatal lynchings and forty-four attempts. It is important to remember that in the period between 1969 and 1979, only forty-one lynchings were reported for Rio de Janeiro.[14]

A close examination of the eighty-two lynch incidents for the 1979–1982 period disclosed some interesting information:

—The majority of reported lynchings took place in urban areas of São Paulo and Rio de Janeiro. There were fewer reported lynchings in rural areas.

—Rio de Janeiro had the most reported lynchings, with twenty-three cases in Baixada Fluminense, a large, poor suburban region on the outskirts of the city. There were six lynchings in Rio's central district, and nine in the rest of greater Rio de Janeiro.

—Only two reported lynchings took place in urban slums.

—There were seven lynchings in São Paulo city outskirts, four in the central district, and eight in rural regions of São Paulo State.

—Taxi drivers constituted the occupational group most involved in lynchings.

—The apparent reason for the majority of lynchings was assault—on people, residences, or commercial establishments.

—The monetary amount or value attached to something was not always a good predictor of whether lynching would occur. Some lynchings resulted from minor thefts—a cheap radio or small amount of food from a supermarket. Other lynchings were responses to rape, murder, or armed robbery.

—Of the eighty-two reported lynchings, in only fifteen had the lynch victim murdered someone or committed an armed robbery.

—Sexual violence against women or children constituted an important stimulus for lynching. Sexual violence was often the stimulus in cases where a whole community became involved in a lynching.

—In seven lynch incidents, the lynchers seized a police station or court building in order to capture their victim from the police. In three of these invasions, the lynching was subsequently carried out.

—In nine lynch incidents the victim of the lynching had been officially judged innocent of the crime for which he was lynched.

—The majority of lynch victims were poor people accused of thievery. These impoverished victims ranged in age from eleven to fifteen.

—In several lynch incidents the mutilated victims could not be identified; they were buried as anonymous indigents in a potter's field.

—Of the eighty-two reported lynch incidents, police inquests had not closed even one case as of 1982.

WHY DO BRAZILIANS LYNCH?

This analysis of press reports of lynching suggests several generalizations about the social perceptions that lead to lynching. Let us first discuss how a population's image of the police and the courts establishes a seedbed for lynching. Rio's Baixada Fluminense district, scene of barbaric activities of death squads, holds the record for reported lynchings. The misery and the political, social, and economic marginality that characterize much of this district are well known. Percival de Souza[15] explains the high rate of lynching there in these terms: There is total police disinterest in small thefts, and there are ample opportunities for private revenge. If the lack of police action against crime seems ridiculous to those who live outside Baixada Fluminense, it is even more ridiculous to Baixada residents who, therefore, do not overlook opportunities for revenge. Lynchings and beatings have become commonplace in Baixada Fluminense.

The most famous lynching incident in Baixada Fluminense occurred in 1970, when residents of its Morro Agudo lynched an insane old man who roamed the bairro streets. The man was tied to a post and severely beaten. He died on the post. There was another lynching in Morro Agudo: Residents who were dissatisfied with an astrologer's predictions (and with his flirting with bairro women) lynched their slum's fortuneteller.[16]

Many lynchings in Brazil seem to be related to a generalized fear and malaise. Significant portions of the Brazilian population live in fear—there is reference to "an hallucinatory climate," "people are in panic," or "there is collective paranoia." Wealthy Brazilians who experience such fear and malaise can hire private security guards. This is clearly not a possibility for poor people, who must devise their own defense against theft, assault, and sexual abuse. As one Baixada Fluminense resident explained, "We have to create justice with our own weapons, and all we have are hoes, sickles, mason's axes, and rakes."[17]

In Brazil, poor people defend themselves with vigilante posses; some women in poor bairros have set up "neighborhood watches" to accompany their husbands and children to bus stops. In poor slums it is commonplace to pay protection money to guard women against sexual abuse. In fact, the lack of police protection for women generates extreme disgust toward the police. It is common for authorities to tell distraught parents of a poor, sexually victimized woman that "the police have no time to defend your daughter."[18]

Rape provides a powerful motivation for lynching. But there are other motives as well. In fact, different combinations of motives are associated with different lynch responses. Let us examine these.

ANONYMOUS LYNCH ACTION AND COMMUNAL LYNCHINGS

Anonymous Lynch Action

The report of social scientists[19] does not explicitly recognize "anonymous lynch action," although the data in that report point to the existence of this type of lynching. In anonymous lynch actions, the lynchers act individually, not as a community, in carrying out the lynching. Such lynchings are almost exclusively urban. The origins of anonymous lynch action are practically unknown. This lynching is usually initiated by cries of "catch the thief" after an alleged criminal act has taken place. Following are some examples of anonymous lynch action.

Downtown São Paulo. It is a busy street at high noon.[20] A pickpocket goes into action. The group of citizens who see him become so violent that the thief's victim protects him from the angry mob until the police arrive. The thief is tubercular and epileptic, a former ward of Brazil's State Foundation for the Well-Being of Minors.[21]

Downtown Rio de Janeiro. A criminal wounded in a shoot-out with the police is pursued by passersby who observed the shoot-out. In addition to trying to lynch the wounded man, the mob attempts to snatch, presumably in order to lynch him, too, another criminal from the police van.

A Busy Urban Street. A taxi driver abandons his cab in the middle of the street and grabs a man in police custody. The taxi driver then beats and kicks the suspected criminal. What this cabbie did not know is that his presumed criminal had just been saved by firemen from committing suicide. The taxi driver explained his behavior to the police: "I've been robbed so many times, I swore that if I got my hands on a thief, I would kill him."[22]

Rio de Janeiro's Central District. Passersby, seeing a poorly dressed young boy standing "suspiciously near a bicycle," grabbed the luckless fellow and tied him to a tree. The police arrived in time to stop the lynching; they proved the suspect's innocence—the bicycle was his own.[23]

São Paulo's Business District. There was a near lynching of an actor who was filming a soap opera scene on São Paulo's fashionable Paulista Avenue. The realistic scenes of this "pickpocket's" assault were taken so seriously by passersby that they began kicking and beating the young actor.[24]

These lynchings reveal two things about anonymous lynch action in Brazil. First, such lynchings occur in social settings outside slums, which are most commonly thought of as scenes of violence. Second, the lynch incidents resulted from the action of anonymous individuals. We can contrast these anonymous lynch actions with what we label "communal lynchings."

Communal Lynchings

These lynchings result from the collective action of people who, in one way or another, besides not trusting the police or courts, deeply feel that "the criminal has to suffer more than [just] death." The Baixada Fluminense lynchings discussed earlier are manifestations of communal lynching; some claim that they represent collective hysteria.

In a communal lynching in the small Brazilian city of Macaè, a large number of townspeople invaded the police station, kidnapped a prisoner accused of sexual violence against a great many women, and lynched and mutilated him. The police commissioner was able to find no fewer than twenty-seven persons who admitted to having participated in the lynching, including women and children. Some of the rape victims went to the police station in a show of support for the lynchers, who were released five days later. No charges were brought against the lynchers.[25] They were respectable residents of the region—carpenters, fishermen, mechanics, and day laborers. Their class origins were very similar to that of the twenty-one-year-old boy they had lynched.

Data in the social scientists' report suggest that in some lynchings there is a "homogeneous and identifiable community behind the lynch action"; such lynchings challenge formal legal structures, representing a demand for "justice that was not forthcoming." Our own data suggest that these communal lynchings occur only in small cities or in contained neighborhoods like bairros, not on city streets where passersby are strangers to one another.

A central feature of communal lynchings is that they manifest strong popular distrust of the judicial system. In some communal lynchings, the lynchers assume the role of police, judge, and executioner. For example, in the lynching of a "pickpocket" by taxi drivers in the city of Curitiba, the cabbies undertook their own "investigations," then "tried," "convicted," tortured, and killed their suspect. The revenge-seeking cabbies hanged their victim—already dead—from a street light.[26] The supposed thief was later shown to have been innocent.

In another example of communal lynching, a fifteen-year-old boy, a former ward of the Brazilian State Foundation for the Well-Being of Minors (FEBEM), was accused of several assaults, armed robberies, and the murder of a bar owner. The boy was lynched by outraged members of the community, who declared: "It [is] the best thing we have done here." "God should help those folks who kill bandits." "We did a good job of cleaning up."[27] The young boy's lynching was preceded by a symbolic punitive ritual: Relatives of the murdered bar owner forced the accused killer to attend the bar owner's funeral service, after which they lynched him. The lynchers then chartered a bus and delivered the victim's body to the police station, where it was presented to the police.

EXPLANATIONS FOR LYNCHING

Most press explanations for lynching are general; they can be categorized into several different sets of theories about lynching:

—Lynching results from lack of access by the lower class to social and political power.
—Lynching grows out of popular disbelief in the effectiveness of the police and the courts, due to perceived police disinterest or even involvement in criminal activity.
—Lynching grows out of the feeling that there is one law for the poor and another for the rich. This feeling contributes to a popular desire to rectify radical inequities in the application of law.
—Lynching represents an imitation of violent police methods by criminals, and by the people who suffer both criminal and police violence.
—Lynching is a natural consequence of extreme repression and arbitrariness at various levels of Brazilian society.

Legal professionals agree with some of these press explanations for lynching. Of particular importance is public disbelief in the effectiveness of the police and courts. Research conducted in 1980 by the Gallup Institute revealed that a a large majority of Brazilians who had been assaulted in Rio de Janeiro and São Paulo did not report such attacks to the police. This failure to report crime is a clear vote of no confidence in police effectiveness. Another contributor to lynching is disrespect for the law, which begins with the government itself and develops into an accentuated public distrust of authority.

THE POLICE, URBAN CRIME, AND VIOLENCE

The press and Brazilian authorities recognize that large segments of the population lack confidence in the courts and in public security agencies. We must discover how such perceptions have come about. Such an examination necessarily begins with an analysis of urban violence in Brazil. In order to place urban violence within the context of Brazilian cities, we must initially distinguish criminal violence (robberies, murder, physical assaults) from violence that characterizes the living conditions of Brazil's lowest-income groups. It is the latter structural violence that does the most physical, mental, and social harm to those subjected to it on a daily basis. This violence of daily life is rooted in Brazil's socio-economic structure. But what about criminal violence?

There is a public consensus in Brazil that in São Paulo and Rio de Janeiro crime has increased since the 1970s. This is widely explained by sociologists, modernization theorists, criminologists, and policymakers as due to the population explosion. The latter is caused by accelerated urbanization, due particularly to a quantitative growth in the number of poor and unattached people. But an analysis of the presumed relationship between urbanization and crime has been generalized into an unparticularized and superficial thesis that is applied to every capitalist metropolis.

According to David Gordon, writing about urban crime in the United States, this generalization is not based on quantitative data.[28] In fact, in the United States the proportion of urban street crime is small compared with all crime. The state, however, influences perceptions about crime through public disclosures about it. Public information about crime comes from police and juridical sources. These focus almost exclusively on the "index crimes" of murder, assault and battery, and nonwhite-collar crimes against property.

But much is left out of such public information about crime. Gordon observes that even official statistics on homicide in the United States record only one-twelfth of all violent deaths; the probability of an individual's being murdered by an unknown assailant is 50 percent less than being murdered by someone known to the victim. And frequently omitted are the crimes of major relevance in terms of their economic impact—financial fraud and the business activities of organized crime. These are not usually the object of official statistics and public disclosure. The state gives priority to crimes against property and persons. It is these that provide the basis for theorizing about the "dangers" of large urban cities and the behavior of the poor populations who live in them.

These facts of official crime reporting are equally observable in Brazil. Helena P. de Melo Jorge[29] found that between 1960 and 1975 there was a 290 percent increase in murders. During that same period, deaths from traffic accidents went up 455 percent. In Brazil the second most frequent cause of death is accidents, of which 30 percent occur at work, primarily at construction sites. Yet police activity in Brazil focuses predominantly on crimes against property.

In April 1981 there were 1,875 reported thefts in greater São Paulo, only 11 of which (much less than 1 percent) resulted in the victim's death. Data from Belo Horizonte for the period 1960–1970 indicate that nonviolent crimes against property grew twice as fast as crimes against persons.[30] But in Brazil, violent urban crime is the great fear.

In fact, the amount of urban crime in Brazil cannot be identified directly by official statistics; such figures reflect only a portion of all crime. And violence cannot be measured only quantitatively: Evaluations about violence must take into account the perceptions of victims and observers.

This brings us to two related questions: Who makes up Brazil's criminal population, and how do the formal institutions of society control and interact with that population? First, the population that is practically the exclusive object of police control is the lower class, the people who live in precarious socioeconomic conditions. The task of police is to repress popular social movements; such movements are always a possibility among those who are exploited. The social conditions in which they live are shaped by social discrimination and class domination.

In Brazil, the presumed relationship among misery, crime, and violence has come to justify arbitrary police repression—torture and the large-scale, heavily armed police dragnets and searches of working-class bairros and slums. The sweeping police arrests "solve" crimes by arbitrarily selecting from a broad base of possible criminal suspects (in practice the greater part of the urban population) those who could "realistically" be claimed to have committed a crime (e.g., the poor). This stigmatizing of the poor by public officials has been taken up by the larger population. This leads it to support police arbitrariness.

The poor victims of such abusive police practices recognize that these police procedures are ineffective in guaranteeing community security. This often provokes popular reactions of disgust, dramatically exemplified by lynchings.

The only real effect of this contradictory and conflictive relationship between police and the people is police terror, a terror that represses personal or collective expression and places each isolated citizen at the mercy of the institutional apparatus. The means employed by the state to control social participation lead citizens—principally, though not only, from the economically neediest sectors—to consider social and political institutions to be superior and external to themselves. Such institutions are seen as impermeable to individual or collective intervention. This represents a condition of maximal social and conceptual distance—in thought or action—between the citizen and the state.

The daily experience in Brazil of inequality and oppression strengthens citizen isolation and vulnerability. Many Brazilians are pressed to the limits of their ability to resist fear and insecurity by the internalization of stigma and by structural impediments to their exercise of civil rights. Lynchings represent moments in which citizens' feelings of impotence and rage reach a peak.

NOTES

This chapter originally appeared as Maria-Victoria Benevides and Rosa-Maria Fischer Ferreira, "Respostas populares e violência urbana: O caso de linchamento no Brasil," in *Crime, violência e poder*, ed. Paulo Sérgio Pinheiro (São Paulo: Brasiliense, 1983). Reprinted by permission.

1. *Justiça popular* in the original text, translated here as "people's justice."
2. *Jornal da República*, November 23, 1979.
3. *Meios populares* in the original.
4. *Jornal do Brasil*, January 16, 1981.
5. TV Globo is Brazil's largest television network.
6. *Jornal da República*, December 12, 1979.
7. Commissioner Waldemar de Castro, *Jornal do Brasil*, August 22, 1980.
8. *Jornal do Brasil*, June 22, 1981. Baixada Fluminense is a large and poor suburban region inside the State of Rio de Janeiro, on the periphery of Rio de Janeiro City.
9. *O Estado de São Paulo*, January 17, 1981.
10. Disturbances such as attacking trains are also forms of collective popular violence with components analogous to lynching.
11. Ongoing research at CEDEC is coordinated by the authors, with financial support from the Ford Foundation and the Comité Catholique de France.
12. There is an ample bibliography on lynchings in the 1920s and 1930s in the United States. Several associations against lynching were founded. There is also a well-documented history of efforts to combat lynching. For example, in the United States an anti-lynching law was enacted. The Commission of Southern Women for the Prevention of Lynching stands out as an organization against lynching. See "Lynching: A National Crime," in *Catholic World*, 127 (1920).
13. The following newspapers were examined: *O Estado de São Paulo, Jornal do Brasil, Folha de São Paulo, Jornal da Tarde*, and *Jornal da República*, along with the weekly magazines *Isto É, Vêja*, and *Movimento*.
14. Ibid.
15. Percival de Souza, *A maior violência do mundo* (São Paulo: Editora Traço, 1980), p. 51.
16. Ibid.
17. *Vêja*, October 31, 1979.
18. *Movimento*, October 27, 1981.
19. Brazilian Ministry of Justice, *Special Report on Urban Violence* (1980).
20. *O Estado de São Paulo*, January 18, 1980.
21. The State Foundation for the Well-Being of Minors (FEBEM) functions more as a reformatory and warehouse for abandoned children than as a social welfare agency.
22. *Isto É*, October 31, 1979.
23. *Jornal do Brasil*, August 25, 1980.
24. *Folha de São Paulo*, October 21, 1980.
25. *Jornal do Brasil*, August 16, 1980.
26. *Isto É*, October 31, 1979.
27. *Folha de São Paulo*, October 21, 1980.
28. David M. Gordon, "Crime," in *Problems in Political Economy: An Urban Perspective*, ed. David M. Gordon (Lexington, Mass.: Heath, 1977).
29. M. Helena P. de Melo Jorge, "Mortalidade por causas violentas em São

Paulo," Ph. D. dissertation, School of Public Health, University of São Paulo, 1979.

30. Antonio Luiz Paixão, "Crimes e criminosos em Belo Horizonte: Uma exploràçao inicial das estatísticas officias de criminalidade", unpublished internal paper, João Pinheiro Foundation (1981).

3
POLICE, PEOPLE, AND PREEMPTION IN ARGENTINA

Laura Kalmanowiecki

Coercion has played a central role in the development of modern states. As Charles Tilly points out, during the long history of state formation, the lines between "legitimate" and "illegitimate" violence were often so elastic that banditry, piracy, policing, and making war belonged on the same continuum. Like racketeers, states created the threat and then, at a price, provided protection against it. If states were not labeled racketeers, it was because their authority was sanctioned as legitimate. This legitimacy is what distinguishes public violence from crime. In the long run, governments succeeded in monopolizing the means of violence within their territories. Eventually this process of state formation led to the "civilianization" of governments and their domestic politics: Coercive state power became contained and constrained by civil bureaucracies and legislatures.[1]

This chapter focuses on a December 31, 1989, rebellion against the police in Tres Arroyos, Argentina. Tres Arroyos is a provincial town of 55,000, 350 miles south of Buenos Aires. The uprising at Tres Arroyos reminds us that "it is not absolutely foreclosed and prescribed that people will lose every contest with power."[2] Moreover, it indicates that people are not inevitably quiescent in the face of abuses of state power. The rebellion at Tres Arroyos—a rural town located in the heartland of Argentina's richest agricultural region—ignited a series of protests throughout Buenos Aires Province; it brought about changes in police organization and eroded not only police impunity from prosecution but also their self-image as above the law.

In Argentina it is not always possible to distinguish the police from common criminals: The frontiers between agents of order and its transgressors are often fuzzy. Police practices in Argentina reveal how easy it is to cross the boundaries between "legitimate" and "illegitimate" violence. The events related in this chapter dramatically demonstrate that the analogy between states and organized crime fits our time.

ARGENTINA'S DEMOCRATIC TRANSITION

The return to civilian government in Argentina was by no means synonymous with the "civilianization of power,"[3] even after free national elections were held, first in 1983 and again in 1989. The elections taught us that democratization of power is not equivalent to democratizing government institutions and the state. Argentina's democratic reconstruction will require containment of the repressive tactics blatantly established during eight years (1976–1983) of military dictatorship. True democratization involves bringing the state's coercive apparatus under public accountability.

Democracy remains fragile and precarious in Argentina. It is continuously threatened by a coup; the laws allow military intervention for "internal commotion," and there are social and economic crises associated with hyperinflation.[4] But democratic institutions are not only blackmailed by the military, they are also undermined by police behavior that, long after the demise of authoritarian rule, continues to be secretive and clandestine. Given that the police learned long ago to disregard the law, one of the crucial tasks of state democratization has been to check police violence and redefine the institutional role of the police. It was an illusion to think that, with the advent of democracy,[5] the police would by themselves cease illegal activities.

The Tres Arroyos uprising must be understood in the context of this democratization process and in light of Argentina's recent violent past.

TRES ARROYOS: THE PEOPLE SPEAK

At 8:30 P.M. on New Year's Eve, 1989, Liliana Fuentes went to Tres Arroyos's Police Station Number 1 to declare that her nine-year-old daughter, Nair, had not returned from an afternoon trip to a swimming club. Even though the desperate woman explained to the police that she had been looking for her daughter for hours, they refused to do anything. They turned the problem back on Mrs. Fuentes: "Do you know how your daughter behaves?" asked one policeman, in a manner reminiscent of a recent past in which the security forces were obsessed by young people's subversive potential.[6] At 10 P.M., still not knowing the whereabouts of her little girl, Mrs. Fuentes returned to the police station, imploring a patrolman parked in front of the station for help. His response was, "Madam, we are celebrating now, come back later." This was the fourth time that Mrs. Fuentes had asked the police for help.[7]

When Mrs. Fuentes could not get the police to look for her little girl, she asked Evaristo Alonso, director and owner of LU 24, the local radio station, to appeal to the people of Tres Arroyos for help. Alonso's plea ignited a massive popular protest. It made public Mrs. Fuentes's private, individual drama.

Perhaps not foreseeing the consequences of his action, Alonso put his radio station at the service of what would suddenly become a collective act of state defiance. The people of Tres Arroyos, many of whom had on their radios for the New Year's celebration, heard Alonso's appeal. They left their dwellings to search for the missing girl. Alonso promptly organized a search. In less than ten minutes, the residents had found the missing child: She had been raped and strangled to death near the railroad tracks—just seven blocks from her home. It was estimated that Nair's death had occurred at 10:30 that evening, two hours after her mother had first reported her missing. The police had had ample time to rescue the little girl.[8]

Nair's dead body ignited a violent reaction among the townspeople. Alonso got into an argument with Subchief of Police Norberto Sosa at the murder scene. Sosa blamed Alonso for the public disturbance, charging that Alonso had incited the people by calling them together. Fearing that they would be lynched, Sosa and his two policemen fled the murder scene; their car was burned. The crowd then moved to the Municipal Building, where it demanded the immediate removal of Tres Arroyos police superiors and the municipal *intendente*.[9] Over 1,000 people eventually gathered around the Tres Arroyos police station; they threw stones and broke windows. The crowd denounced the police as "bribe-takers, thieves, killers." The police, who were no longer sober after their New Year's Eve celebration, attacked the crowd with tear gas and plastic bullets; shots were fired into the crowd. The intendente was almost wounded trying to subdue the police.

Before the uprising at the Municipal Building had ended, more than fourteen police cars had been turned upside down and burned. By 6 A.M. New Year's Day, the tension had decreased, thanks to the efforts of the council members and judges who mediated between the police and the people. But within four hours the police–citizen confrontation had erupted again. This time police from neighboring cities were called in. Within twenty hours the city had been turned into a police garrison.

The *puebleada*, as the Tres Arroyos uprising was called, left twenty-seven wounded (nineteen from gunfire); twenty cars were burned (police cars or cars in police custody). The uprising resulted in replacement of the town's entire police force. Provincial authorities eventually attempted to transfer Tres Arroyos police to other towns. These transfers were rejected.

On Tuesday, January 2, 1990, two days after the Tres Arroyos uprising had begun, the people were still incensed: They booed angrily when Provincial Governor Antonio Cafiero proposed, in an attempt to calm them, that council members and a commission of neighbors elect a new chief of police. Tres Arroyos residents summarily rejected this proposal on the grounds that they did not know enough about police work to select a police chief. The City Council later concurred that choosing a chief of police was not its job. At the same time, the people questioned the proposal to appoint Ramón Venancio Vega as the town's new chief of police. His past, they alleged, made him untrustworthy. In the end it was decided that the Municipal Council and a commission of Tres Arroyos residents would draw up a list of three candidates for police chief; the provincial government would then appoint a person from this list.[10]

POLICE CORRUPTION

For the people of Tres Arroyos, the violent uprising had grown out of police corruption, especially after Chief of Police Carlos Fusco had assumed responsibility for the police station.[11] Indeed, the Tres Arroyos police were involved in all kinds of criminality: clandestine banking, prostitution, thefts of cattle and cars, and drug trafficking.[12] In the period immediately following the Tres Arroyos uprising, more than 350 testimonies to police corruption were presented to prosecutors. These testimonies brought to light a good deal of police involvement in corruption and racketeering. For example, in January 1986 the police failed to solve a murder involving charges against the son of a powerful local landowner. In a subsequent case a police patrol car had been seen parked one mile from a burglarized house, suggesting that those police were in league with the burglers. In a third suspicious case, a man who had been robbed had to pay the police to investigate the alleged crime.

Citizen disgust at police corruption had actually come to a head eight months before the *puebleada* when LU 24, the Tres Arroyos radio station, and the daily newspaper, *La voz del pueblo*, launched a campaign against it. Just four months before the uprising, in August 1989, 400 Tres Arroyos neighbors presented a petition of public insecurity to the provincial deputy that denounced Tres Arroyos's police for involvement in cattle rustling, farm thefts, and the stealing of telephone lines.[13] A Council of Neighborhood Security was set up to investigate these allegations. Thus, there is no doubt that Tres Arroyos authorities had ample knowledge about police corruption. At the same time, no official action was taken until it was too late.[14] For the people of Tres Arroyos, the rape and murder of nine-year-old Nair Fuentes, and police unwillingness to respond to her mother's pleas for help, were the last straw.

In the face of police unwillingness to search for Nair, Tres Arroyos residents took collective action. But this was out of character for them. Tres Arroyos residents had always liked to think of themselves as "moderates"; they were proud of their respect for order and authority. New Year's Eve 1989 became the unexpected beginning of a new age for Tres Arroyos.

DISSENT AND ACCUSATIONS

Argentina's national authorities did not anticipate Tres Arroyos's violent reaction and, understandably, were alarmed by the uprising. By taking justice into their own hands, the people of Tres Arroyos had rejected the state's monopoly over violence and justice; they had, in the words of Argentina's minister of the interior, Julio Mera Figueroa, violated a "basic principle of Western civilization, which is not to do justice with one's own hands."[15]

The successful action carried out by Tres Arroyos residents against the police was contagious. Mass protests spread rapidly, although less violently, to several other provincial towns. There, local police also were accused of corruption and laziness. In San Vicente, a town of 20,000 people about 35 miles from Buenos Aires, the police chief was removed after a crowd of several hundred disrupted a council meeting to protest the police. The San Vicente police had caused public outrage by taking high school girls to the station on charges of boisterous conduct and forcing them to take off their clothes. The people of San Vicente also were incensed about police racketeering—the police were charging fees to prevent cattle theft and were failing to investigate crimes.[16] There was similar unrest over the quality of police services in at least two other towns in Buenos Aires Province: Médanos and General Alvear. In Médanos, the police chief denounced the president of the Chamber of Commerce as a "bomb-thrower."[17]

In Argentina, public authorities were so accustomed to dismissing the complaints of poor people that the authorities failed to recognize early enough that this protest was different. This time, the challenge was not from poor, starving people who were looting grocery stores in order to survive. On the contrary, the protesters were upper-middle-class rural dwellers and urban merchants.

The provincial governor's representative saw the Tres Arroyos uprising as "a product of the general moral and social crisis that Argentina is experiencing because of [its] grave economic crisis." The governor's short-term solution was for the people of Tres Arroyos to elect their own police chief. This reflects political authorities' shortsightedness about the ability of legal and administrative mechanisms to assist in conflict management.

"GOOD" PEOPLE RISE UP

The people who participated in collective action in Tres Arroyos were astonished by their behavior. Such action would have been unimaginable some hours earlier. They were obsessed with maintaining their self-image as moderates. They did not want their behavior misunderstood, even though some hours earlier they had dared to burn cars. In reports on the uprising, the people of Tres Arroyos were emphatic that "no activists [had] participated [in it]." They explained, "We are not savages who dedicate ourselves to burning cars." Indeed, this seems to be true: According to witnesses, it took the residents more than twenty minutes to burn a car, because they did not know how to do it. Only police property was damaged.[18]

Both Alonso and the director of *La voz del pueblo* reasoned that since no looting had occurred during the protest, it was safe to conclude that there had been "no professional agitators present."[19] As for the radio station director, this was the first time in twenty years that he had personally taken an issue or problem to the public. No one could accuse Alonso's radio station of being manipulated by left-wing forces: During the period of military rule it had never even referred to the twenty-five Tres Arroyos residents who had disappeared, among them the son of Jorge Foulkes, who in 1983 became intendente of Tres Arroyos.

The people of Tres Arroyos were shocked and frightened by what they had done. They had always subscribed to a Hobbesian pact because of their fear of "societal chaos," symbolized by people gathering together and, even worse, making claims on the state and its authorities.[20] The people of Tres Arroyos had usually preferred to disengage themselves from any kind of direct confrontation and mass mobilization. This time, however, they took over the streets and challenged the authorities.

The Tres Arroyos protest involved people who had previously found certain levels of state violence acceptable, or at least tolerable. What made them rebel against the state this time? The experience of authoritarian rule was still present in their collective memories—vaguely glowing in some and burning fiercely in others. How was it possible for these ordinary people to lose their fear of the state and its repressive apparatus? How was it possible for them to overcome their depoliticized modus vivendi—"Do not bother, it is none of your business"—and directly confront the police, an "armed extension of the state in the street"?[21]

WHY THE PEOPLE REBELLED

The rape, torture, and murder of young Nair Fuentes was the catalyst that triggered the collective outburst in Tres Arroyos. The Tres Arroyos uprising was a community protest. The people knew each other, and there were solidarity networks among them. It is worth pointing out that ten years prior to the Tres Arroyos uprising, there was a popular protest there against an increase in electric tariffs. This protest was directed against municipal authorities. The loss of a neighbor's child reinforced the bond of solidarity that existed among the residents. This bond gave them the strength to do the unthinkable: to strike out against the state forces that had deprived Liliana Fuentes of her only daughter through their laziness and arrogance. By disregarding Mrs. Fuentes's plea for her daughter's safety, the police struck a blow at the child's right to life. This made the community see that no one's life was safe.

The people of Tres Arroyos suddenly found themselves able to "break the law" through an extraordinary act of defiance against local authorities. Their mass protest erupted both as a reaction and as a defense against police abuses. In fact, the Tres Arroyos uprising combined a negative evaluation of the police with a strong demand for "law and order"—for *more* "police protection."[22] The people denounced police misbehavior and demanded an honest police force and the restoration of order. The Tres Arroyos uprising was a reactive collective protest against police who had consistently violated citizens' established rights; it was a local issue fought by local people.[23] Clearly, the people of Tres Arroyos would have preferred a more peaceful means of reclaiming their rights, but such alternative means had been shown to be ineffective. The unwillingness of authorities to listen to the people's continuous denunciations of police misbehavior forced Tres Arroyos residents to engage in collective protest.

While some participants in the Tres Arroyos uprising may have been unclear about their motives for becoming involved, all knew that Mrs. Fuentes had lost her only child. They also knew that the police bore a great responsibility for the young girl's death. Moreover, they considered the police responsible for many robberies and "unresolved" crimes. As citizens, they expected honest police and wanted police protection. When the police failed to protect the people and also participated in criminal acts, they violated the people's right to justice.

The people of Tres Arroyos wanted police power with citizen accountability. They were in a battle against the impunity and arrogance of a police force that had been bred to exercise unlimited power. According to Fagen,[24] long before the military coups of the 1960s, Argentina's military and police had been reorganized and redirected along counterinsurgency lines. It was risky to act against that organization, from either the inside or the outside. In the report *Nunca Más, The Report of the Argentinian Commission on the Disappeared,* we learn that one policeman who objected to police corruption had to seek other employment. The policeman in question denounced an officer for keeping a car that had been taken in a police raid.

> I . . . went to the Area Chief of Federal Security . . . to report the occurrence, and he replied that I had to understand that we were "at war." When I went to collect my salary, I was put under twenty days of arrest, with no reason given. I was unable to get any explanations from my superiors. When I appealed I was arrested again, my performance assessment was lowered from 9 to 4 points and finally I was forced to take retirement in November 1981.[25]

The Tres Arroyos uprising represented a demand for the police to perform their necessary and legitimate function—to enforce the law and protect citizens against offenders.[26] In fact, the people of Tres Arroyos might actually have preferred order at the expense of legality. They might have been tolerant of a police "shoot to kill" policy toward the "dangerous classes," or of police mistreatment of political activists.[27]

How, then, did the people of Tres Arroyos overcome their conservatism and the imprint of fear left by years of authoritarian rule? How did they become able to strike out against police arbitrariness? A cynic would say that the middle- and upper-middle-class participants in the Tres Arroyos uprising were more immune from fear than poorer Argentinians. That is, the greater economic resources of Tres Arroyos participants may have made them less fearful of state violence. But this is not true: The clandestine and secretive state of Argentina's recent military dictatorship demonstrated the vulnerability of even middle- and upper-middle-class citizens to State repression. The repressive state was blind to the personal, professional, or political influence of its victims.[28]

THE ROOTS OF UPRISING: OPPORTUNITY AND SOLIDARITY

Opportunity seems to have been a major determinant in the Tres Arroyos collective action. The people faced threats to their life and security from the corruption, inattention, and arrogance of local police. At the same time, changes in the structure of the state provided a new opportunity to act successfully on their grievances. Under the military regime, all categories of the population were "suspect" and targets of state repression. The people of Tres Arroyos seem to have estimated that the new democratic regime was less likely to repress them, making the cost of their action much lower. Nonetheless, such collective action always has a price. In Tres Arroyos, twenty-seven people were wounded. Two weeks after Evaristo Alonso had triggered the Tres Arroyos uprising, he died in a suspicious car accident.[29]

The opportunity to strike out against the police—a symbol of state authority—also resulted from general political and economic chaos in Argentina. Such chaos made the state more vulnerable to the collective action, which grew, in the first place, out of its inability to channel and act upon people's demands. In Tres Arroyos, the target of people's defiance was not merely police corruption and arrogance; it was the larger political institutions. The people struck out against not only the way that state power was exercised by the police but also the lack of responsiveness of political authorities to denunciations against the police. Since there were no legitimate channels for changing corrupt police practices, people turned to the media and then took to the streets. Rather than a middle- and upper-middle-class protest for democracy, the Tres Arroyos puebleada was a protest against the unjust state practices against a whole community. The Tres Arroyos uprising unintentionally triggered collective quests for improved police practices in other Argentine communities.

Solidarity networks seem also to have played a role in the Tres Arroyos collective action. In Tres Arroyos, the murder of a young girl resonated throughout the community *because* the community was already involved in a discussion of police corruption and violence. This discussion, in which the police were portrayed as brutal and corrupt, made challenging the police more possible.

In any case, in Tres Arroyos traditionally compliant people went to the streets when they felt that their community's life and identity were being threatened. This has also occurred in Brazil, where, as Paul Chevigny has shown, people have acted against the police when police action was directed against the community rather than being used to control criminals.[30] In one instance of repressive policing, the Brazilian police "[ran] after suspects in the streets, pushing open doors and searching rooms." In June 1987, a force of 3,000 police closed Rio de Janiero's Baixada Fluminense slum to look for criminals. Brazilians have other good reasons to distrust their police. According to Americas Watch, the Brazilian police usually do not respond to calls for help. This is, of course, more true for poor neighborhoods than for rich ones. Repressive policing against the poor in Brazil is so widespread that people refer to two groups of police—those for the rich (*policia da gente*) and those for the poor (*policia de moleque*).[31]

POLICE VIOLENCE AND COLLECTIVE RESPONSES

In Brazil, as in Tres Arroyos, Argentina, police violence against a community has contributed to the creation of a sense of shared grievance.[32] A community's reaction to police violence seems often to vary with the degree of police abuse; reactions are strongest when many citizens are killed, or when a child is victimized. For example, in July 1987, a thirteen-year-old girl was killed during a police blitz in Tuiti, a Rio de Janeiro slum. At the girl's funeral there was a great demonstration against police brutality. In another case, mass protests have erupted in Brazilian *favelas* (slums) after the arrest of a local leader, or when an innocent bystander is killed in a street sweep.[33] Likewise, in Argentina in 1987, a mass protest erupted after police killed three men "resisting arrest" in the poor Ingeniero Budge neighborhood in the Buenos Aires suburbs.

The elements that may promote collective action in the first place—changes in state structure, shifts in a group's relationship to authorities, inefficient political institutions—can also contribute to different collective responses. Public knowledge of police corruption, of their involvement in criminal rackets, and of police inefficiency may help to create shared grievances. Of course, this does not mean that people will act collectively on those grievances. As the articles on Brazil in this book demonstrate,[34] collective responses can also take the form of lynching, whereby actors resort to illegal forms of punitive justice. In Brazil, the combination of negative attitudes toward the police, judicial inaction against crime, and a demand for "law and order" has resulted in increasing numbers of lynchings. Lynching and vigilante justice are beginning to occur in Argentina. In 1990 a thief was almost lynched, and two thieves were killed by a man whose tape deck had been stolen.[35]

As we can see, the people's resistance to the police is complex. The complexity of this problem raises questions about the capacity for democracy in formerly authoritarian societies. Indeed, how can state power be brought under public accountability in such political situations? An equally important question is what makes state authorities take public protest seriously.

Obviously, protests by middle- and upper-middle-class people are more acceptable to Argentina's national authorities than protests by less powerful people. For example, in the poor Buenos Aires suburb of Ingeniero Budge, collective action was more likely to be repressed, making the costs of such action higher for the participants. One witness to the Ingeniero Budge protest was savagely tortured; defense lawyers for relatives of protest victims were repeatedly threatened.[36] In Ingeniero Budge, the protest did not alter police use of deadly force against the "dangerous classes." In 1990, three years after the Ingeniero Budge killings, the policemen implicated in it were still on trial.[37]

In Tres Arroyos, by contrast, even though the actors may not have foreseen the consequences of their action, mass protest became the catalyst for a far-reaching battle against state abuse of power. In the first four months of 1990, 700 members of the Buenos Aires police force had been arrested and were under prosecution. This is a step toward rejection of the authoritarian presupposition that the rule of law equals the rule of people by the police.[38]

NOTES

I would like to thank Charles Tilly and Luis Fleischman for their intellectual support. My thanks also to Gloria Fernández for her helpful suggestions on a draft of this article.

1. See Charles Tilly, "War Making and State Making as Organized Crime," in Peter Evans et al., *Bringing the State Back In* (Cambridge: Cambridge University Press, 1985). Tilly links the process of state formation to warfare. War making requires the state's fiscal and extractive capacities to develop. See Charles Tilly, *Coercion, Capital and European States* (Cambridge: Basil Blackwell, 1990), Ch. 3.
2. E. P. Thompson, *Writing by Candlelight* (London: Martin Press, 1984), p. 155.
3. Alain Rouquie, "Demilitarization and the Institutionalization of Military-Dominated Politics in Latin America," in *Transitions from Authoritarian Rule*, edited by Guillermo O'Donnell et al. (Baltimore: Johns Hopkins University Press, 1986).
4. Juan Corradi, "A Difficult Transition to Democracy," *Telos*, no. 75 (Spring 1988); International League for Human Rights, "Argentina: The Human Rights Record. Comments on the Government of Argentina's Official Report to the Human Rights Committee" (New York: The League, 1990).
5. The work by Paulo Sérgio Pinheiro is very illuminating in regard to the problems of policing during the transition to democracy in Brazil. See *Escritos indignados: Policia, prisões e política* (São Paulo: Editora Brasiliense, 1984); and *O controle da policia no processo de transição democrática no Brasil* (São Paulo: Temas Imesc, 1985), vol. 2, no. 2, 77–96.
6. *Gente*, 1–11–90; *Somos*, 1–20–90; *La Nación*, *Página 12*, and *Clarin*, 1–2–90 and following days.
7. *Noticias*, 1–7–90.
8. Ibid.
9. In the province of Buenos Aires, the intendente, who governs the municipality, is elected every four years.
10. *Página 12*, 1–7–90.
11. Police corruption in Tres Arroyos is old. More recently, in 1983, when *intendente* Jorge Foulkes took power, he asked for the removal of the heads of the police. However, police corruption has continued. *Clarin*, 1–4–90.
12. Evaristo Alonso, director of LU 24, whose call to the citizens precipitated the New Year's Eve uprising, claimed that the police charged a fee for their services—to find a stolen car—to initiate an investigation, or to alter a police file. A common joke after the uprising was that after the police had fired against the people on New Year's Eve, and had been subsequently dismissed, many unexplained thefts had stopped: "The police had been either removed [from their jobs], or [were] under arrest in the police station." *Página 12*, 1–7–90.

13. Perhaps as a premonition of what was to come, the citizen petitioners added, "We do not want to reach the point in which we have to fight for our patrimony and lives." *Página 12*, 1–4–90; *Clarin*, 1–10–90.

14. Three weeks before the uprising, during a visit to Tres Arroyos by Vice-Governor Luis Macaya, six petitions denouncing corruption were brought to him by more than 400 people. Even though Macaya asked for the removal of the police station heads, nothing was done. *Noticias*, 1–7–90; *Gente*, 1–25–90.

15. *La Nación*, 1–4–90, p. 10.

16. *La Prensa*, 1–18–90; *Sur*, 1–17–90 and 1–19–90; *Página 12*, 1–16–90; *Clarin*, 1–16–90 and 1–18–90; *La Nación*, 1–17–90. People who accused police of corruption were often threatened by policemen involved in the crimes.

17. *Sur*, 1–17–90.

18. See the note by Martin Granowsky, "La puebleada chacarera," *Página 12*, 1–7–90. Also *New York Times*, 1–19–90.

19. *Clarin*, 1–4–90.

20. In "The Culture of Fear in Civil Society," Juan Corradi refers to processes that lead to societal support for practices of state repression and terror (in *From Military Rule to Liberal Democracy in Argentina*, edited by Monica Peralta Ramos et al. [Boulder, Colo.: Westview Press, 1987]). See also, in the same volume, Javier Martinez, "Fear of the State, Fear of Society: On the Opposition Protests in Chile and the Problem of Fear."

21. As Guillermo O'Donnell calls it in *Y á mí qué me importa? Notas sobre sociabilidad y política en Argentina y Brasil* (Buenos Aires: Estudios CEDES, 1984).

22. In his analysis of crime and violence in Brazil, Antonio Luiz Paixão states that the reaction of the population which daily experiences the effects of crime and violence is translated into intense feelings of fear. On the other hand, it also expresses strong demands for law and order, generally intermingled with negative evaluations of police and judicial institutions. See his "Crimes e criminosos em Belo Horizonte, 1932–1978," in *Crime, violência e poder*, edited by Paulo Sérgio Pinheiro (São Paulo: Brasiliense, 1983); and "A distribução de seguranza pública e a organização policial," *Revista OAB—A institução policial* (1985).

23. On collective action see Charles Tilly, *From Mobilization to Revolution* (Reading, Mass.: Addison-Wesley, 1978); and "European Violence and Collective Action Since 1700," *Social Research* 53, no. 1 (Spring 1986); and Sidney Tarrow, *Struggle, Politics and Reform: Collective Action, Social Movements and Cycles of Protest* (Ithaca; N.Y.: Center for International Studies, Cornell University, 1989).

24. Patricia Fagen, "Repression and State Security" (undated, unpublished paper).

25. *Nunca Más, The Report of the Argentinian Commission on the Disappeared* (New York: Farrar, Straus and Giroux, 1986), p. 243.

26. As E. P. Thompson points out, the functions of police are as necessary and legitimate as those of firemen and ambulance men. "These legitimate functions include not only helping old ladies across the road . . . but also enforcing the law and protecting the citizens against offenders." In his *Writing by Candlelight*, p. 174.

27. As Provincial Governor Antonio Cafiero has pointed out for the La Tablada uprising (January 23, 1989), when a left-wing group attacked the La Tablada

army barracks, the provincial police were cheered on by the population as the police battled the barracks attackers. According to the International League for Human Rights, numerous human rights violations occurred during La Tablada, including the disappearance of unarmed prisoners. See International League for Human Rights, *Argentina, the Human Rights Record* (New York: The League, 1990). For more on the problem of order, see Allan Silver, "The Demand for Order in Civil Society," in *The Police,* edited by David Boruda (New York: Wiley, 1967); *La Nación,* 1–10–90.

28. See Juan Corradi, *The Fitful Republic* (Boulder, Colo.: Westview Press, 1985), Ch. 9; and Marysa Navarro. "The Personal Is Political: Las Madres de Plaza de Mayo," in *Power and Popular Protest,* edited by Susan Eckstein (Berkeley: University of California Press, 1989). Navarro cites the example of Adriana Landaburu, the daughter of a former air force minister. Even though almost immediately after her abduction her father had an interview with the president, General Videla, any attempt to rescue her was useless. According to CONADEP, she was imprisoned in the navy mechanics' school (ESMA) and dumped into the sea. CONADEP, 1985: 250–51.

29. *Clarin,* 2–21–90. In a televised interview Mrs. Fuentes pointed out the strange circumstances of Alonso's accident and implied that his death was not accidental.

30. In Chapter 12 of this volume.

31. Americas Watch, *Police Abuse in Brazil: Summary Executions and Torture in São Paulo and Rio de Janeiro* (New York: Americas Watch, 1987); See also Chapter 12 in this volume.

32. Chapter 12 in this volume.

33. Amnesty International, *Guatemala* (London: Amnesty International, 1987).

34. See Chapters 1 and 2 in this volume. See also Maria-Victoria Benevides and Rosa-Maria Fischer Ferreira, "Repostas populares e violência urbana: O caso do linchamento no Brasil (1979–1982)," in *Crime, violência e poder,* edited by Paulo Sérgio Pinheiro (São Paulo: Brasiliense, 1983); Alba Zaluar, "Condominio do diablo: As classes populares urbanas e a lógica do ferro e do fumo," in *Crime, violência e poder,* edited by Paulo Sérgio Pinheiro (São Paulo: Brasiliense; 1983); Antonio Luiz Paixão, "Crimes e criminosos em Belo Horizonte, 1932–1978," in *Crime, violência e poder,* edited by Paulo Sérgio Pinheiro (São Paulo: Brasiliense, 1983).

35. *Página 12,* 5–1–90; *New York Times,* 7–16–90.

36. Jorge Luis Ubertally, *Al suelo señores . . . !* (Buenos Aires: Puntosur, 1987).

37. *Clarin* and *Página 12,* 5–15–90.

38. Inter Press Service, 6–6–90.

4
AUTHORITARIAN SOCIETY: BREEDING GROUND FOR *JUSTICEIROS*

Heloísa Rodrigues Fernandes

> He was an outlaw. He didn't deserve to live. I'm in favor of the death penalty. If of one hundred who die in the electric chair, ten are innocent, how many are the ninety not going to kill? *Someone has to pay!*[1]

These are the opinions of Florisvaldo de Oliveira, better known as Cabo[2] Bruno, also as a *justiceiro*[3] and killer. A bricklayer, the son of a family of rural workers from Catanduva in rural São Paulo State, Cabo Bruno entered the São Paulo State Military Police (PMSP[4]) in late 1978 at the age of twenty. In 1979, he was assigned to the capital's southern district and was promoted to corporal in 1980.

In 1982 the São Paulo press carried a series of almost daily articles labeling Cabo Bruno the "killer from the Southern District." In September 1983, he was arrested by the PMSP Disciplinary Service and expelled from the force. Convicted and sentenced during several trials, Cabo Bruno began serving time in Romão Gomes Prison.[5] In June 1984 he escaped, and in August, while still at large, he granted a television interview in which he admitted killing scores of people: "I remember that I stopped [counting] at thirty-three. Even today, I remember that is where I stopped. After that, I don't know . . . I lost count. But I know, more or less, that it must have been at least fifty, more or less, or more."[6]

Thanks to ample coverage by the press, Cabo Bruno became known in the 1980s as one of Brazil's most famous justiceiros. His concept of justice as revenge represents a deep subversion of juridical order. But such personal revenge can never be understood as merely deviant or abnormal. Much to the contrary, justiceiros often find very passionate supporters in broad segments of the Brazilian population, including urban workers, who see them as protectors of the poor. In 1984, while Cabo Bruno was at large, a day laborer from a *bairro* on the city's outskirts emphatically stated, "There are many crooks here. What the Corporal [Bruno] did was right. Outlaws must die. I wouldn't lay a hand on the Corporal. . . . He doesn't deserve to be a prisoner. He did only good for all of us here."[7] Vengeful private justice does not disturb people with its paradox: Outlaws who kill *must* die, but those who murder outlaws do not deserve to be in jail!

The public certainty about the moral legitimacy of private justice arises from a social perception that divides the world into the two antithetic camps of good and evil. Justice is ruled by the dictum of an eye for an eye: two weights, two measures, two sentences. Within this conception of justice, "the moral maxims that determine social behavior and constitute some religious commandments—Thou shalt not kill!—virtually disappear."[8] Justice becomes superfluous; the law of retaliation reigns.

The social phenomenon of justiceiros must be studied on multiple levels. Within the confines of this chapter it is possible to suggest only a few of its contemporary dimensions. First, justiceiro justice in Brazil is rooted in a particular conception of justice, "to give unto Caesar that which is Caesar's," which has its origins in rules and structures mandated by the dominant class, and in the dominant class's conceptions of, and control over, public order.[9] Another element for understanding justiceiro justice is to recognize how and why such justice is embraced by broad segments of Brazil's lower classes.[10] Still another element is national security ideology, traditionally justified by the "Communist threat," which has had the impact of subverting citizenship by dividing Brazil's population into "true citizens" and "internal enemies." This negation of citizenship establishes terror and fear: In principle, everyone is, or can be considered, suspect. National security ideology strives to create a public order dominated by silence, as evidenced by an assertion made in 1975 by the commander of Brazil's 3rd Military Region:

> "It seems that security and silence are two concepts which admirably complement each other. *Silence is* probably *a good barometer for measuring security.* It would be sufficient to compare Brazil today with the Brazil of strikes, agitation, fear and intranquillity that, after twelve years, was happily transformed into the past, into history and fog"[11]

This conception of public order formed the seedbed after 1969 for the reorganization of Brazil's state military police—under the army's control and coordination—after which the previously civil military police began combat against urban guerrillas. This transformation of Brazil's military police spared "the armed forces the inconvenience of a conspicuous and prolonged presence in large urban centers."[12]

Even after the defeat of armed dissent in Brazil, national security ideology has remained, though its target has been modified: The public "enemy" is no longer the "terrorist," it is poor *marginais*. In police discourse, this extremely vague and imprecise category, "marginal," identifies people suspected of being dangerous to public order. It often includes the mass of Brazil's urban working class.

It is not by chance that in Brazil poverty and unemployment are associated with "marginality." For example, in 1976, the PMSP carried out an operation called "*Tira da Cama*" ("Drag from the Bed"), in which the police surrounded one of São Paulo's slums at dawn, gathering up and arresting "suspects." The newspaper *O Estado de São Paulo* reported that 98 percent of those arrested were unregistered workers—in Brazil, a great number of businessmen do not register their employees. Those arrested lost at least one day of work before being freed.[13] In effect, the discourse of suspicion produces a juridical inversion—it presupposes that workers are "outlaws," not "good citizens." The workers are then forced to prove that they are not criminals.[14]

A discourse of suspicion and secrecy covers Brazil's urban space. The population is subjected to the conspicuous and violent police practices of investigation and surveillance, including the police dragnets that bring with them large numbers of civilian deaths. In 1976, in justification of such police violence and as evidence of police frustration about "lawlessness," the São Paulo State secretary of public security argued: "Our city has twenty thousand outlaws on the loose, but it is evident that the police cannot see 'I am an outlaw' or 'I am a good citizen' written on anyone's forehead."[15] Thus, in principle, everyone is under suspicion and constrained by fear. Social space is divided into "outlaws" and "good citizens." This kind of public order is a breeding ground for justiceiros.

THE "DEMOCRATIC TRANSITION"

The 1984 indirect election of Tancredo Neves as president of Brazil, to succeed General João Batista Figueiredo, is thought to symbolize Brazil's transition from dictatorship to democracy. Nothing better expresses Brazilians' expectations about that transition than the words selected to commemorate it: The democratic "opening" or *abertura*. There was to be an opening of the dictatorship's "basements," of civil society's space; a freeing up of speech and political expression.[16] This symbolic discourse about the political "opening" allowed Brazilians to imagine that national security ideology was little more than an armor that had been manufactured to dress citizenship with a skin other than its own. But that way of thinking was a trap: Stripped of its armor, society had a second skin—authoritarianism, the legitimate father of national security ideology.

Our hypothesis is that in this, the second period of dominance by national security ideology (the first was during the military dictatorship), the urban space has been divided between "citizens" and "outlaws." During the first period, urban space was divided between "terrorists" and "good citizens." National security ideology has thus allowed the preservation intact of the military dictatorship's apparatus of repression; also intact are the social forces that sustained dictatorship.

Violence and terror are not as dominant in today's authoritarian social order as they were during the period of military rule. Instead, what dominates is an authoritarian conception of society that makes citizens' discourse unequal. This inequality of discourse is manifested in such phrases as "Do you know with whom you are talking?" or "All are equal, but some are more equal than others."[17] Such phrases produce silence among those against whom they are directed. This inequality of discourse both reflects and perpetuates social hierarchy. It represents a public order characterized by "differentiated citizenship," in which there are first-class citizens, second-class citizens, and those who are excluded. Forms of discourse that create and enforce silence run the gamut from pity—"He doesn't know what he is saying"—to condemnation—"Human rights are for human beings, not those who only *look* human."[18] This authoritarian division of public order is the great breeding ground for justiceiros.

As Marilena Chaui very aptly observed, Brazilian society is authoritarian because it

> is a society in which differences and social asymmetries are immediately transformed into inequalities, and these into relationships of hierarchy, power, and obedience. . . . In Brazil all relationships take the form of dependence, tutelage, concession, [and] authority and favor, making symbolic violence the rule of social and cultural life."[19]

This symbolic violence and the "differentiation" of citizenship present the state's repressive apparatuses with an irremediably divided public order.

In authoritarian public order, first-class citizens are protected, except in cases of excess police zeal. Those below first-class citizenship are the population at risk: They are considered dangerous to public order. It is not by chance that the poor, the badly dressed, the black are suspect until proven otherwise. And someone who carries all three stigmas is triply suspect—in Brazil, that means the overwhelming majority of the population.[20] But there is no way to distinguish a second-class citizen (the worker) from the outlaw because, as a former military police ROTA sergeant explained, "The suspect is not he who does something. At times, it is he who doesn't do anything."

For those excluded from first-class citizenship, society appears to be sharply polarized between rulers and ruled, rich and poor, powerful and weak. In short, society tends to present itself as divided. This division is marked by an idealized morality—"good" on the one hand, "evil" on the other. And this idealized moral order is highly personalized—remember Cabo Bruno's statement that "Someone has to pay" for crime. In such a morally divided public order, the idea of punishment does not remain abstract or formal; it is personalized in a Manichaean fashion. The search for quick, personal justice, combined with a belief that the law has failed—"Oh, the law never favors the poor, only the rich"[21]—acts as a breeding ground for justiceiros.

But justiceiro justice also has structural roots. Brazil's dictatorship stripped workers of the means of mediation and political organization. The latter could have facilitated the creation of institutions for common defense and collective political projects. Brazil's process of capitalist modernization, particularly since 1970, has aggravated the secular processes of usurpation and exclusion and has created an "amorphous (and fermenting) violence" within working-class daily life.[22] The working class has thus been condemned to a true urban periphery where violent patterns of social relation are a basis for their position outside first-class citizenship.

In today's Brazil

> There is no rest, . . . no truce, . . . no compensation in life's trajectory for broad segments of the population. Fear and violence accompany workers and their families from cradle to grave. In the street, at home, on the way to work, there is always a toll to be paid with part of the body or even with life itself."[23]

In Brazil's slums residents give legitimacy to the action of *their* justiceiro; he is the outlaw from *their* turf. This justiceiro is contrasted with the "true outlaw," who is "blood-thirsty," "perverse," and cowardly." He is from *another* slum![24]

In short, the poor classes' authoritarian conceptions of society and social relations, which are functional for the dominant class, divide social space into workers and outlaws. These authoritarian conceptions include a thirst for vengeance, defense, torture, and the extermination of outlaws.[25] This view of society operates as a breeding ground for justiceiros. However, simply to interpret the punitive nature of this authoritarian discourse as working-class conservatism is to conjure away the amorphous but massive violence to which the true "wretched of the earth" are condemned.

Whether society sees the justiceiro as hero or villain—thanks especially to interpretations given by the press, radio, and television—the social imagination creates an image of justiceiros as active and creative: responsible for their *individual* decisions and actions. Society is then allowed to evaluate and judge the justiceiro, rather than the social order from which he comes. But this individualized image of the justiceiro inhibits society from recognizing the phantom that lurks within authoritarian social order.

JUSTICEIROS SPEAK

In 1986, I was given permission to conduct a series of interviews with three justiceiros. They are sons of working-class families, members of the PMSP's lower ranks. They were expelled from the PMSP, then arrested, convicted, and sentenced for murdering civilians. They are now in São Paulo's Romão Gomes Prison.[26] In the discourse of these justiceiros, society is antithetically divided into the rich and powerful, the poor and weak. Within this division, justiceiros identify with the poor, whom they see as "weak" and exploited. One justiceiro maintained:

> In Brazil, the worker is exploited, *sacrificed*. He works extremely hard and earns only a pittance. . . . What can you do with that, with the minimum wage?[27] And many earn a lot. Some with much and many with nothing. I can't fight against the shark, the industrial barons. I *protect the poor*. He is robbed in everything, is robbed in everything he buys, is robbed in his rent . . . robbed by the government and by the boss. . . . But I can't do anything. What is within my direct reach is to combat evil: that robbery there. I went as far as I could.

For another justiceiro, societal divisions are rigid, unfair, and irremediable:

> As much as things change, they don't get better, principally for the lower class. The powerful always get theirs; today they lose, tomorrow they earn twice as much. *They* never managed to do anything. They keep fooling the people; and the people believe them.

A third justiceiro manifested strong identification with the workers:

> I was always sickened by [having to use] the shock battalion.[28] Me, break up the workers' movement! He's the one who is hungry, needy.

One former PMSP justiceiro argued that social plundering lays the basis for class polarization and culminates in the violence of the worker's daily life:

Have you been to Interlagos,[29] over there? It is poverty; there I ran across many things. It's really shocking. The poor are robbing the poor! That's what's really upsetting! If they robbed the rich, but [they rob] those poorer than themselves. They grab the working stiff, poor fellow, go and assault him. They assault the poor worker. And they even kill him! They rape and murder girls! All of that was really messing with me.

The plunder, violence, and injustice to which the poor are exposed stand as justifications for the justiceiro's defense of the poor. As another justiceiro put it:

I was a worker for a long time, I know. I preferred working in the slums. I preferred the outskirts, the poorest barrios. There are already a lot of police on the asphalt.[30] It's the slum dweller, the worker, who needs police, because the poor *aren't protected* at all. I didn't like to work in rich neighborhoods. The rich, if he's robbed, is going to lose a little bit of what he has, but life goes on. But if somebody earns a pittance, lives in a poor barrio, in a *favela*, no matter how little is stolen from him, that makes a big difference. I was class conscious. I went there to protect the slum dwellers.

Social polarization, mediated by unmet demands for "justice," justifies a Manichaean division of society into good and evil. This view of society transforms the poor: They are good but weak; the worker is seen as "*Zê-Povinho*,"[31] a "working stiff," "exploited," "sacrificed," "injured," "foolish," a "poor guy," an "unfortunate fellow." In short, the poor are exploited, weak, and unprotected. The justiceiro struggles for Zê-Povinho and in his name, deciding in the process who among the poor deserves to live—"the good working stiff"—and who must die—the poor, wretched "marginal." The latter is outside first-class citizenship.

Justiceiros are the product of an authoritarian social order in which those who do not speak—second-class citizens—need spokesmen who act in their name. In this sense, it is not by chance that in Brazil there is a socially constructed, amorphous, degraded image of the poor and "oppressed." This image coincides with how justiceiros (and the dominant class) expect the poor to behave. Indeed, justiceiros prefer that the poor remain unorganized: They believe that working-class unions and other worker organizations create disorder and agitation.

The justiceiro's conception of society involves a negation and deep subversion of the State. The justiceiro substitutes himself for the police, displaces the judiciary, and threatens the "social contract" that underpins the State. In a television interview Cabo Bruno stated, in response to a question about how he selected his victims, "It's not a choice. I don't try to choose. I . . . try to do my own investigation to see who the person is. And if I thought he should be killed, I would kill him."

A society that is exclusionist and violent is reinforced and sustained by authoritarian conceptions of public order. Within an exclusionist, authoritarian society, the "marginal" is an "emissary victim," a scapegoat for all that is wrong with society. The marginal becomes an escape valve for the hostility and aggressiveness of the excluded and violated masses who exhaust themselves in resentment and revenge against one another. The Brazilian sociologist Florestan Fernandes has argued that "Brazil [provides] an extreme historic case for coexistence between . . . very unequal and rigid classes, with a high concentration of institutionalized and organic violence at the top, [and a dense concentration] of 'anomic' and inorganic violence [among] the mass of the poor and oppressed population." This violence is released upon the poor by a social order that is "practically blind to the disinherited's luck; [the poor are] made to 'stew in [their] own juices.' "[32] For Fernandes, these two forms of violence not only coexist but also complement one another; this relationship of coexistence and complementarity shapes a bourgeois–autocratic form of domination.

The poor second-class citizen recognizes himself as such and identifies his interests with "his" justiceiro. In a classic example, Cabo Bruno's June 1984 escape from prison was celebrated by small businessmen and workers in São Paulo's outskirts: "Here, no one sees him as guilty of anything." "He should really walk down the street with his head held high." "We need ten Brunos here. If he wanted to return, I would hide him in my shack, because outlaws must die." "He made some mistakes, but at least we had peace. Now, we don't. It's keep your eyes open and your heart in your hand."[33]

Authoritarian society lays the seedbed for justiceiros. It produces second-class citizens with their eyes open and their hearts in their hands. It incites the desire for vengeance and makes the marginal into an "emissary victim"—someone who has to pay. This process of social production can only reproduce—in a vicious circle of steel—the authoritarian society.

NOTES

1. Interview of Florisvaldo de Oliveira by Mônica Teixeira, *TV Gazeta*, Abril video, 1984.
2. *Cabo*, literally, corporal.
3. *Justiceiro*, literally, "justice maker."
4. Acronym for Policia Militar de São Paulo, a civil state police force.
5. A prison reserved for members and former members of the PMSP.
6. Interview given to the journalist Mônica Teixeira, whom I thank for access to the tape. Florisvaldo was captured in March 1985. In December 1985, he escaped a second time and was recaptured in late May 1986. Currently he is in Romão Gomes Prison and his sentence, after being convicted in five trials, now totals eighty-four years.

7. *Jornal da tarde*, 12–20–84.

8. H. Arendt, *Eichmann em Jerusalem* (São Paulo: Editora Diagrama e Texto, 1983), p. 302.

9. To track that conception down, we must turn to the slaveholding order in Brazil; to the constitution of a bourgeois order incapable of conceiving of workers and strikes as anything other than vagrancy and a case for the police.

10. *Classes populares* in the original text, translated here as "lower classes" in order to avoid confusion over the meaning of "popular," which signifies "of or pertaining to the common people" in Portuguese.

11. Quoted in A. Affonso and H. Souza, *O estado e o desenvolvimento capitalista no Brasil: A crise fiscal* (Rio de Janeiro: Editora Paz e Terra, 1977), p. 33. Emphasis added.

12. P. S. Pinheiro, "Policia e crise politica," in Maria Paoli, Maria-V. Benevides, P.S. Pinheiro, and Roberto da Matta, *A violência brasileira* (São Paulo: Editora Brasiliense, 1982), p. 59.

13. "*A guerra rondando as rondas*", *Estado de São Paulo*, 10-5-76. See also H. Fernandes, "Rondas a cidade: Uma coregrafia do poder," in *Tempo social* (Department of Sociology, University of São Paulo) 1, no. 2 (2nd semester 1989), 121–134.

14. Fernandes, "Rondas a cidade."

15. "O secretario determina o fim das metralhadoras. E explica," *Jornal da tarde*, 11–30–76.

16. The very same general, João Batista Figueiredo, referring to the constitution adopted in 1988, predicts, "It is going to have a very short life. The child is going to die before learning to speak." "Nova Carta podera ter vida 'curtinha,' diz Figueiredo," *Folha de São Paulo*, 7–4–88, p. A–5.

17. See Roberto da Matta, *Carnavais, malandros e herois*, 4th ed. (Rio de Janeiro: Zahar Editores, 1979), esp. pp. 139–93, where he explores the thesis of the ambiguous and ambivalent coexistence of two ideals—hierarchy and equality—in Brazilian culture.

18. Declaration by a state representative made during a television debate. J. Araújo, "Debates na TV, uma tristeza," *Folha de São Paulo*, 6–17–84.

19. M. Chaui, *Conformismo e resistencia: Aspectos da cultura popular no Brasil* (São Paulo: Editora Brasiliense, 1987), p. 54.

20. P. S. Pinheiro, "Política e segurança na transição democrática," *Folha de São Paulo*, 3–25–85.

21. Chaui, *Conformismo*, p. 78. Chaui proposes the "failure of law" in order to explain another course—not the one I pursue in this chapter—that of the "search for justice" functioning as a pole of resistance and rebellion, producing unity and solidarity among the oppressed.

22. The concept of "amorphous violence," taken up again later, is that of Florestan Fernandes, *A ditadura em questão* (São Paulo: T. A. Queiroz, 1982), pp. 133–34.

23. L. Kowarick and C. Ant, "Reflexos sobre a banalidade do cotidiano em São Paulo," in R. Boschi, ed., *Violência e cidade* (Rio de Janeiro: Zahar Editores, 1981), p. 72.

24. A. Zaluar, *A maquina e a revolta* (São Paulo: Editora Brasiliense, 1985), sensitively analyzes that spatial process of division in detail.

25. A. L. Paixão, "Crime, controle social e consolidação da democracia: As metaforas da cidadania," in F. W. Reys and G. O'Donnell, eds., *A democracia no Brasil, dilemas e perspectivas* (São Paulo: Editora Vertice, 1988).

26. I accepted the condition of not revealing their names, since the subjects of the interviews are prisoners awaiting further trials.

27. The monthly minimum wage in February 1990, NCz $2,004.37, was equivalent to U.S. $30.96 as of February 20, 1990. Due to inflation, running then at over 70 percent per month, the minimum wage was adjusted monthly.

28. *Batalhão de choque*, a type of highly mobile police unit, in the original text.

29. Interlagos is a bairro on the southern outskirts of São Paulo.

30. "Asphalt" is a reference to the fact that streets, if they exist, are not paved in the *favelas*, the slums.

31. "Zê-povinho," an expression equivalent to John Q. Public or John Doe, in the original text.

32. Fernandes, "Rondas a cidade," p. 125.

33. R. Lombardi, "Periferia comemora a fuga," *O Estado de São Paulo*, 6–10–84.

II
PARAMILITARY AND PARAPOLICE DEATH SQUADS

5
GUATEMALA: THE RECOURSE OF FEAR

Carlos Figueroa Ibarra

To my parents, Carlos and Edna, murdered by the Guatemalan dictatorship, June 6, 1980

In recent decades Latin America has seen a long, ascending spiral of violence. The mass media continually inundate us with its horrors. Today our societies bleed. Their deep social wounds result from age-old violence, social scars, unresolved social problems, dependency, and underdevelopment—and such new social traumas as narcotraffic.

Guatemala has the sad distinction of having the highest figures for political violence and State terror in Latin America. It measures 108,000 square kilometers. Between 1954 and 1989, Guatemala's population increased from 3 million to 8 million. In slightly more than three decades, Guatemala has witnessed the death of about 150,000 people through political violence.

These facts call for a study of political violence, particularly as it manifests itself in State terror. But such a study is complicated: In Guatemala, State terror reaches beyond national borders.

GUATEMALAN HISTORY AND VIOLENCE

A historical fact of Guatemalan society, which forms a fundamental component of the history of political violence, is the 1954 overthrow of the Jacobo Arbenz Guzmán government. This counterrevolution left social questions unsolved and political and economic projects unfinished. It also left in its wake severe political instability in which military coups, cycles of popular mobilization, and surges of guerrilla activity alternate. After repeated bloodbaths, Guatemalans find themselves with a guerrilla movement that has more or less successfully besieged the Guatemalan state since 1963. That movement has not been victorious, but it has not been strategically defeated. This is why guerrilla activity and the constant struggle against it continue to be one of the principal manifestations of political violence.

Since 1960, Guatemala has been a sort of laboratory—a pilot plan—for testing and carrying out counterinsurgency tactics and strategies.[1] During that entire period the army, educated in counterinsurgency and in national security doctrine, has been the State's backbone. Guatemala's geopolitical position makes it the inevitable recipient of multiple forms of U.S. intervention, one of which is counterinsurgency assistance.

TERROR WAVES

In *The Prophet*, Khalil Gibran wrote that to dethrone a despot, one must first destroy the throne that all who surround it have erected within themselves. In one sense, a State's strength rests more on consensus than on force. But when, for whatever reason, consensus cannot be created, or has been destroyed, then force—the resource of fear—becomes necessary.

In Guatemala, since 1954, terror has been the fundamental component of State domination. State terrorism is not solely the work of a group of sick or heartless people—although it needs them. In reality, it is a political option. It is coldly calculated and exercised in a manner deemed appropriate to achieve its objectives. Political terror is used in Guatemala to guarantee State survival.

But Guatemala has not experienced simple State repression—an inevitable function of all States, however democratic they may be—rather, a specific and perverse form of repression: State terrorism. In a socio-political situation in which insurgency has been a historic fact of life, this terrorism results in the State's entire repressive apparatus being directed at the creation of passive consensus. Such passive consensus is created by annihilating through terror any existing will for social transformation.

In Guatemala, State terror takes several forms: It can be open or clandestine. In the case of *open terrorism*, the State assumes public responsibility for its repressive acts, with the objective of punishing and discouraging behavior considered contrary to its interests. *Clandestine terrorism* is carried out by the repressive apparatus (the army, police, and tolerated extralegal paramilitary groups) outside the realm of law; the State assumes no public responsibility. Clandestine State terror is carried out behind society's back.

State terror can be *selective* or *massive*. It is *selective* when terrorist action is discriminatory—exercised against specific persons because of who or what they are, the dangers they allegedly represent, or the confusion their liquidation could bring about. State terror is *massive* when its action is indiscriminate. With massive terror, a group or large segment of the population is targeted.

The preceding distinctions—between State terror that is open and clandestine, selective and massive—are useful for making a causal interpretation of State terror. Having now established these parameters, we can discuss the structural and conjectural roots of State terror.

Since 1954, Guatemala has seen three "massive terror waves"; these are conjunctures of intensive, open, and widespread terror. The first terror wave occurred in 1954, at the height of the counterrevolution against President Jacobo Arbenz. The second unfolded between 1967 and 1971; it was used to dismantle the guerrilla surge that began in 1962. The third massive terror wave developed between 1978 and 1983; it played a key role in the partial defeat of the guerrilla movement that had surfaced in the 1970s.

But such massive terror waves are only a blatant outcropping of the daily exercise of State violence in Guatemala: State terror as a *structural phenomenon*. Such structurally rooted terror is most easily observable between the three massive terror waves. At that time, State terror was predominantly *clandestine* and *selective*.

THE STATISTICS OF TERROR

Massive terror and structurally rooted terror can be documented statistically. Between 1966 and 1980, around 25,000 people in Guatemala were murdered or disappeared. Approximately 4,000 of these deaths and disappearances occurred in a seven-month period spanning 1966 and 1967, at the beginning of the second terror wave. According to our figures, from July 1978 to June 1981 (at the beginning of the third terror wave) another 5,000 people were victims of State terror. This was during the Romeo Lucas García government (1978–1982).[2] These figures indicate that up to 40 percent of the total number of deaths and disappearances reported in Guatemala between 1966 and 1980 occurred during the last two massive terror waves.

What makes the previous statistics so striking is the percentage increase in citizen deaths over time. In 1979, there were 56 percent more victims than the preceding year; in 1980, the State terror death toll rose 65 percent; in 1981 it increased by 51 percent. Using the accumulated total, between 1979 and 1981, the death toll in Guatemala from State terror was 800 percent above that reported for 1978.[3]

The high-water mark of Guatemala's third State terror wave occurred during the Efraín Ríos Montt government (1982–1983). During the Ríos Montt presidency, the Guatemalan State (and particularly its army) committed more than 15,000 murders, was involved in over 1,000 forced disappearances, and ordered 15 executions by firing squads—the product of summary trials. As a result of such massive and open terror, which took place over a 17-month period, more than one million people were displaced in Guatemala; 90,000 of them sought refuge in neighboring countries.[4]

Rather than seeing this State terror as historically isolated, we can speak of it as occurring in spiraling phases. That is, State terrorism under Ríos Montt was quantitatively and qualitatively greater than during the previous Lucas García government. Quantitatively, the Ríos Montt government carried forward the massive terror that had been used by Lucas García: Data obtained by the author show that 249 massacres, costing nearly 7,000 lives, were carried out in 1982 by Ríos Montt's security forces. In 1983, the Ríos Montt government carried out 82 massacres, causing almost 1,000 deaths and disappearances. In 1984, under the government of Oscar Humberto Mejía Victores (1983–1985), such state massacres slackened notably. But the victims of selective and clandestine terror came to outnumber victims of massive and open State terror.[5]

A qualitative feature of terror during the Ríos Montt regime is that it was associated with attempts to establish political consensus—in contrast with the methods employed by the Lucas García government. During the Ríos Montt presidency, as in an Orwellian fantasy, State massacres and demagoguery were accompanied by a discourse of populism and talk about "democratic transition." There were efforts to link the masses with the State through Protestant religion, and attempts to create a State party and to institute parastate syndicalism, the development of "poles,"[6] and self-defense patrols.[7]

To summarize, during the Ríos Montt period, the State sought to resolve the chronic crises of consensus both by pushing State terror to its limits and by institutionalizing it in ways that gave political terror a more visually subordinate place in the State's arsenal of domination. The State terror that is being meted out by the current Guatemalan government is uninterpretable and inexplicable without an understanding of this change in the nature of State repression after 1982. State repression in Guatemala today reflects both the real and the illusionary components of past State terror.

STATE TERROR IN GUATEMALA: THE THEORIES

One theory about the roots of Guatemalan State terror sees it as a proportionally direct result of capitalist development. Such theorists argue that regions where capitalism had been implanted had the most extreme class exploitation and tension. Such exploitation resulted in political violence, and called forth State terror in retaliation. According to the "capitalist development" argument, the most fundamental causes of State terror are not only class inequality and struggle but also the exacerbation of political and social tensions provoked by capitalism.[8]

The data presented by adherents of the "capitalist development" thesis have seemed to support it. For example, in Guatemala those departments with the least capitalist penetration, where the *minifundio*[9] (Sacatepequez, Chimaltenango, Totonicapán, Huehuetenango, El Quiché) or the more traditional *latifundio*[10] predominates, or those areas with relatively low population (Baja and Alta Verapaz), never experienced more than 1 percent of the total violence.

However, the data that support the "capitalist development" thesis cover only the period of the second massive terror wave and the years following it (1966–1976). Statistics on the third terror wave call that thesis into question: From 1966 to 1976, the more capitalistically developed departments in Guatemala contained only 5 percent of the victims of political violence, whereas in 1980 those departments had 40 percent of the State terror victims.[11] Even though capitalist development in the aforementioned departments was significant between 1976 and 1981, it is impossible to explain the vertiginous increase in political violence in those departments through capitalist development alone. State terrorism has causes reaching beyond that explanation.

This suggests another explanation for State terror in Guatemala. The departments with the greatest violence were locations of the most intense guerrilla activity, which suggests that State terror was a response to revolutionary armed struggle.[12] That is, it was a clear effort to destroy the insurgents' social base. It is recognized that State terror has been present in Guatemala in historical periods in which there was no significant insurgent activity. Indeed, this possible disjunction between the absence of guerrilla insurgency and use of State terror points to an analytical disadvantage in not distinguishing between massive and selective terror. The government's terror waves have certainly been linked to guerrilla successes, but they have also occurred in the absence of it.

Still another explanation for State terror in Guatemala is that it results from "institutionalization, consolidation, and the crisis of a counterinsurgent model." This argument proposes that the program of genocide in Guatemala results because the State and bourgeoisie are weak and incapable of confronting social contradictions by means other than terror.[13] The disadvantage of this explanation is that it indicates neither the sources of State and bourgeois weakness nor the roots of bourgeois hegemony. It is tautological to declare that genocidal repression exists in Guatemala *because* the State and bourgeoisie are incapable of resolving social contradictions by means other than terror. This argument is circular: Terror exists because there is an inevitable need to use terror.

From our point of view, the preceding explanations fail to locate Guatemalan State terror historically and structurally. Consequently, the sources of dominant class and State weakness remain a mystery. The historical and structural roots of violence also remain unexplained. But there is another explanation for State terror, one that incorporates components of previous explanations into a new one.

THE HISTORICAL ROOTS OF VIOLENCE

Guatemalan capitalist development has involved the accumulation and exacerbation of contradictions that are sustained by the maintenance of latifundio, peasant misery, decreasing salaries, and increasing emisseration. The dual realities of dependency and underdevelopment make it necessary to buttress the capitalist model of accumulation with State authoritarian determination. Capitalist accumulation, and the terror necessary to achieve social reproduction, have been combined into a political culture of terror. This culture of terror is fortified by the dominant class and the State.

But why is politics in Latin America a daily exercise in ferocity? The explanation for political violence and State terror in Guatemala should go beyond conjecture and the simplistic application of one theory to all politico-economic circumstances. For example, it is obvious that in Guatemala's last terror wave, regional political conflicts—the spread of war and revolution throughout Central America—contributed to the use of State terror. But State terror existed in Guatemala before the Central American conflict. And the Central American crisis did not generate terror waves in all Central American countries. Moreover, while capitalist reproduction has often made coercion (and on occasion extreme coercion) necessary, capitalist functioning has not always and everywhere required the permanent use of terror to guarantee its continuity.

What aspects of Guatemalan history explain why that country's dictatorial regimes have been among the most ferocious in the world? In the first place, Guatemalan State terror has colonial roots. The colonial legacy of terror and racism, necessary for the reproduction of colonial society, is an element in State terror today. The territory that is now Guatemala was the region of Central America with the largest Indian population. It was, therefore, in this region that Creole overlords had the greatest need to use physical force and terror.[14]

State terror also has roots in Guatemalan independence. In 1821 the Creole oligarchy created a reactionary design for independence: It guaranteed the continuity of colonial order even in the absence of a semi-centralized Spanish imperial regime. The discouraging defeat of the Creole liberals in 1838 was followed by a "dictatorship of order" headed by Rafael Carrera.[15] The Carrera dictatorship (1838–1865) reinforced barriers against mestizos' upward mobility, fortified the self-sustaining latifundio, and bolstered the cumbersome Guatemalan economy, which was weakly linked to the foreign market. Colonial terror was perpetuated by the paternalistic and despotic Carrera dictatorship, and reinforced by the reactionary obscurantism inherited from the colonial period.

The Liberal regime of Justo Rufino Barrios (1871–1885) reproduced and fostered previous regimes' dictatorial baggage. The Barrios regime launched a program of massive capital accumulation aimed at accelerating capitalist transition. This economic program, which was linked to the need to make the Guatemalan economy responsive to the world market coffee boom, meant pillaging church property, confiscating Indian communal lands, and reinforcing servile forms of exploitation. Indeed, the great contradiction of this politico-economic strategy was the illusion that the rule of law could be created while forced labor remained the cornerstone of Guatemala's economic position within the world capitalist system. The democratic State was a juridical fiction; it masked an iron-fisted "dictatorship of progress" that was nothing more than a dictatorship.

The Guatemalan Revolution of October 1944 and the dismantling of the Jorge Ubico dictatorship (1931–1944) tore at the sutures of this "dictatorship of progress." The 1944 revolution included first the liberal presidency of Juan José Arévalo Bermejo (1945–1951) and then the democratically elected government of Jacobo Arbenz Guzmán (1951–1954). The latter, in particular, established a domestic policy against labor extortion, racism, dictatorial rule, and government obscurantism. The politically progressive decade in Guatemala from 1944 to 1954 saw a transition from a capitalist-oriented, democratic–bourgeois State to a State with a national and popular content. This transition involved agrarian reform and other redistributive measures, the growth of popular and peasant organizations, an anti-imperialist domestic and foreign policy program, and a radical political presence in State and civil institutions. These deep-cutting social, economic, and political changes gave rise to the specter of anticommunism.

The 1954 U.S.-orchestrated overthrow of Jacobo Arbenz Guzmán fueled existing anticommunist elements within Guatemalan political culture, creating anticommunist paranoia. Although Guatamalan anticommunism had strong internal reinforcement, it was also richly cultivated by McCarthyism and Cold War ideology. In fact, the 1954 counterrevolution had anticommunism as its ideological backbone. This anticommunist ideology clarified and consolidated a Manichaean vision of politics: Just as the international order was divided between "good" and "evil," so was Guatemala's internal order. Anticommunism and the Manichaean world view are key components of Guatemala's political culture of terror.

THE CULTURE AND COUNTERCULTURE OF TERROR

Guatemala's 1944 revolution began a deactivation of the contradictions that had accumulated since the colonial period. The 1954 coup against Arbenz, which quashed efforts at resolving fundamental political, economic, and social contradictions, turned Guatemalan politics into a Gordian knot. Since 1954 there have been interlocking cycles of social conflict, including periods of massive popular agitation (1956–1962, 1973–1978) and guerrilla activity (1962–1967, 1979–1983) and the application of State terror. Such terror has grown, in part, out of the dominant classes' lack of political determination to examine the structural and political roots of social unrest. In any case, a "counterinsurgent monster" has been created within the Guatemalan State; this monster both breeds and feeds upon a culture of terror.

Guatemala's political culture of terror seeks to secure domination through labor extortion, racism, dictatorship, the specter of communism and anticommunism, reactionary obscurantism, and raw physical force. This culture of terror is inherited from the colonial past and nourished by the present: The Guatemalan model of capitalist accumulation broadly reproduces it; the State's structurally based and permanent instability makes State terror an economic necessity. State terror—through its continual use—becomes essential to the perpetuation of an exclusivist economic model. In turn, Guatemala's accumulation model breeds and is threatened by the precariousness of labor and economic fluctuations. That model creates chronic instability within the Guatemalan State. The State cannot address the social, economic, and political needs of broad segments of the Guatemalan population and, thus, cannot construct solid and lasting legitimacy and consensus.

Certainly, human misery in itself does not generate permanent State instability. But Guatemala's specific brand of "oligarchical–dependent"[16] capitalist development, which is inserted into and fortified by a political culture of terror, has created a "culture of insubordination" among the subaltern[17] classes. The accumulated and exacerbated contradictions of Guatemalan society, which have been created and fostered by capitalist development, have generated cultures in opposition to one another: a State "culture of terror" and the oppressed's "culture of insubordination." It is between these opposing cultures that social conflicts are expressed.

The modern, structurally based roots of State terror in Guatemala grow out of a weak and unstable State, on the one hand, and a civil society that demonstrates a refusal to obey, on the other. These factors in combination establish state terror as a structural phenomenon in Guatemala today. The cyclical crises of terror which emerge from that structural base are components in the State terror equation. These cyclical crises reveal State terror as a conjuncturally massive fact.

The cardinal necessity in Guatemala today lies in closing the disjunction between the State and society. We need to achieve an interactive and mutually supportive relationship between the State and civil society.[18] The facts are demonstrating that the key to transforming Guatemalan politics from a violent struggle for life and death into democratic practice lies in resolving the social question.

EPILOGUE

The objective of *State modernization* is to construct a meaningful consensus within civil society. Political stability is a goal of State modernization. Such modernization also involves a distancing of the State from unilateral terror and a preference for, and reliance upon, consensus-creating measures. Accomplishing these objectives has often involved a redefinition of the relative importance of civilians and military in the State.

In January 1986, with the ascension of the Christian Democratic candidate, Vinicio Cerezo, to the Guatemalan presidency, State modernization and its associated cycle of State terror reached a third phase. The two previous cycles occurred during the governments of Ríos Montt and Mejía Victores. The Ríos Montt government exercised massive terror to carve out an enlarged political and geographical space for a new type of State. Mejía Victores embraced this operational space and endowed his State with new juridical and institutional scaffolding. The Cerezo government is the beginning of a new State action that is attempting to resolve chronic weaknesses in the Guatemalan state.

There is a misconception that the Cerezo government is little more than a civil facade for military dictatorship, or that it is a puppet of the military. These are fallacious simplifications. In reality, we see in Guatemala today an alliance between modernizing sectors within the political class and the modernizing sector of the armed forces. This alliance is against those who continue to view politics as total war. There is an abandoning of unilateral terror, as the essence of political modernization, and there are efforts to construct political parties, albeit within a limited spectrum of choice. There are also moves to create a network of reformist political parties, and even a modern right wing. These efforts lend credibility to state modernization efforts. Another legitimizing factor is the existence of a foreign policy that seeks new political alliances and relative autonomy from the United States.

But such modernization efforts have their Achilles heel. On the one hand, the Guatemalan economy has a fragile position within the world economic order. Economic downturns affect the State's ability to address social and economic needs, thus creating a threat to its legitimacy. On the other hand, Guatemala's dominant class often opposes any redistributive measures that would resolve social, economic, and political inequalities. Within such a political–economic context, State terror is indispensable. And the Gordian knot of democracy remains without any prospects of being untied.

Democracy is not something that can be achieved through purely political procedures. It will come to Guatemala only after a variety of social and economic issues have been addressed and resolved. Only then will State recourse to terror—and the resulting fear—be a painful memory, slowly lost in the labyrinth of time. Real democratic practice will make national prosperity flower in Guatemala.

NOTES

This chapter originally appeared as Carlos Figueroa Ibarra, "Guatemala: El recurso del miedo," *Nueva Sociedad*, no. 105 (Jan.-Feb. 1990). Reprinted by permission.

1. Susan Jonas Bodenheimer, *Guatemala: Plan piloto para el continente* (San José, Costa Rica: EDUCA, 1981).

2. These figures came from, among other sources, the following Amnesty International documents: *Guatemala* (London: Amnesty International, 1977); *Los derechos humanos en Guatemala*, published with the Democratic Front against Repression; *Guatemala: Programa gubernamental de asesinatos políticos* (Mexico City, 1981). See also Juan Maestre, *Guatemala: Violencia y subdesarrollo* (Madrid: IEPALA, 1969).

3. There were 879 victims of state violence in 1978; between 1979 and 1981 the number reached 7,061. These figures are based on newspaper research done by the Association of University Students and by the author. The author also used statistics collected by the anonymous authors of *Violencia política en Guatemala* (1979).

4. This estimate was arrived at by the Guatemalan Human Rights Commission (CDHG). See its *Boletin internacional*, no. 5 (August 1983), p. 5.

5. The data for these calculations came from laborious investigations by the Guatemalan Human Rights Commission, the Peace and Justice Committee, the World Council of Churches, the Central American Institute of Social Research (ICADIS), and diverse newspaper sources.

6. *Polos de desarrollo*, in the original text. The "poles" were part of a strategy that also included "model villages," a more recent version of the "strategic hamlets" instituted in South Vietnam by the United States during the Vietnam War. Self-defense patrols, *patrullas de autodefensa*, in the original text, also had their counterpart in Vietnam in the form of the Civil Guard and the Self-Defense Corps.

7. While these "patrols" during the Lucas García regime involved more than 15,000 people, under the Ríos Montt government they had between 300,000 and 500,000 members. See Carlos Figueroa Ibarra, "La centaurización estatal en Guatemala (El golpe de estado de 1983)," *Polémica* (San José, Costa Rica), no. 19 (January–April 1986).

8. See Central American Research and Documentation Center (CIDCA), "Marco general de la violencia en Guatemala," *Alero* (University of San Carlos), no. 3 (September–October 1979). CIDCA's work is a forerunner of Gabriel Aquilera Peralta, Jorge Romero Imery, et al., *Dialéctica del terror en Guatemala* (San José, Costa Rica.).

9. *Minifundio*, literally "small farm."

10. *Latifundio*, literally, "large landed estate."

11. These figures are based on research in newspaper articles done by the author and, therefore, are not exhaustive. They refer only to the victims of terror who are reported in various Guatemalan newspapers.

12. Gabriel Aguilera Peralta, "El estado, la lucha de clases y la violencia en Guatemala," master's thesis, Department of Sociology and Administrative Sciences, Universidad Iberoamericana, Mexico City, 1980, pp. 1, 10, 40.

13. Susana Medina, "Guatemala: Contrainsurgencia y revolución," *Territorios* (UNAM-Xochimilco), no. 15 (November–December 1980).

14. Severo Martínez Peláez, "La violencia colonial en Centroamérica y Chiapas," in *Cuadernos de la Casa Presno* (Puebla, Mexico: Universidad Autónoma de Puebla, 1985), esp. Ch. 3. This same author examines terror during the colonial period in *La patria del criolla* (San José, Costa Rica: EDUCA, 1981), esp. Chs. I and II.

15. Rafael Carrera was the general who headed the conservative forces that defeated the liberal Francisco Morazán in 1840. He served as head of state from 1844 until his death in 1865.

16. Augustín Cueva, *El desarrollo del capitalismo en América Latina* (Mexico City: Siglo XXI Editores, 1977), Ch. 5.

17. "Subaltern" is taken to mean the poorest, marginalized groups of Guatemalan society.

18. For more on the fluid relationship between State and society, the "social options," see René Zavaleta Mercado, *La nacional popular en Bolivia* (Mexico City: Siglo XXI Editores, 1986).

6
ALL THE MINISTER'S MEN: PARAMILITARY ACTIVITY IN PERU

Elena S. Manitzas

> The sole existence under its jurisdiction of nonsubversive terrorist [paramilitary] groups is severely compromising for the State, especially if we take into account that the discourse of these groups aims to justify their actions declaring that they favor the democratic system that the government represents.[1]

The terms "paramilitary group" and "death squad" are often used indiscriminately to describe criminal actions characterized by human rights violations and a right-wing ideology supported by the acquiescence—if not outright involvement—of the State. "Paramilitary," the term used for such phenomena in Peru, can refer to death squads, private justice, armed "self-defense" groups, "cleanup operations" (aimed against prostitutes, beggars, homosexuals, etc.), or simply an extension of official State repression against civilians—known as the "dirty war."

Paramilitary activity in Peru is rather difficult to analyze. The investigation into such groups is relatively recent, and it is still unclear where they are headed. But a preliminary analysis of the victims of paramilitary violence has allowed some conclusions, although it is apparent that this form of political violence is still in its initial stages. Thus far, two general trends have been identified; these have led specialists to conclude that State institutions are deeply involved in paramilitary activity.

THE BEGINNINGS

The assassination of Manuel Febres Flores on July 28, 1988, marked the first officially recognized case of paramilitary activity in Peru. Febres

Flores was a defense attorney and member of the Association of Democratic Lawyers (AAD), an organization that defends people accused of terrorism, primarily members of the Shining Path (Sendero Luminoso). The AAD is considered by many to be the legal arm of this guerrilla organization, which characterizes itself as Marxist–Leninist–Maoist, following "the teachings of Gonzalo" (Pensamiento Gonzalo). Gonzalo is the nom de guerre of its main leader, Abimael Guzmán. Persons who have studied the writings and actions of Sendero have suggested that it most resembles the Khmer Rouge of Pol Pot in Cambodia, especially with respect to its ruthless and extreme violence.

At the time of his assassination, Febres Flores had gotten his client, Osmán Morote Barrionuevo, exonerated of one charge against him. This exoneration of Morote, who is considered Sendero Luminoso's second in command, once again brought into question the Peruvian judicial system's commitment to punish people accused of terrorism.[2]

According to Americas Watch, each courtroom in Peru hears 120 to 180 criminal cases daily; 20 percent of such cases involve terrorism. In the majority of them, "it is concluded that the evidence is insufficient or . . . that the accused are innocent."[3] Peru's former minister of justice, César Delgado Barreto, acknowledged during his term that only 20 percent of all persons in detention have actually been tried and sentenced by the courts.

Recent measures to remedy such judicial irregularities have included the "law of repentance" and calls for using military tribunals to try people accused of terrorism. The "law of repentance," which was approved on October 4, 1989, states that persons who have participated in crimes of terrorism may be eligible for a penalty reduction, exemption, or remission upon voluntarily abandoning the criminal organization, or by disclosing information "that reveals details of the terrorist organization . . . and its structure, facilitating the identification of its leaders and/or members," or by testifying and offering "material information which allows the discovery of the organization and structure of terrorist gangs . . . facilitating their capture."

But many jurists have found this law defective. First, it violates res judicata by permitting modification of an already rendered sentence where the "law of repentance" applies. Second, the law does not take into account the structure of guerrilla groups: The people most frequently captured are lower-level cadres who are normally unable to provide sufficient information to be eligible for a penalty reduction, exemption, or remission. Finally, the "law of repentance" does not provide the necessary security for the "repentant," who would undoubtedly face revenge from former "comrades" and even the police.

Another proposed solution to the handling of political violence in Peru (often interpreted, at least tacitly, by the government as solely left-wing) is the use of military tribunals, which presumably would speed up terrorism trials. The issue of military tribunals resurfaced after President Alan García's July 28, 1989, address commemorating Peruvian independence. Arguments against using military courts to try people accused of terrorism include the inability of such tribunals objectively to try and punish their own members who are accused of human rights violations. The impartiality of military courts has been severely questioned, as has the threat they pose to the administration of justice and basic principles of democracy. And there are fears that military courts might summarily imprison alleged "terrorists," including members of legal left-wing parties or organizations.[4]

Although the July 28, 1988, murder of Manuel Febres Flores was the first official case of paramilitary activity in Peru, the AAD has been under attack for several years by members of the police forces or unidentified groups, thus suggesting a precursor to what later came to be called "paramilitary violence." Several such precursors brought to light by the media and human rights reports include the cases of José Vásquez Huayca, Jorge Cartagena Vargas, and Martha Huatay. Vásquez Huayca, a lawyer and AAD member, was kidnapped on October 29, 1986, from Lima's Palace of Justice. According to Americas Watch, "prisoners in the jails of Lima's DIRCOTE (Administration Against Terrorism, of the National Police) saw Vásquez [in jail] on November 7 and again on November 19."[5] Vásquez Huayca is still considered "disappeared." Jorge Cartagena's car was involved in an assault attempt on August 7, 1987, in Lima, while he was defending alleged members of Sendero Luminoso. On September 23, 1988, Cartagena, who took on the case of Osmán Morote after Febres Flores's death, reported having received constant death threats: He and his client had been marked for "liquidation."[6] Finally, approximately one month prior to Febres Flores's assassination, Martha Huatay, former president of the AAD, was accosted while walking down a busy Lima street. She resisted the assault by calling out to pedestrians. The assailants then identified themselves as members of the Peruvian Police of Investigations (PIP). Huatay subsequently went to the DIRCOTE, where she was informed that there was no arrest order out for her. She was then set free.[7]

These cases, among others, give important insight into the composition of Peru's paramilitary groups, to be detailed later.

SENDERO VIOLENCE AND PARAMILITARY ACTION: THE WAR AND THE DIRTY WAR

Peru's May 1980 elections, in which Fernando Belaúnde Terry of the Popular Action Party (AP) won the presidency, marked the end of a twelve-year military dictatorship. On May 17, a group of armed rebels entered the town of Chusqui, in the department of Ayacucho (located in the central sierra, and considered the birthplace of Sendero Luminoso), burned election ballots, and declared war against the State. The self-proclaimed "Communist Party of Peru–Sendero Luminoso" had carried out its first armed attack. These initial Sendero sabotage actions were directed primarily at power pylons and similar strategic energy and power sources. By the end of 1982, however, Sendero activity in the department of Ayacucho had become more frequent and more violent. The government of President Belaúnde Terry (1980–1985) declared the department and a few neighboring provinces in a state of emergency. Article 231 of the 1979 Constitution provided for the limiting of such constitutional guarantees as personal freedoms, the right to privacy, the right to assemble, and the right to travel freely in national territory. The "dirty war" had begun.

The government's strategy for combating guerrilla subversion was detailed in a January 1983 interview with retired General Luis Cisneros Vizquerra. This strategy still applies today: "In order for the police forces to succeed, they would have to kill members and nonmembers alike of Sendero, because this is the only way to ensure success. The police kill 60 people and maybe three are Senderistas."[8] According to Amnesty International, over 3,000 people have "disappeared" in Peru—the majority of them peasants—in a war that has cost over 17,500 lives in less than 10 years and U.S.$15 billion in economic losses.[9]

Instead of stopping guerrilla activity, State repression has actually strengthened the largely rural-based Sendero Luminoso. The political situation became even more complicated in January 1984, when the pro-Cuban Tupac Amaru Revolutionary Movement (MRTA) began operating in urban settings. Neither the elected government of Fernando Belaúnde Terry nor that of President Alan García Pérez (1985–1990), of the populist American Popular Revolutionary Alliance (APRA), has been able to stop the activities of the MRTA and Sendero. A state of emergency has now been declared in more than eight departments, with over 40 percent of the estimated 20 million Peruvians.[10] These emergency zones have been placed under the control of Political–Military Commands and are locations of grave human rights abuses. Far from stopping guerrilla activity, such emergency actions have facilitated its consolidation.

It is perhaps this expansion of left-wing guerrilla activity that strengthened the determination of some Peruvians to take justice into their own hands. The day that Manuel Febres Flores was kidnapped and killed in Lima, the "Rodrigo Franco Democratic Command" (CRF) claimed responsibility for his assassination. In its communiqué, the CRF maintained that it was "tired of the demagoguery of Alan García and the indecisiveness of the security forces," and vowed that "for each assassinated mayor, soldier or police officer, a leader of Sendero Luminoso, or of groups that aid and protect it, will die."[11]

Febres Flores's murder was not given very much attention by the police assigned to investigate such homicides. According to Americas Watch, "in a meeting with high members of the PIP in July [1988], a close advisor of General Reyes[12] argued insistently to Americas Watch [representatives] that the democratic lawyers [AAD] were an integral part of Sendero's structure."[13] This presumably was a justification for the foot-dragging in the Febres Flores murder investigation, which cannot be taken to court until the police determine the assassin's identity.

Certain human rights groups, some media, and sectors of Peruvian public opinion also assumed that those targeted by the CRF were people associated with the guerrillas, such as members of the AAD and correspondents for *El Diario*, the pro-Sendero weekly, now distributed clandestinely. It was apparent that certain people were tired of the inefficiency of the legal and repressive mechanisms of the State at confronting left-wing insurgents. But this way of thinking began to turn in November 1988, when the paramilitary CRF delivered death threats to Javier Silva Ruete (senator of the Solidarity and Democracy party), César Hildebrandt (anchor of "En Persona," a Sunday news program similar to Ted Koppel's "Nightline"), and Roxana Canedo (anchor of the TV show "Panorama"). Because all three were on the center-right of the political spectrum, it was difficult to argue convincingly that they were associated with left-wing guerrilla groups. It seemed that the reason behind the threats was their call for the resignation of President Alan García.[14]

It is worth noting that before late 1988, when the centrist politician and the two news anchors received CRF death threats, there had already been numerous incidents in Peru of paramilitary activity: death threats, bombing attempts, threats spray-painted on buildings, and assassinations. The pervasiveness of such incidents between July and November 1988 underscores that paramilitary activity could not be considered sporadic and was rather well developed. Furthermore, at the time of the November 1988 death threats one trend had become very clear: Those who opposed the regime in power were potential targets of paramilitary groups. As Peru's paramilitary mystery unraveled, the panorama became more complex: More than one group was acting in the name of the CRF.[15] One fact suggesting this is that across Peru, violence has been attributed to the CRF. Such cases are as follows:

On November 17, 1988, in Tingo María (department of Huánuco, in the central region of the country), the home of Professor Ramiro Alvarado Celis, a council member for the United Left Party (IU), and the home of a medical doctor, César

Picón, were dynamited. Also bombed were the Provincial and the Criminal Instruction (Juzgado de Instrucción) Courts; the latter is assigned to hear cases of terrorism. The CRF was held responsible for these bombings.[16]

On January 17, 1989, in Huamanga, the capital of the department of Ayacucho, the body of Luis Antonio Guerrero Vargas was found at a university dorm entrance. Guerrero had been kidnapped on January 12. A placard left by the body stated, "This is for the Republican . . . the CRF keeps its promises," referring to the previous assassination by Sendero Luminoso of Walter Dulce, a member of the National Police Republican Guard (Guardia Republicana).[17]

On February 13, 1989, in Zárate (department of Lima), Saúl Cantoral Huamaní, secretary general of the Peruvian National Federation of Miners and Metallurgical Workers, and Consuelo García Santa Cruz, a community leader and educator of the miners' wives, were assassinated. The two had been kidnapped prior to their deaths. Sendero Luminoso denied responsibility for these deaths. But it is difficult to place responsibility: In Peru, the mining sector is caught in a cross fire between left- and right-wing extremists. However, many people feel that the CRF is the most likely perpetrator: Sendero is not generally known for kidnapping its victims, or for shooting them in the back, as happened to Cantoral Huamaní.[18]

The above violence suggests that there are numerous paramilitary groups in Peru, all acting in the name of the CRF. While it is unclear how they might be related (if at all), specialists on the issue have concluded that the various CRF act autonomously, particularly in areas under a state of emergency, and may be linked to government security forces. In emergency zones, the actions of paramilitary groups (using the name of the CRF) have aimed primarily at what the CRF considers left-wing guerrillas or their advocates. These "advocates" include judges, lawyers, labor leaders, journalists, and human rights activists. Due to the political situation in Peru and the lack of political will truly to investigate paramilitary groups, it is possible only to speculate on the composition of these groups. The Cayara massacre sheds light on the composition of one such paramilitary group that uses the name CRF.

CAYARA: A TOWN DRAPED IN IMPUNITY

On May 14, 1988, an army patrol entered the town of Cayara, in the department of Ayacucho, and massacred twenty-nine peasants. Their bodies disappeared. Initial army reports stated that the peasants were actually guerrillas who had died the day before in a Sendero Luminoso ambush of a military convoy. Witnesses to the massacre exposed the truth: The army had killed the peasants in an act of revenge for the Sendero-led ambush. In the days following the May 14 massacre other peasants were killed; their bodies also disappeared. Key witnesses to the Cayara incident were executed or disappeared during investigations into the massacre.[19]

Few cases of human rights violations have been brought to justice since the beginning of Peru's dirty war. Briefs on human rights cases have been archived, there are scapegoats, or, in some cases responsibility cannot be established because of existing legislation.[20] Numerous cases of peasant executions are claimed by the armed forces to be deaths in combat. In such cases, the names and identities of the dead are rarely given and the causes of death are never investigated.[21] The Cayara massacre, however, is the epitome of government impunity: Events surrounding it, and the makeup of the government's investigative commission, ensured the conclusion that the massacre never occurred. In fact, this was the majority ruling of the APRA senators who formed the congressional investigative commission on the Cayara massacre.[22]

On August 8, 1988, Carlos Escobar Pineda, the ad hoc special attorney for the Public Ministry who was investigating the case of Cayara, received a CRF death threat: He was warned to stop the investigation into responsibility for the massacre of the commander of the Political–Military Command in Ayacucho, General José Valdivia. Twelve days later, a dead dog was left for Escobar as another warning.[23] The judge hearing the Cayara case, César Amado Salazar, suffered two assaults on his home. He was warned: "All who support terrorist delinquents will die. This is only a warning; the next time you won't have time to denounce [having been threatened]."[24]

Other cases of paramilitary violence in Ayacucho department, such as the threats received by and assaults against human rights lawyers and journalists, have led specialists to conclude that CRF paramilitary activity in the Ayacucho emergency zone has connections with the military barracks there.[25]

INVESTIGATIVE COMMISSIONS: THE OFFICIAL LINE

On April 27, 1989, Eriberto Arroyo Mío was murdered while driving his son to school in Chaclacayo (Lima). Arroyo Mío was an opposition IU representative in the Peruvian Congress. Nine days later, Pablo Norberto Li Ormeño, a representative for the governing APRA, was killed.[26] The scandal in Peru over these assassinations led to the resignation of Minister of Interior Armando Villanueva del Campo. There was even a proposal to arm members of Congress. Public fury resulted over the lack of police protection for civilian authorities.[27]

At the insistence of the IU Party, led by Representative Manuel Piqueras Luna, on May 25, 1989, the Peruvian Congress formed a fact-finding commission to investigate these murders and to look into other violence carried out in the name of the CRF. Piqueras Luna and the IU had for some time sought a mandate to investigate paramilitary violence. The murder of the two members of Congress provided an impetus for demanding an official investigation, with commission representatives from the political opposition.

It was unclear at the time of Arroyo Mío's assassination whether the CRF or Sendero Luminoso was responsible. In Peru today, where many people are caught in violent cross fire, neither Sendero nor the CRF can be eliminated as possible assassins. However, there was an initial feeling that Li Ormeño's murderers were common criminals, since the assailants stole his car.[28]

In any case, the proposed investigative commission would have thirty days to turn in its report. Since there was suspicion that members of the APRA ruling party and the police were involved with paramilitary groups, the opposition wanted the commission to be presided over by someone from an opposition party. In the end, the majority party decided that Abdón Vílchez Melo, of the APRA, should chair the proposed commission.[29]

Those close to the commission's investigations claim that the political opposition, primarily IU Representatives Manuel Piqueras Luna and Gustavo Espinoza Montesinos, in fact did most of the work on the preliminary report, published July 27, 1989.[30] These opposition leaders were given neither the material nor the administrative support for their investigations, but they were also not blocked by APRA investigative commission members.

This first report did not end investigations into paramilitary violence in Peru. The congressional minority urged that the investigative period be extended. But before the extension was granted, the commission chair, Vílchez Melo, resigned to assume a post on the House's Directive Board (Junta Directiva de la Cámara). After his resignation, no one was assigned to preside over the commission; it was shut down.[31]

Representative Piqueras Luna demanded the appointment of a new commission chair and a reopening of investigations. His calls were reinforced by the mass media. On August 22, 1989, the investigative commission was given another thirty days to complete its work. The new chair, César Limo Quiñónez, was, like his predecesor, from the APRA governing party.[32]

Limo Quiñónez announced on October 4, 1989, that the commission's investigations into the murders of Eriberto Arroyo Mío and Pablo Li Ormeño, and into CRF paramilitary activity, had been completed.[33] However, he did not turn in a report at the time that he closed the investigation. His "report" was presented four months after the deadline given by the House. Piqueras Luna called Limo Quiñónez's effort to close the investigations a manuever to obstruct his committee's work. The right-leaning magazine *Oiga*—one of the more audacious with respect to reporting on paramilitary violence in Peru—even accused Limo Quiñónez of a cover-up. Weeks earlier, the same magazine had published an interview with a former CRF member who had claimed that former commission chair Vílchez Melo was linked to paramilitary groups.[34]

On October 26, 1989, IU Representatives Piqueras Luna and Espinoza Montesinos—who had received death threats as a result of their investigations into paramilitary activity—and Representative Celso Sotomarino Chávez of the Popular Christian Party presented their own Minority Report to Congress.[35] This report could not be discussed by Congress until the majority had presented its report.

The Minority Investigative Report brought to light some interesting facts. The first public and official appearance of paramilitary activity in Peru was the CRF's July 28, 1988, assassination of Manuel Febres Flores. Nevertheless, the Minority Report was able to document a chronology of cases of political violence dating at least to the July 1985 inauguration of President Alan García. These cases are considered the work of paramilitary groups, if not of the CRF itself. The Minority Report documented the illegal use, appropriation, or possession of weapons by paramilitary groups. Evidence was also given that civilians (presumed to be tied to paramilitary groups) had been trained in courses for State security forces.[36] Finally, the Minority Report charged that paramilitary violence had been aimed at eliminating subversives or dissidents, as well as wiping out opposition to, or criticism of, the García government.[37]

The Minority Report presents evidence of 220 cases of paramilitary violence, in 82 of which (37 percent) the CRF has claimed responsibility. Of such cases, 103 took place in Lima and 42 in the department of Ayacucho, location of the Cayara massacre. Of the paramilitary violence in Lima, thirty instances were claimed by the CRF (29 percent); in the department of Ayacucho the CRF claimed twenty-five of the forty-two cases (59 percent). The Minority Report also pointed out that of the total number of violent acts for which the paramilitary CRF has claimed responsibility, sixty-four occurred in regions under control of the government's Political-Military Commands.[38]

Among the paramilitary groups named in the Minority Report are the CRF, the Anti-Senderista Command (CAS), the Peruvian Punitive Platoon (PPP), the Haya Vive Movement (referring to Víctor Raúl Haya de la Torre, the founder of the APRA), the Manuel Santana Chiri Command (referring to the APRA mayor of Ica killed by Sendero Luminoso in 1986), the Cipriano Gil Regional Annihilation Command, and the Braulio Zaga Pariona Command (referring to the APRA leader killed in Huancayo in 1986; this group first appeared in Ayacucho).

Since the July 28, 1988 assassination of Febres Flores, the violent incidents reported by the Peruvian press are largely those for which the CRF and the Manuel Santana Chiri Command have taken responsibility. This has led some analysts to speculate that the abrupt appearance and disappearance of various paramilitary groups reflects the degree to which politicians or armed forces support them. Persons working closely with the commission minority suggested that paramilitary groups could not exist without support from the State or its institutions. Although the Manuel Santana Chiri Command operates 306 kilometers south of Lima, in the city of Ica, and does not formally associate itself with the CRF, the Minority Report claims that it is linked to the Lima CRF. This Lima CRF—which differs from the one operating in Ayacucho, for example—has close ties to the ruling APRA, to the Ministry of Interior, and to members of the police forces.[39] The report substantiates these claims with some very disturbing facts:

Jesús Miguel Ríos Sáenz is accused of complicity in a failed bombing attempt on October 2, 1987, in Lima, against the pro-Sendero newspaper *El Diario*. Ríos Sáenz, who is thought to be a CRF member, is linked to the APRA from his years at the University Inca Garcilaso de la Vega, where he was an activist in the Revolutionary Student Alliance, an APRA youth group. Ríos Sáenz was also a member of President Alan García's personal guard during the 1985 presidential campaign. The Minority Report suggests that perhaps Ríos Sáenz was never charged for the 1987 attack on *El Diario* because he has close connections to members of the García government.[40]

Investigations have shown that the CRF has taken "direct orders" from Minister of Interior Máximo Agustín Mantilla Campos, and that Mantilla Campos has "utilized the Ministry to obtain weapons for [CRF] members."[41] The Ministry of Interior oversees the police forces.

Public enterprises have given aid and cover to members of the Lima CRF.[42]

Members of the CRF have been recruited from the Revolutionary Student Alliance at the University Inca Garcilaso de la Vega; it was there that Mantilla Campos met Ríos Sáenz.[43]

A building on Lima's Dos de Mayo Avenue was utilized by President García during his presidential campaign; that same building was later used by members of the CRF.[44]

The Technical Police, part of the Peruvian National Police and under the jurisdiction of the Ministry of Interior, have been unable to formulate any conclusions with respect to the July 28, 1988, murder of Manuel Febres Flores—nor, for that matter, have they arrived at any conclusions about any other paramilitary activity in Peru. In fact, the Technical Police have overlooked key evidence in the Febres Flores assassination.[45]

Generals who head the National Police ought to be investigated, "in order to determine whether their cover-ups of [paramilitary] terrorist groups is due to [the Generals' actually] forming a part of [such groups] or because of the support given to [paramilitary activity] by [police] institutions." Retired General Edgar Luque Freyre, head of the National Intelligence Service, is also implicated in this cover-up—for not carrying out his duty to investigate charges of paramilitary violence.[46]

Minister of Interior Mantilla Campos, who is thought to be connected with the CRF, "has arranged . . . that dollars confiscated in police . . . narcotics . . . raids, be directly turned over to him." While there is little evidence in Peru of links between drug traffickers and paramilitary groups, this denunciation could suggest the establishment of such ties in the future.[47]

One issue not covered by the Minority Report is that on August 15, 1985—when paramilitary activity is thought to have begun in Peru—the government of Alan García reorganized the police forces, ostensibly to eliminate corruption and abuses. Because of the alleged ties between members of the National Police and the CRF, it is possible that this reorganization may have been motivated by political interests and/or that it may have had some relationship to the eventual formation of paramilitary groups. In any case, as the press has reported, "This weeding out [of the police], far from eliminating crime, has allowed [crime] to increase by leaps and bounds."[48]

It is necessary to address the conclusions of the Minority Report with respect to the assassinations of Arroyo Mío and Li Ormeño. In the case of Arroyo Mío, the Minority Report concludes that his assassination was a "symbolic crime," a warning, a show of muscle by those responsible for his death. The modus operandi of those who committed the Arroyo Mío murder suggests CRF involvement. The murder of Li Ormeño was directed at more explicitly political ends, as suggested by its timing: It happened at a rather delicate political moment in Peru when former Minister of the Interior Villanueva was being heard before Congress. Villanueva resigned when the assassination took place and was replaced by Mantilla Campos. In view of Mantilla Campos's ties with the CRF, the Minority Report suggests that "The political moment, thus, is sufficient for this to be considered . . . an assassination that seeks political ends."

The Minority Report further pointed out that there was no real evidence against the common criminal held in the Li Ormeño murder. In the first place, the evidence against him had been obtained illegally. He had been held incommunicado beyond the fifteen days legally mandated for terrorist investigations, and only then was charged with Li Ormeño's murder. Furthermore, the alleged assassin testified that his confession had been obtained under torture. Because of the questionable nature of the police case against this common criminal, the Minority Report concluded that Li Ormeño's assassination by a paramilitary group could not be ruled out.[49] It had already concluded the probable involvement of paramilitary groups in the murder of Arroyo Mío.

The Minority Report labeled the paramilitary groups "nonsubversive terrorists" and recommended that they be handled under existing antiterrorist legislation. While this legislation does not make a distinction between left- and right-wing political violence, it also does not specify paramilitary violence as terrorist. Putting aside a discussion about the efficacy of current legislation and of the Peruvian judicial system in general, the antiterrorist legislation, in itself, could be fairly adequate for handling cases of paramilitary violence, with two exceptions. First, as noted earlier (see note 20), Peruvian law requires full identification of the presumed perpetrator of a crime in order to prosecute. The nature of paramilitary organizations makes this nearly impossible. The law, however, could be modified to make identification of the institution or organization behind a crime (the intellectual author) sufficient to initiate prosecution. The other factor inhibiting the efficient use of existing antiterrorist legislation for handling paramilitary violence is that the institution assigned to investigate these cases—the National Police—is thought to be a part of the structure of the paramilitary CRF.

The Minority Report's other recommendations were the following:

Congress should cast a vote of censure against Interior Minister Mantilla Campos to protest his political involvement in paramilitary activity.

A special commission should be formed to bring charges against Minister Mantilla Campos for taking leadership in a "terrorist organization." Piqueras Luna had, in fact, accused Mantilla Campos of heading the paramilitary CRF before the 46th Session of the U.N. Human Rights Commission. He also accused the Peruvian government of complicity in the covering up of paramilitary activity.[50]

Peruvian National Police Generals Edgar Luque Freyre, Fernando Reyes Roca, and Raúl Jares Gago should be dismissed for their involvement in and/or covering up of paramilitary activity.

The Minority Report and other related documentation on paramilitary violence should be turned over to the office of Peru's attorney general, who should "initiate an investigation that can lead to the preparation of criminal charges" against paramilitary groups.

A special commission should be formed to investigate CRF activities in regions under a state of emergency, and to look into the possible connections between the CRF and Peru's armed forces.[51]

COVER-UPS AND FURTHER HARASSMENT

Peru's news media announced on January 22, 1990, that the police had captured eleven Sendero Luminoso members—the alleged assassins of Arroyo Mío.[52] But this accusation is called into question by several conflicting strands of evidence. People who had investigated Arroyo Mío's murder questioned whether there was sufficient evidence to assert conclusively that the CRF had assassinated him. Those same investigators were also skeptical that the Sendero had murdered Arroyo Mío. In fact, the pro-Sendero newspaper *El Diario* flatly denied Sendero complicity:

The Communist Party of Peru communicates to the nation and the world that it is not responsible for the assassination of Representative Eriberto Arroyo Mío and [assigns responsibility] to APRA's fascist and corporatist government. . . . The government does not hesitate to kill [its] representative . . . as part of its . . . counterinsurgency war . . . centered on genocide and generalized repression.[53]

While the truth of this newspaper's claim could not be verified, the nature of this guerrilla organization has led analysts to conclude that *El Diario*'s version is rather likely, at least with respect to its denial of Sendero involvement in the Arroyo Mío murder. Furthermore, the fact that Sendero Luminoso has been accused of killing other IU leaders and that *El Diario* has not denied the guerrillas' responsibility (and in some cases has even lauded their assassinations) adds more weight to the claim with respect to the Arroyo Mío murder.

The accusation of Sendero involvement in the Arroyo Mío assassination is also brought into question by the fact that, as of March 1, 1990, the Congressional Minority Commission had not been allowed to see the police report on the eleven Senderistas alleged to have participated in the Arroyo Mío murder. Another "preoccupying contradiction [of the Sendero arrests] . . . is that the main witness, Crelia Burgos, the widow of Arroyo Mío, did not recognize any of the accused [assassins]. . . . None [of the detainees] matched the descriptions of witnesses."[54] The police seem to have overlooked these facts. It has also been suggested that if the captives were indeed Arroyo Mío's murderers, and not Sendero members, and assuming that Arroyo Mío's assassination was ordered by paramilitary groups, the CRF has sufficient resources to pay assassins to keep quiet, guaranteeing its immunity from prosecution.

While the Minority Commission, represented by Piqueras Luna, was presenting its findings on paramilitary activity in Peru before the U.N. Human Rights Commission, the chair of the investigative commission announced the completion of its deliberations. On February 16, 1990, Representative Limo Quiñónez appeared on national television and presented to the media a voluminous stack of paper and binders that, he stated, was the Majority Investigative Commission's report on paramilitary activity in Peru. The Limo Quiñónez Report, which came out four months after the expiration date set by the House, charged three IU representatives were connected with left-wing guerrilla groups—this allegation did not include the names of the three, nor was evidence given for this charge. Limo Quiñónez claimed to be withholding any inflammatory evidence so as "not [to] play with the honor of people." Limo Quiñónez, however, asked Congress to investigate his charges.

Limo Quiñónez's 4,050-page report found the CRF responsible for only 7 terrorist actions, and claimed that none of those actions bore any relationship to the others—suggesting that they represent isolated acts of violence. The CRF, according to the Limo Quiñónez Report, could be made up of three types of people: former police officers whose colleagues had been killed by guerrillas; relatives of the victims of violence; ideologically motivated conservative groups. Limo Quiñónez denied that Ríos Sáenz, a suspected CRF member, and Mantilla Campos, who has been implicated in paramilitary violence, had had any such involvement. He also maintained that Saúl Cantoral, leader of the Peruvian Miners' Federation, was assassinated by Sendero Luminoso with the aid of Consuelo García Santa Cruz—who died in the assault—rather than by paramilitary groups.[55]

IU Representative Gustavo Espinoza Montesinos, after challenging the Limo Quiñónez Report and denouncing its cover-ups, demanded a reexamination of Limo Quiñónez's findings. Espinoza charged that the government was covering up paramilitary violence until a new government could be installed after the April 8, 1990, presidential and congressional elections. Espinoza's examination of the Limo Quiñónez Report disclosed that the House had no knowledge of it; Limo Quiñónez had not turned it over to the House. Even APRA's congressional representative, Fernando Ramos Carreño, who allegedly signed the Limo Quiñónez Report, did not know that it existed. Espinoza therefore charged that the Limo Quiñónez Report, which had been "presented publicly," was a fake.[56]

Evidence disclosed by the opposition parties' Minority Report, along with the accusations against Limo Quiñónez and his predecessor, Vílchez Melo, by the newsmagazine *Oiga* and by other media, human rights reports, and witnesses' statements, make it clear that Limo Quiñónez's report on paramilitary violence is a cover-up. His behavior as chair of the investigative commission leads to questions about the impartiality of the ruling party members who formed the commission.

DO PARAMILITARY GROUPS FADE AWAY?

Paramilitary activity is pervasive in Peru in spite of the investigations carried out by members of Congress. The investigative commission's role, however, was not to eradicate this violence; it was to uncover leads on the composition of paramilitary groups and present sufficient facts to permit judicial proceedings.

A look at paramilitary violence in other Latin American nations suggests that there is little reason to think it will be eradicated unless governments demonstrate a firm resolve to remedy the socioeconomic and political conditions that lead to social dissent and armed insurrection. Such conditions inevitably encourage the creation of paramilitary organizations. Latin American governments also must demonstrate a serious determination to pursue, try, and punish those involved in paramilitary violence.

Colombia is a case in point. The government did not seriously confront the fact that paramilitary groups were assassinating members of the Patriotic Union Party, perhaps because such paramilitary "dirty work" against the legal left-wing and amnestied guerrillas favored the interests of the Colombian government. The government has already identified over 100 such paramilitary groups—linked, in some cases, to drug trafficking and to police and military forces. Now it is not only the left that is being targeted: The government itself and the traditional Conservative and Liberal Parties are also being attacked by paramilitary groups. Eliminating paramilitary violence in Colombia at this point would be a herculean effort.

In *El Salvador*, the Nationalist Republican Alliance (ARENA), headed by the notorious Roberto D'Aubuisson, is behind the "Mano Blanco" death squad. ARENA currently holds power in El Salvador. President Alfredo Cristiani gives the appearance of having broken ties with ARENA's most violent faction, but the death squad's activities continue. In fact, even the most dramatic and well-publicized cases of violence attributed to the "Mano Blanco"—the assassinations of Archbishop Oscar Romero and the three North American Maryknoll nuns and a layperson—remain unresolved and unpunished to this day.

In *Brazil* there have been recent media reports of death squads summarily executing people in Rio de Janiero and São Paulo slums, with little to no government action.

Peru is still at a point where it can take steps to eliminate paramilitary activity; before long it will be too late. The emergence of new and disturbing trends underscores that something must be done immediately. There have been media reports of new paramilitary groups, including one named for Calderón Cafferata Marazzi, retired vice-admiral of the Peruvian Navy killed in October 1986. The press has also disclosed that "thugs" are entering Lima's shanty towns, terrorizing the populations, burning their homes, and killing. An event on January 18, 1990, involved 600 civilians violently raiding a settlement of 10,000 people: 25 homes were burned, and 6 residents suffered bullet wounds. A similar incident occurred in September 1989, when 400 "paramilitaries" occupied a Lima shanty town, "decreed" a curfew, and set up their own "police patrols." Witnesses stated that in the evenings these paramilitary patrols—who set one resident afire and kidnapped another—shouted pro-CRF slogans.[57]

There are also reports of civilians taking up arms against left-wing guerrilla groups. Such is the case in Peru's Pasco department, where the Ashnaninkas Indians declared war on the MRTA after the latter assassinated their spiritual leader, Alejandro Calderón Espinoza. In retaliation, the Ashaninkas executed seven alleged members of the MRTA and twenty peasants who were considered MRTA collaborators. The Peruvian press reported that this incident represented a laudable effort by Ashaninkas Indians to force guerrillas and drug traffickers out of their territory. Peruvian political leaders and military officers praised this action as well: They supported the Indians' right to self-defense. The Ashaninkas, however, have also executed natives of neighboring tribes, presumably for collaborating with the MRTA. This case illustrates the seriousness of arming civilians and the danger posed to human rights enforcement.[58]

There are also peasant defense groups in Peru—*rondas campesinas*, as they are called. One such group in Ayacucho department, led by the notorious "Comandante Huayhuaco," has received arms from President Alan García's government. IU Senator Javier Diez Canseco and Juan Rojas Vargas, general secretary of the Peruvian Peasant Federation, have charged that Comandante Huayhuaco's *ronderos* are a paramilitary group responsible for human rights abuses. Diez Canseco and Rojas Vargas maintain that these *ronderos* have used "abuses, assaults, robbery, illegal and unconstitutional acts . . . to control the production of coca [the plant used to produce cocaine]" on the banks of the Apurímac River in the Ayacucho department.[59] And the opposition newsweekly *Cambio*, in an examination of both Ashaninkas Indian violence against the MRTA and civilians, and the violence of Comandante Huayhuaco's *ronderos*, has asserted that "there is reason to believe that [the Ashaninkas] . . . are a [type of] paramilitary force similar to [the one] led by Comandante Huayhuaco." *Cambio* suggests that Peru's government party (APRA) and the military seek and encourage bloody confrontations between the Ashaninkas and the MRTA. In the words of *Cambio*, this confirms the government's "desire to use civilians as 'prey' in its counterinsurgency war."[60]

In order to demonstrate its political will, the Peruvian government must take seriously the recommendations of the Congressional Minority Report. Only by investigating and punishing paramilitary violence will the government eliminate it. The "dirty war" must be short-circuited before it becomes a free-for-all.

NOTES

1. Comisión Investigadora de los Asesinatos de los Señores Diputados Eriberto Arroyo Mío y Pablo Norberto Li Ormeño, así como de las Actividades Desarrolladas por el Grupo Terrorista que Desarrolla Acciones Criminales Incompatibles con la Vida Democrática del País y que Indebidamente Utiliza el Nombre de un Mártir, "Informe final" (Lima, October 26, 1989), p. 4.

2. Comisión Andina de Juristas, "Grupos paramilitares," working paper, (Lima, 1989).

3. Americas Watch, *Derechos humanos en el Perú: Primer año del Presidente García* (Lima, 1986), p. 76.

4. "Military Tribunals and the Law of Repentance," *Andean Newsletter* (Lima) no. 35–36 (November 9, 1989).

5. Americas Watch, *Derechos humanos en el Perú: Cierta pasividad frente a los abusos* (Lima, 1987), pp. 55–56.

6. Centro de Estudios y Promoción del Desarrollo (DESCO), *Resumen semanal* no. 431 (August 7–13, 1987); and *Resumen semanal* no. 487 (September 23–29, 1988).

7. Comisión Andina de Juristas, "Grupos paramilitares."

8. Centro de Estudios y Promoción del Desarrollo (DESCO), *Violencia política en el Perú: 1980–1988* (Lima, September 1989), p. 569.

9. "Comisión Especial de Investigación y Estudio sobre Terrorismo y Otras Manifestaciones de Violencia," edited by Senator Enrique Bernales Ballesteros, President of the Senate (Lima, January 1990, Mimeograph).

10. DESCO, *Violencia política en el Perú*, pp. 347–53.

11. Comisión Investigadora, "Informe final," p. 4.

12. General Fernando Reyes Roca, head of the Technical Police of the National Police.

13. Americas Watch, *Tolerancia frente a los abusos. Violaciones a los derechos humanos en el Perú* (Lima, October 1988), p. 55.

14. "Amenazan de muerte a senador Silva Ruete y Hildebrandt," *La República* (Lima), November 12, 1988; "Roxana Canedo recibe amenaza de muerte," *Expreso* (Lima), November 13, 1988.

15. President García stated to the press: "In one case it is lethal and murderous; in others only letters are sent. I do not think it is the same people. . . ." In "Alan García expresó desacuerdo con amenazas a periodistas," *El Comercio* (Lima), November 14, 1988.

16. Comisión Investigadora, "Informe final," p. 25.

17. "Asesinan a estudiante huamanguino a quien consideraban desaparecido," *La República* (Lima), January 18, 1989.

18. "Asesinan a secretario general de los mineros," *Expreso* (Lima), February 14, 1989; "Unánime repudio por alevoso asesinato de Saúl Cantoral," *La República*, (Lima), February 15, 1989; "Dos hipótesis sobre un crimen," *La República* (Lima), February 15, 1989; "Crimen es político," *Cambio* (Lima), February 16, 1989: "All seems to indicate, . . . by the characteristics of the kidnapping and the position . . . in which the bullets were found, the same position as those found in . . . Manuel Febres Flores, that the crime was committed by paramilitaries, presumably the 'Rodrigo Franco Command.' "

19. Amnesty International, *Perú: La matanza de Cayara* (London: International Secretariat, September 1989), pp. 11–20.

20. During its 45th session, the U.N. Working Group on Enforced or Involuntary Disappearances stated: "Despite the fact that many people have reappeared and have given extensive testimony, . . . criminal proceedings have been initiated in only one case [of disappearances]. This is due to the fact that in order to initiate criminal proceedings, the legislation of Peru requires that the person presumed to be guilty be fully identified, something which is very difficult to do as such acts are carried out generally by persons who remain completely

anonymous. With respect to the legal protection against disappearances, the mandate of habeas corpus on behalf of detained or disappeared persons has little effect; although the formalities are followed, the results are generally negative and the cases are not investigated efficiently." Comisión Andina de Juristas, *Boletín*, no. 20 (April 1989), 32–33.

It should be noted that the Peruvian Constitution states that the mandate of habeas corpus does not apply in emergency zones (article 38 of law no. 23506 on habeas corpus), thus contradicting itself because the Constitution accepts the American Convention on Human Rights as part of its national legislation (article 105), which holds that habeas corpus applies even under the state of emergency (Consultative Opinion no. 08/87 of the Inter-American Court of Human Rights).

21. Amnesty International, *Derechos humanos en el Perú: Cierta pasividad*, p. 37.

22. Amnesty International, *Perú: La matanza de Cayara*, pp. 21–22.

23. Ibid., p. 20.

24. Comisión Investigadora, "Informe final," p. 26.

25. "Matan periodista, a su familia y dos de sus hijos," *La República* (Lima), January 31, 1989; Comisión Investigadora, "Informe final," pp. 22, 24.

26. "Asesinaron a un diputado izquierdista," *El Comercio* (Lima), April 28, 1989; "Viuda describe detalladamente al que mató a diputado Arroyo," *La República* (Lima), April 28, 1989; "El presidente ordena exhaustiva investigación, *Expreso* (Lima), April 28, 1989; "Abrieron la puerta de su camioneta y lo asesinaron," *La República* (Lima), May 7, 1989; "Otro diputado asesinado," *Expreso* (Lima), May 7, 1989.

27. "Cerca de 40 parlamentarios en lista de amenazados de muerte," *La República* (Lima), May 12, 1989; "Norman uso de armas para defensa personal," *Expreso* (Lima), May 17, 1989.

28. "Ubican camioneta de diputado asesinado Pablo Li Ormeño," *El Comercio* (Lima), May 9, 1989; "Esclarecido crimen del diputado Li Ormeño," *Expreso* (Lima), June 8, 1989.

29. Comisión Investigadora, "Informe final," p. 7.

30. Comisión Investigadora, "Informe preliminar" (Lima, July 27, 1989).

31. Comisión Investigadora, "Informe Final," p. 8.

32. Ibid., p. 9.

33. Ibid., p. 10.

34. "Confesión de un desertor del CRF," *Oiga* (Lima), no. 447 (September 4, 1989); "Mantilla busca un milagro" and "El diputado parapsicólogo," *Oiga* (Lima), no. 453 (October 16, 1989).

35. Comisión Investigadora, "Informe final," ibid.

36. Ibid., pp. 15–19.

37. Ibid., p. 46.

38. Ibid., pp. 37–38.

39. Ibid., p. 52.

40. Ibid., pp. 55–59.

41. Ibid., p. 59.

42. Ibid., pp. 60–61.

43. Ibid., pp. 61–62.

44. Ibid., pp. 63–64.

45. Ibid., p. 42.

46. Ibid., pp. 59–60.
47. Ibid., p. 65.
48. "Policía violenta en el banquillo," *La República* (Lima), September 3, 1989.
49. Comisión Investigadora, "Informe final," pp. 67–69.
50. "Diputado peruano acusa ministro ser jefe grupo terrorista," EFE wire service, February 15, 1990.
51. Comisión Investigadora, "Informe final," p. 80.
52. "Cayeron los asesinos de diputado Eriberto Arroyo Mío," *La República* (Lima), January 20, 1990.
53. "Sobre asesinato de diputado Eriberto Arroyo. El PCP aclara," *El Diario*, no. 546 (May 3, 1989).
54. "Caso Arroyo Mío. Dudas que matan," *La República* (Lima), January 28, 1990.
55. "Acusan a 3 parlamentarios IU de vinculación con terrorismo," *La República* (Lima), February 17, 1990.
56. "El informe fantasma," *Oiga* (Lima), no. 471 (February 26, 1990).

The majority commission led by César Limo Quiñónez presented its report on paramilitaries to Congress in April 1990. The report upheld the February press statements of the Congressperson and included the names of three United Left congresspersons whom Limo Quiñónez accused of being "terrorists." Unofficial and public information on these congresspersons indicates that the three not only were adament supporters of an investigation on paramilitary activity, but also had been threatened by the CAS.

Just prior to the change of government, both the minority and majority reports were heard before the Peruvian House of Representatives. To the surprise and outrage of the opposition parties (both right- and left-wing), the APRA majority approved the Limo Quiñónez report, leaving at bay any serious discussion of paramilitary groups for the remainder of the García administration. (Instituto de Defensa Legal, Area de Información y Promoción en Derechos Humanos, *Informe Mensual*, no. 13, May 1990, pp. 28–29; *Informe Mensual*, no. 14, June 1990, p. 26).

57. "A balazos intentan desalojar a diez mil en cuatro asentamientos humanos," *La República* (Lima), January 19, 1990; "Matones implantan 'toque de queda' en barriada de Comas," *La República* (Lima), September 21, 1989.
58. "Ashaninkas Declare War on the MRTA," *Andean Newsletter* (Lima), no. 39 (February 12, 1990); "Ashaninkas invaden valle de Palcazu y asesinan a 5 nativos Yaneshas," *La República* (Lima), February 18, 1990.
59. "Ashaninkas Declare War on the MRTA."
60. "Quién se beneficia?" *Cambio* (Lima) no. 99 (January 18, 1990).

7
INSTITUTIONAL CRISIS, PARAINSTITUTIONALITY, AND REGIME FLEXIBILITY IN COLOMBIA: THE PLACE OF NARCOTRAFFIC AND COUNTERINSURGENCY

Germán Alfonso Palacio Castanêda

Colombia is in the throes of an institutional crisis. It would be risky to present a blanket explanation for that crisis. There is, in fact, an explosion of phenomena shaking the organic and functional scaffolding of the State. Such phenomena include the following:

1. Collapse of the administration of justice, frequently described in terms of criminal impunity from prosecution, government inefficiency, high levels of crime, rampant corruption, and lack of security and protection for judicial officials, many of whom have been assassinated.[1]
2. Inability of political parties and parliament to act as vehicles for expressing social demands.[2]
3. Inability of juridical–institutional mechanisms to integrate and channel social struggles.[3]
4. A growing, though dispersed, guerrilla challenge to the State and the military.[4]
5. A breakdown of the State's monopoly over legitimate physical force, not only by guerrillas but also by "narcoparamilitary" groups.[5]
6. Permanent tension between successive governments and cocaine entrepreneurs that has brought about paramilitary and "parapolice" justice.[6]
7. A generalization of forms of conflict, expressed in growing manifestations of physical violence from diverse social actors.[7]

INSTITUTIONAL FRAGMENTATION AND ECONOMIC DEVELOPMENT

Colombia's violent and fragmented institutional and political foundation does *not* exist alongside a similarly troubled economic situation, at least not according to traditional economic indicators. Colombia's GNP has grown at a rate of between 3 and 6 percent since 1984. Colombia is, in fact, an excellent example of how extreme and generalized physical violence can exist alongside high indices of economic growth. This combination might seem paradoxical, if not contradictory, in other countries.[8] But as Fabio Echeverry has pointed out, in Colombia "the economy is doing well, and the country poorly."[9] In fact, common sense based on Keynesian political economics has led to the mistaken assumption that a relatively harmonious social situation will be associated with economic development and vice versa.[10] This is definitely untrue in Colombia. Today in Colombia, as in earlier periods of original capital accumulation elsewhere, capitalist development is associated with open physical violence.[11] Colombia has experienced the violence of development for some time, yet it is not a "backward" traditional agricultural country.

It is now common to say that Colombia—where positive (formal) economic development indicators are associated with massive political violence—is one of a kind. Economic development has not been associated with the development of regulated institutional mechanisms. Instead, it has been associated with the emergence of noninstitutional paths of *parainstitutional creativity*.[12]

By "parainstitutional" we mean a series of mechanisms of social regulation and conflict resolution that do not rely on formal constitutional or legal means, but are governed by informal arrangements and ad hoc mechanisms. They can be legal or illegal. They are manifestations of, and alternatives to, an institutional inability to respond to both social conflict and the State's need to accumulate capital. They have become parainstitutional to the extent that they (a) have ceased to be exceptional and (b) are present in any country and are frequently used.

This chapter proposes that one of the key factors in Colombia's institutional crisis, and a predominant explanation for much of the parainstitutionality, is the search by a new fraction of capital for political expression. This new capital fraction has its economic and political base in international cocaine traffic, the "narcotraffickers."[13] This chapter shows that the parainstitutionality employed by this new fraction of capital in fact complements State designs and strategies for social reinstitutionalization. The State is forced to recognize the reality of parainstitutionality and to enter into negotiations with parainstitutional actors.

Such negotiations take the State beyond the legal limits of State action. In other words, the State itself engages in parainstitutionality.

PARAINSTITUTIONALITY

Colombia offers many examples of parainstitutionality. The labor regulations, known as "de facto labor reform," which have been slowly imposed since the mid–1970s, without any accompanying legal reform (due to procedural difficulties and opposition by different sectors, particularly organized labor), represent parainstitutional change. It does not seem to matter that such "de facto labor reform" ignores or occasionally violates the Colombian Labor Code.

Another set of parainstitutional manifestations centers on extralegal violence. Paramilitary repression is one type of parainstitutional expression. The growth of *sicarios* (paid assassins) is another. The sicarios arise from the illegality of the cocaine business, which demands mechanisms for settling accounts without having to go through legal channels. The paid sicarios, who are from Medellín's poor barrios, have become celebrities. They solve problems that formal, regulated institutions cannot. Guerrilla struggles are parainstitutional manifestations: The guerrillas do not use electoral or other established means within the political system. Urban protests are another type of parainstitutionality.

Wildcat strikes also represent parainstitutionality. Unlike organized labor strikes, the wildcat strikes do not usually adhere to established regulations or rely on formal negotiations with authorities.

But these are just a few examples of parainstitutionality. This chapter concentrates on the parainstitutionality generated by Colombia's cocaine economy. The first section gives some critical premises for understanding narcotraffic, the vague and imprecise name that U.S. government authorities have been able to plant in national and international public opinion. The second section describes changes in the institutional fabric of the Colombian State and the parainstitutional crises that have been associated with the development of a new fraction of capital. This fraction's source of accumulation is illegal cocaine traffic.

"NARCOTRAFFIC"

"Narcotraffic," to use the word in vogue in the 1980s, refers to "juridical and police transnationalization of drug discourse."[14] The abundant literature dealing with this theme shares several characteristics: It is dominated by sensationalism; it comes from sources with little interest in objectivity; it reduces the phenomenon to a single explanatory dimension. In short, much information about narcotraffic is distorted and manipulated.

In fact, most information about narcotraffic is furnished by the *Miami Herald* and other U.S. newspapers that use the U.S. DEA (Drug Enforcement Agency) as their information source. Such media tend to follow the DEA's strategic orientation, which is empirically unacceptable. The theoretical and political importance of one of the most profitable and politically important businesses in recent decades makes it necessary to remove contaminated information from healthier data. This is difficult: The line between perception and reality is tenuous.[15]

Undoubtedly the nature of narcotraffic business lends itself to easy manipulation. For example, establishing its precise size is arduous. Its illegality makes official accounting difficult. We do know that in proportional terms for Colombia, the narcotraffic business is enormous, to the point of being compared with income earnings from coffee.[16] *Fortune* magazine listed Pablo Escobar and Jorge Luis Ochoa among the world's wealthiest people, along with Queen Elizabeth II, Queen Beatrix of the Netherlands, The Sultan of Brunei, the Rockefellers, and other magnates.[17] There is no doubt that *Fortune* has overestimated the economic position of "cocaine billionaires." In fact, this is part of the manipulation we spoke of. But, in any case, the fortunes of Escobar and Ochoa are still significant. The *New York Times*, writing about "coca billionaires," stated in 1989 that Pablo Escobar cannot be bought for less than $2 billion.[18]

Carlos Caballero,[19] a prestigious Colombian economist, has shown that the juiciest cut of this business is not produced in cultivation, refining, or transport, but in direct sales to the consumer—on the streets of large U.S. cities.[20] If this is true, it casts doubt on the contention that Colombian drug cartels are the major beneficiaries of narcotraffic. This could occur only if they were in business with U.S. authorities. If the latter is true, it must be shown that U.S. police have collaborated with Colombian *capos* on the streets of Miami, Los Angeles, Atlanta, New York, and Chicago.

In fact, evidence suggests that such collaboration has occurred in the past. It is well known that Havana was the hub of illegal drug traffic before the 1959 revolution. Once Cuba's new revolutionary State was consolidated, Cuban capos established themselves in Miami and continued their operations.[21] On occasion, the capos were protected by the CIA, since they represented an important bulwark in the anti-Castro struggle.

On several occasions in the 1960s the CIA was accused of being involved in heroin traffic. The CIA is shown to have allowed heroin sales to finance pro-American, anticommunist political movements.[22] Alfred W. McCoy, a U.S. university professor and ex-collaborator with the CIA, has documented this connection in *The Politics of Heroin in South East Asia*.[23] The CIA has responded that such methods "are no longer being employed." As a consequence of such denunciations, President Richard Nixon attempted to centralize the struggle against illegal drugs by establishing the DEA, a special agency attached to the Department of Justice. The DEA took some heat off the CIA, whose nefarious reputation across the Third World was not initially transferred to the DEA. Thus, while the CIA must still enter foreign countries under cover—which is not difficult—DEA agents are invited by many foreign governments. The DEA presumably comes to carry out a laudable mission. It is not yet clear how far the DEA carries its mission beyond the struggle against "narcotraffic."[24]

Let us return to the concept of "narcotraffic." It forms the basis of public knowledge about international drug trafficking. The expression "narcotraffic" is totally ambiguous. In fact, its success is based largely on its vagueness. In the first place, narcotraffic covers the commercialization of different types of drugs, both legal and illegal. We know that in reality "narcotraffic" refers to all illegal drugs, even though currently cocaine is the dominant image conjured up by the term. As Rosa del Olmo demonstrates,[25] in the 1960s heroin was the villain in the drug war; in the 1970s it was marijuana. These drugs were targeted in antidrug repression. When narcotraffic is spoken of in the 1980s, one thinks primarily of cocaine. In the 1990s "crack" has entered the public consciousness.

Other elements create conceptual confusion about narcotraffic. Cocaine, a stimulant, is equated with all narcotics, some of which are depressants.[26] Another area of conceptual confusion is that coca is considered equivalent to cocaine. But coca is a plant linked to Andean Indian communities' mythic–cultural tradition, whereas cocaine is the industrial product of an illegal capitalist economy. To employ the language of political economy, while coca is characterized primarily by use value, cocaine has exchange value—it is merchandise.

Discussions of the narcotraffic economy (cocaine) tend to globalize disparate and diverse social actors and sectors without being overly specific about each. "Narcotraffic," quite misleadingly, includes or suggests the traditional Indian population that has cultivated coca for thousands of years. It also encompasses the tenant farmers and peasants who plant it (as a more profitable agricultural product). It embraces small-scale, urban-based couriers ("mules"), whose work in the drug economy helps them escape poverty. It includes medium- and large-scale merchants and businessmen who refine and transport cocaine on a large scale. It also incorporates international financiers and money launderers. Government policies to combat narcotraffic attempt joint criminalization of this arbitrarily grouped and disparate variety of actors.

Moralistic rhetoric about narcotraffic has been able to mobilize U.S. public opinion; there has been a "demonization" of narcotraffic. In the United States this demonization has some footing in reality: The high consumption of drugs has very probably contributed to reducing U.S. work productivity; it has affected a young population ready to be integrated into the productive work force. Moralistic rhetoric may be aimed at arresting the perverse effect of drugs on the work ethic. But the moralist argument has gone beyond this, to stigmatize all drugs and drug users. Such generalized demonization is not unheard of in American political culture. Communism, which has been demonized by successive heads of state, has been used to discredit socialist governments. However, at this moment when "truly existing socialisms" are being restructured and capital has become interested in penetrating those countries, it is difficult to continue making communism a demon.

COCAINE TRAFFICKING AND NARCOTRAFFIC

We must distinguish between the business of cocaine trafficking and narcotraffic. Cocaine trafficking is an illegal, internationalized business that supports and contributes to capitalist accumulation. Narcotraffic is a political device used by governments, particularly though not solely the United States, to justify repressive, disciplinary social control operations.

Once the distinction between cocaine trafficking and narcotraffic has been made, we can use it in social and political analysis. In the first place, this distinction cuts down on sensationalism, the manipulation of information, and demonization. The illegality of cocaine traffic makes possible its political and ideological manipulation, particularly when powerful interests control information. Second, recognizing that cocaine trafficking is a form of capitalist accumulation allows scholars to draw from the literature on political economy. Such scholarship assists in the recognition that the "illegality" of drug trafficking is both the principal factor behind its profitability and the reason for keeping secret relations between cocaine traffickers and governments. Third, the distinction between cocaine trafficking and narcotraffic highlights the international dimension: When cocaine traffic becomes international, illegal business relations reach beyond national sovereignties. The 1989 assassination of Luis Carlos Galán, senator and primary Liberal Party candidate for the Colombian presidency, made it clear that the Colombian–U.S. war on narcotraffic had transformed the capitalist cocaine business into a mechanism of U.S. control. The war on drugs was being used to counteract social turmoil in Colombia.

CRISIS, INSTITUTIONAL CHANGE, AND PARAINSTITUTIONALITY

Colombia's political institutions can be classified, at first sight, as representative and liberal–democratic. The Colombian government is founded on a constitution that directs the separation of government powers into three branches: Legislative, Executive, and Judicial. In principle, the organic and functional divisions between the branches guarantee the independent functioning of each in relation to the others.

Colombia has been one of the most stable democracies in Latin America. Since the end of General Rafael Reyes's government in 1910, it has had a representative democracy except for the regime of General Gustavo Rojas Pinilla (1953–1957), which was overthrown by a military triumvirate. In 1958, control of the State was turned over to civilians. For the rest of the century (from 1910 until 1953 and from 1958 to date), the Colombian government has been controlled by the traditional Liberal and Conservative parties, which have alternately been in power.

At the same time, Colombian political life has been punctuated by severe political and social convulsions. During these periods of extreme social turmoil, the formal division of powers has been little more than a fiction. Political analysts have pointed out that, in reality, the Executive has assumed prerogatives that weaken the independent functioning of other branches of government; this has created an imbalance in public power. This imbalance is particularly apparent in the authority exercised by the Executive branch: Order maintenance has been administered in Colombia by successive executives through the state of siege. The latter is allowable only under specified conditions, through Article 121 of the Colombian National Constitution.[27]

Other factors call into question Colombia's supposedly democratic–representative government. An important proportion of voting in Colombia is tied to political patronage; abstention is normal in elections, sometimes reaching more than 50 percent of all eligible voters.[28] Thus, even though Colombians formally have a multiparty democratic system, the government often seems to be run by a single party. In fact, the seeming differences between Liberal and Conservative parties actually hide an underlying unity that combines the factions into a single group.

Up to this point our characterization of Colombia's political system has been restricted to its formal components. We have not discussed social inequalities or imbalances in capitalist development—not because they are not important, but because they do not distinguish Colombia from other Latin American countries. What is peculiar to Colombia's political system, and also represents its strength, is the *combination* into one frame of "formal democratic" and "repressive authoritarian" mechanisms. Repressive mechanisms function to the extent that they exist *simultaneously* with democratic–formal ones and vice versa. In fact, the centerpiece of democratic functioning in Colombia is a set of highly repressive social control mechanisms. Let us examine how these repressive mechanisms are inserted into Colombia's formal political system.

Both the Liberal and the Conservative parties have governed Colombia through the state of siege,[29] initially justified as a safeguard for democracy. When the state of siege lost popularity in the early 1980s, paramilitary and parapolice control operations—already under development—came to be used more frequently. But the State had to dissociate itself from these actions while allowing them to substitute for a state of siege. The State, of course, actually worked hand in hand with parapolice and paramilitary violence.[30] The Colombian State is, therefore, able to wear a clean face for the outside world; its legitimacy appears to have democratic foundations. Its representative democratic features present to the international community an image that makes internal repression less noticeable.

In fact, in the 1980s (particularly with disuse of the state of siege), the "dirty war"[31] being waged by paramilitary and parapolice groups expanded in Colombia.[32] It manifested itself as threats, bombings, and selective assassination or collective massacres of government officials (principally but not exclusively from the left), and of popular political leaders, workers, peasants, professors, human rights activists, and members of nongovernmental organizations. The Colombian government did not do much to stop such paramilitary and parapolice violence. In fact, the State and its military were charged with complicity in this violence and terror.[33] Government officials countered that the State was not wholly responsible for such terror: The narcotraffickers and guerrillas were very difficult to control. The State maintained that these groups were responsible for a good deal of the political violence and terror.

Such widespread violence and terror have fostered the hypothesis that Colombia's "institutional crisis" can be resolved only through a reform of the political system.[34] One popular reform proposal includes revising the Colombian Constitution. However, participants in this debate differ on how to achieve constitutional reform—oscillating between using constitutional mechanisms to accomplish it and relying on "exceptional mechanisms" such as plebiscites and/or referenda.[35]

It would be comforting to believe that Colombia's violence could be eliminated by piecemeal reforms of the political system. Many reformers seem to assume that the formal "democratic" political dimension and the formal and informal authoritarian ones are distinct from (and contradictory to) one another.[36] But this assumption is incorrect.

In fact, what is peculiar to Colombia is the combining of democratic political institutions with highly repressive ones. In an earlier period, repressive social control was administered directly by the Colombian armed forces, with institutional support from a constitutionally legitimated state of siege. Now, extraofficial armed groups do the army's job though they seemingly have no organic links to the army.

PARAINSTITUTIONALITY AND POLITICAL CRISIS

Colombia's two-party, patronage-based political system has been weakened by, but has shown itself resistant to, pressures for political and social transformation. In the late 1960s, parainstitutional mechanisms that mediate, block, and take the place of legitimate social change were developed and streamlined. Without doubt such parainstitutional mechanisms existed prior to the 1960s, though not with their current magnitude and capacity for innovation.

The use of parainstitutional means to accomplish institutional reform became most prevalent during the presidency of Alfonso López Michelsen (1974–1978). The most obvious example of parainstitutionality during that regime was Michelsen's proposal that a Constituent Assembly direct social reforms, thus bypassing the Colombian Parliament. By the end of Julio César Turbay's presidency (1978–1982), the highly visible government violations of civil and political rights, through excessive parainstitutionality, had begun to erode Colombia's international image. In response, special commissions were organized to study the peace process and to negotiate an "amnesty" with guerrillas. These "peace initiatives" failed, but they did set a foundation for President Belisario Betancur Cuartas's "peace process" that included the participation of guerrilla organizations. Under Betancur, the "peace process" generated numerous study, discussion, and negotiation commissions.[37]

The failure of this entire process allowed the initiation and refinement, during the Virgilio Barco government (1986–1990), of additional parainstitutional experiments, including paramilitary and self-defense groups, the application of extradition treaties under vague constitutional or legal circumstances, and the implementation of work groups for peace and negotiation with the M–19, Colombia's major and perhaps best-known guerrilla organization.

PARAMILITARISM AS PARAINSTITUTIONALITY

In Colombia, the administration of justice is in crisis. This crisis had led Eduardo Farias, a specialist in juridical sociology, to question whether, in light of "the growing socioeconomic complexity of recent years, the [Colombian] courts and their respective magistrates [are] functionally and technically fit to deal with class conflicts and massive transgressions that involve groups and collective entities."[38] In other words, are the different judicial levels capable of effectively performing their basic functions, of absorbing tension and reducing the political and economic systems' uncertainties, limiting conflicts, and impeding generalization?

In the second half of 1989, the existence in Colombia of guerrillas, paramilitary groups, and the government's war on narcotraffic placed Colombia's Penal Code in question. Under the Penal Code, criminals are to be rehabilitated; suspects are considered innocent until proven guilty. In Colombia, this principle is frequently inverted, and institutional functioning has become unclear. The proper functioning of modern law implies a clear distinction between "peace" (when the law functions) and "war" (when it legitimately does not). This distinction has become vague in Colombia. If we are at war, as it is said, then criminals are enemies to be vanquished rather than rehabilitated. Such a lack of institutional delimitation is open territory for the emergence of parainstitutionality.

While Colombia's justice crisis is not exclusively Colombian, it acquires peculiar dimensions and characteristics in South America's northwestern corner. In Colombia the justice crisis is characterized by (1) a breakdown of the rule of law without installation of a military dictatorship, which allows maintenance of a democratic–representative facade that functions to legitimize the system of domination; (2) a neoliberal government restructuring that limits resources for "unproductive" expenses; (3) the conspicuous presence of social and guerrilla struggles; (4) development of alternative juridical formulas that rely on popular "juridical services," the latter producing alternative forms of justice (parainstitutionality) which are not subject to state monopoly.[39] Some of this parainstitutionality manifests itself as paramilitarism.

Paramilitarism is not new to Colombia. Colombian history, since the period known as *La Violencia* (1948–1962), has been plagued by it.[40] During La Violencia paramilitary groups acted as agents of the group in power. But Colombia's current paramilitary phenomenon is different. It does not have an explicitly defined *political* affiliation. Its origins are traced to cocaine entrepreneurs, who have had trouble establishing themselves within Colombia's formal political system. An anecdote illustrates the relationship of some paramilitarism to the cocaine entrepreneurs. In a 1983 fund-raising operation, M–19 kidnapped the daughter of Jorge Luis Ochoa, an important businessman. In order to obtain the young girl's release, the cocaine entrepreneurs created an antikidnapping group called MAS (Muerte a Securstradores) to which they donated money and manpower.[41] However, MAS was not dissolved once it had succeeded in punishing M–19 audacity. In fact, MAS paramilitary groups continued their cleanup operations against guerrillas in the central section of Colombia's northernmost department of

Magdalena. Links between MAS and the Colombian army have since been established.[42]

But, to return to the subject, how else can current paramilitary violence be distinguished from La Violencia? Today's violence is impregnated with internationalization. The existence in Colombia of Israeli mercenaries training paramilitary forces reveals the international influence on "paragovernmental" forces in central Magdalena. There is another example of international connections with Colombia's paramilitarism: The increased privatization of security by multinational companies has led to scores of people being incorporated into private security groups. This, according to del Olmo,[43] is one of the bases of parapolice groups. The privatization of security by multinational corporations is nourished by their lack of confidence in local police forces. "Parapolice" groups have come to be active in recent years in urban "cleanup" operations. Such operations result in the deaths of criminals, scrap dealers, indigent children, prostitutes, transvestites, beggars, and the unemployed.

The paramilitary groups do what official justice has been unable to do: They combat political crimes and attack the real or fictitious connections between guerrillas and popular and working-class sectors of the Colombian population. And, thanks to the myth of narcoterrorism, the Colombian army has established wartime rules for the application of social control. The army had difficulty legitimating wartime standards in its struggle against communism. Now, thanks to the war against narcotraffic, its job will not seem quite so "dirty."

PARAINSTITUTIONALITY AND REINSTITUTIONALIZATION

Even as parainstitutional mechanisms are being employed, the Colombian government is taking steps to "win the peace" through institutional reforms. Some of these reforms include the following:

—The creation of special judges, initially assigned to try only crimes against public order and, later, narcotraffic

—Establishment of a specialized antinarcotics police force

—Development of a new penal code and penal procedures

—The creation of a human rights agency subordinated to the president of the Republic

—Renewal of proposals for judicial reform, including mechanisms for release and elimination of juries; the latter are considered an anachronism in Colombia today

—Making it illegal to publicize formerly secret criminal investigations

—Creation of "peace advisers," principally responsible for peace negotiations with guerrilla groups but probably open as well to conversations with paramilitary "self-defense" groups

—Institutional changes aimed at "winning the peace," focusing on constitutional reforms associated with political decentralization and greater popular participation in mayoral elections.[44]

Today, the Colombian government is preparing for "peace" while encouraging parainstitutional forms of domination and repression that seemingly are not organically tied to the government. Narcotraffic provides both the impetus and the support for the seeming dissociation between the formal, democratic structures of control and the "informal," extrainstitutional ones. However, the variety and wealth of parainstitutional measures that the Colombian government has developed and deployed have become a source of resistance for subordinated classes. In response to State parainstitutionality, subordinated groups have come up with extrainstitutional devices of their own.[45]

Are paramilitarism and other forms of parainstitutionality transitory or permanent? In the case of paramilitarism, the Colombian government seems to have been involved with it long before Luis Carlos Galán's 1989 assassination. The Colombian government was perhaps encouraged that its paramilitary and parapolice groups were becoming autonomous of the government. If the government's formal repressive apparatus were able to intersect *informally* with such groups, the State might better be able to influence paramilitary groups toward government-supported ends.

COCAINE ENTREPRENEURS, PARAMILITARY GROUPS, AND THE PARASTATE

Cocaine entrepreneurs came into being in Colombia in the mid–1970s. At that time, the profitability of marijuana had fallen, following successful antinarcotic operations in Mexico (Operation Intercept) and in Jamaica (Operation Buccaneer).[46] These operations allowed a considerable part of marijuana cultivation, and the commercial operations associated with it, to be taken over by entrepreneurs on Colombia's Guajira Peninsula. But such prosperity was short-lived: Colombian President Julio César Turbay (1978–1982) allowed paraquat spraying of marijuana. Turbay left office amid accusations of complicity with the Mafia and of government corruption and patronage. The paraquat spraying ended marijuana production on the Colombian coast. Little by little, the illegal cocaine businesses of Antioquia and Cali (the Medellín and Cali cartels) grew to dimensions well beyond that of the marijuana barons. The political aspirations of cocaine entrepreneurs became obvious when they attempted to enter the formal political arena.

The cocaine entrepreneurs attempted to enter politics in two ways: by trying to join traditional parties, and through the financing of political campaigns. This gave new life to political patronage. But the early efforts by cocaine entrepreneurs to join traditional political parties miscarried when Colombia's minister of justice, who was Luis Carlos Galán's political rival, disclosed that "dirty" money was entering Colombian politics. The entrepreneurs responded by attempting to create their own political party. Carlos Ledher, one of the Medellín cartel's most important figures, founded the Movimiento Renovador Nacionalista. Ledher was later arrested and extradited; his party was dissolved. But this did not stop the cocaine entrepreneurs from attempting to move into traditional politics, as many new wealthy class factions have done. They continued to attempt to influence politicians and infiltrate traditional parties. To a large extent the cocaine entrepreneurs succeeded in infiltrating Colombian politics, although they were kept from running for political office. With much greater effectiveness, they moved into the formal economy, laundering dollars and becoming linked to it in various other ways.

But how is paramilitary action related to cocaine entrepreneurs? The 1984 assassination of Colombia's minister of justice set off an explosion of tensions between cocaine entrepreneurs and the State. Another source of tension was the late August 1989 assassination of Luis Carlos Galán. In both cases, the Colombian government took a tougher stand and implemented more drastic measures against the most visible cocaine capos—extraditing some and declaring war on the others. In the period between these two assassinations, the "narcos" continued to earn black marks with various sectors of the Colombian government. In a 1987 parliamentary debate, Minister of Justice José Manuel Arian Caizos and Minister of Defense General Rafael Samudia defended the citizens' right to form "self-defense" committees to protect life and property. The army, the Right, cattle ranchers, and national businessmen already supported paramilitary defense groups; the assassination of two key Colombian political figures lent added legitimacy to such groups.

Today, paramilitary connections reach throughout Colombian society: The cattle ranchers' professional organization, banana growers, and other business associations have been shown to associate with paramilitary groups. The former minister of justice, a champion of "self-defense" by private armed groups, is director of the banana growers' professional organization.[47]

Little by little, a type of parainstitutional parastate has emerged in Colombia. One segment of this parastate includes an alliance between cocaine entrepreneurs and the Colombian army. Cocaine entrepreneurs who saw their land investments threatened by guerrilla activity were willing to work with the army and vice versa. The repressive capacity that has resulted from this marriage is highly effective. Today, cocaine entrepreneurs need not become involved in direct combat with guerrilla groups. Instead, they use terrorist tactics to frighten the population. Their targets are labor, peasant, and popular leaders, and political activists and militants (principally from the Unión Patriótica, but also from the Frente Popular and others), as well as important human rights workers. The social control operations that are used against these groups are terrorist: They combine assassination with collective massacres.

Another important component of the Colombian "parastate" is cocaine entrepreneurs—a fraction of capital that has gained a stronghold within the dominant class. The cocaine entrepreneurs, through alliances with other fractions of capital, have gained territorial control and established social and political bases in some Colombian regions. Some Colombian analysts have labeled such an expansion of territorial control "narcofascism." This "narcofascism" exists in central Magdalena, part of Urab, some regions of Córdoba, and Colombia's eastern plains. Recently the parastate has attempted to launch a political party, Morena.

The parastate also provides "narcowelfare." In Envigado, an industrial town in Antioquia where the Medellín cartel enjoys great influence, there is a cartel-supported social security system that includes unemployment compensation. The latter is unheard-of in Colombia. And the cartel's Pablo Escobar has constructed a residential area for the poor.[48] In central Magdalena, groups of residents have held marches supporting their leaders, who have paramilitary connections.

The Colombian parastate is dominated by a powerful capitalist fraction, the cocaine entrepreneurs. It is fortified by a repressive military and paramilitary apparatus. The parastate engages in social welfare spending, has regional territorial control, and enjoys restricted but effective popular support. This parastate is not an "antistate." That is, it does not represent the subversion of state institutions, as the U.S. government often claims. Colombia's cocaine entrepreneurs contribute to the accumulation of capital in Colombia, not just to the expansion of cocaine-related businesses. They also contribute to State legitimacy by doing the job that State welfare and political institutions and the armed forces and police have proven incapable of doing. And the parastate has helped to promote the Colombian government's democratic image internationally: Violations of human rights are said to have been caused by "malevolent forces," guerrillas, or "narcotraffickers." The State uses the guerrilla threat to control popular struggles. The confusion generated by all of the discourse about "narcotraffic" has helped the Colombian army accomplish its dirty work: Seemingly nongovernment groups, rather than official police and military violence and the judicial system, have been used against unarmed progressive forces.

We could mistakenly conclude that in Colombia parainstitutional methods, which are separate and distinct from formal institutional ones, are most effective at controlling popular disturbances and guerrillas. If this is true, the State should deepen and consolidate the parainstitutional structures, particularly those responsible for repression. But to conceptualize parainstitutional mechanisms as separate from formal institutional ones gives the mistaken impression that a real dividing line exists between them. On the contrary, the Colombian State's effectiveness lies precisely in its ability to combine seemingly opposed structures and mechanisms. This is why we argue that in Colombia parainstitutionality points to State flexibility. Colombia's particular style of democracy requires such flexibility.

But the Colombian State's reliance on parainstitutionality has forced a turn in the road. We must remember that parainstitutionality was produced, in part, by the growth of a class fraction that, along with multinational capital, represented a challenge to the oligarchy. The illegality of cocaine, the high rates of economic accumulation associated with it, and the high levels of political profitability from it make it necessary for the Colombian State to come to terms with this new fraction of capital, albeit discreetly and secretly. This is why we argue that the position of this new class fraction within Colombian national life results from "subterranean corrosion."

However, we must not conclude that the relationship between the Colombian State and its parastate is totally harmonious. It is not. The 1989 assassination of an important Colombian politician points to an erosion of the seemingly amicable relationship between the Colombian State and the parastate. In fact, the Barco government "declared war" on cocaine entrepreneurs, with the U.S. government's blessing. After this declaration of war the United States announced new (principally military) aid to the Colombian government. This aid—planes, military equipment, and advisers—does not seem to be the appropriate way to combat narcotraffic.

Colombia's State–parastate conflict has clearly taken on a greater international tone infused with military characteristics. There are, besides U.S. military advisers in Colombian territory, foreign mercenaries: Israelis and some British have trained paramilitary groups in central Magdalena, a zone under the narcos' control. The military nature of this conflict was driven home in early 1989 by the seizure of arms that were supposedly for the Colombian armed forces. But, according to recent disclosures, those arms were really earmarked for paramilitary groups. It appears, to paraphrase Clausewitz, that narcotraffic is the continuation of politics and war by other means.

FROM NARCOGUERRILLAS TO NARCOTERRORISM

Relations between the Colombian government and cocaine entrepreneurs at times have been close, and at other times tense and distant.

Tension existed after the 1984 and 1989 assassinations of Ministers of Justice Rodrigo Lara Bonilla and Luis Carlos Galan, respectively. Both assassinations were said to have been carried out by narcotraffickers, though they did not totally originate there. Nevertheless, the takeover in 1985 of the Colombian Supreme Court by M–19 marks a clear shift in State–parastate relations. Since then, the Colombian government and narcotraffickers have joined together against guerrillas. In the midst of this shift, the United States and the DEA have promoted new definitions of the sources of conflict. There has been a shift in discourse about the enemy—from a war against "narcoguerrillas" to one against "narcoterrorism."

But why is "narcoterrorism" a more effective national and international rallying cry than guerrilla insurgency? First, the guerrillas are seen by many as Colombia's internal problem. Second, many Colombians still consider the guerrillas politically "altruistic" (i.e., they aim at changing society). Terrorism, on the contrary, "threatens national foundations and the international community." It "should be condemned" by the Right and the Left. Combating terrorism is "in the common interest of humanity." The threat of "narcoterrorism" has breathed new life into demands for paramilitary action. Moreover, charges that a group is "narcoterrorist" delegitimize it. Such charges are frequently lodged against groups that refuse to participate in the Colombian government's "peace negotiations."

CONCLUSIONS

This chapter proposes a critical analysis of the relationship between cocaine entrepreneurs and the Colombian State. A central premise is that the Colombian State has developed a parainstitutional dimension which is founded on a new and powerful fraction of capital: cocaine entrepreneurs. However, parainstitutionality cannot be attributed to the cocaine entrepreneurs alone. An anticapitalist parainstitutionality manifests itself in the social struggles by subordinated classes and guerrilla groups. The latter has barely been mentioned in this chapter, which has focused instead on the repressive parainstitutionality that has grown out of narcotraffic and State crisis. It is within this parainstitutionality that various sectors of the State coincide and form a "right wing" supported by business sectors (in addition to some cocaine entrepreneurs) and outside interests (Israelis are now being replaced by U.S. military advisers). The internationalized nature of the Colombian State crisis leads to a rejection of the hypothesis that two or three Colombian capos (e.g., Pablo Escobar and Gonzalo Rodríguez Gacha) provide the key to understanding narcotraffic in Colombia. Concentrating attention exclusively on them is bound to distract us from struggle and social transformation in Colombia.

In Colombian political science it is now common to argue that the two-party political system is limited and does not allow broad participation by the population. Many Colombian political scientists call for a broadening of the system to create new parties and factions. This presumably would represent multiparty modernity. Without doubt, the Colombian political system—understood in terms of parties—is limited. But we have demonstrated that in spite of such formal political limitations, the regime is very flexible. Its elasticity comes from the emergence of parainstitutionality to control social struggles. Only occasionally does this reinstitutionalizing elasticity open up party politics.

Underneath State flexibility and parainstitutionality lie struggles of resistance by popular groups. Added to these is the work of human rights activists to bring about social and political transformation in Colombia. All such groups of resistance, though they lack a common strategy, have been developing their own forms of parainstitutionality. This parainstitutionality not only confronts state institutions, it also challenges the State's repressive parainstitutionality.

NOTES

1. G. Palacio (1988), "Democracia y crisis de la justicia en Colombia," in *La reforma del estado en América Latina*, Pedro Medellín, ed. (Fescol, Bogotá).

2. E. Pizarro (1988), "Democracia restringida y desinstitucionalización política," in *La reforma del estado en América Latina*, Pedro Medellín, ed. (Fescol, Bogotá).

3. F. Rojas (1980), "El estado en los ochenta: Hacia un régimen Político," in *Controversia*, no. 5 (CINEP, Bogotá).

4. A. Vargas (1989), "Guerrilla y régimen político en Colombia," paper presented at Seminario Crisis Institucional y Violencia (ILSA, Bogotá); A. Reyes (1988), "Conflictos agrarios y luchas armadas en la Colombia contemporánea: Una visión geográfica," in *Análisis político*, no. 5, pt. I (Nacionál, Bogotá).

5. Americas Watch (1988), *The Killings in Colombia* (New York).

6. Palacio, "Democracia y crisis de la justicia."

7. CINEP (Centro de Investigación y Educación Popular) (1988–1989), *Documentos: Conflicto social y violencia* (CINEP, Bogotá); Comisión de Estudios sobre Violencia (1987), *Colombia: Violencia y democracia* (Universidad Nacional de Colombia, Bogotá); G. Palacio (1989), "El discurso sobre la violencia: Hacia la reconstrucción de la neutralidad del Estado," paper presented at Seminario Crisis Institucional y Violencia (ILSA, Bogotá).

8. R. Uprimny (1989), "Politiques d'ajustement et recompositions sociales en Amérique Latine," *Revue du tiers monde*, 30, no. 117 (January–March).

9. Prospects for 1990 are not very promising. The drop in the price of coffee, sabotage of oil pipelines by guerrillas, the "war on narcotraffic," and violence

in the country—factors that do not attract transnational capital—do not allow us to be very optimistic.

10. C. Offe (1984), *The Contradictions of the Welfare State* (MIT Press, Cambridge, Mass.).

11. K. Marx (1941), *El capital, crítica de la economía política* (F.C.E., México, D.F.).

12. F. Rojas (1989), "Hacia la construcción de nuevos conceptos para entender la política en Colombia," paper presented at Seminario Crisis Institucional y Violencia (ILSA, Bogotá).

13. *Narcotráfico*, in the original text, that is, drug trafficking or narcotraffic. Due to a conceptual distinction that Palacio later develops, *narcotráfico* and its derivatives are consistently translated as narcotraffic, narcotraffickers, and so on.

14. R. del Olmo (1987), *La cara oculta de la droga* (Temis, Bogotá).

15. R. del Olmo (1989), "Drogas: Distorsiones y realidades," in *Nueva sociedad* (Caracas), no. 102.

16. N. Hardinghaus, (1989), "Droga y crecimiento econónuci: El narcotráfico en las cuentas nacionales," en *Nueva sociedad*, no. 102, pp. 94–106; M. Arango and J. Child (1985), *Los condenados de la coca: El manejo político de la droga* (J. I. Arango, Medellín).

17. "The Pols and Pariahs: The Wealth That Leaves No Tracks," *Fortune* 116, October 12, 1987, p. 189.

18. *The New York Times* (1987), "Colombian Cocaine Route," 3/15.

19. *El Tiempo* (1987), 3/20.

20. P. Reuter (1989), "Documento de trabajo preparado para el Diálogo Interamericano," in *Las Américas en 1989: Consenso para la acción* (Queenstown, Md.: The Aspen Institute).

21. Arango and Child, *Los condenados*.

22. Arango and Child, *Los condenados*; del Olmo, "Drogas."

23. A. McCoy (1983), *The Politics of Heroin in South East Asia* (Harper Books, New York).

24. Some authors maintain that while the DEA emphasizes police intelligence operations against major figures, the CIA is capable of carrying out military operations. However, a large part of the activities traditionally associated with the CIA are being assumed by the DEA. A. Henman (1989), *Mama Coca* (Bogotá: El Ancora), pp. 107–8.

25. R. del Olmo (1985), *La sociopolítica de las drogas* (Faces, Caracas).

26. P. Laurie (1970), *Las drogas: Aspectos médicos, psicológicos y sociales* (Alianza, Madrid).

27. G. Gallón (1979), *Quince años de estado de sitio en Colombia, 1958–1978* (América Latina, Bogotá); F. Leal (1984), *Estado y política en Colombia* (Siglo XXI-Cerec, Bogotá).

28. E. Díaz (1986), *El clientelismo en Colombia: Un estudio exploratorio* (El Ancora, Bogotá).

29. The need to restore the mechanism of the state of siege is officially recognized, as outlined in the constitutional reform project establishing levels of civil threat (state of alert, internal commotion, etc.). We do not consider its use to be over. Its permanence and use by the government is one evidence of "regime flexibility."

30. Americas Watch, *The Killings in Colombia;* Amnesty International (1988), "Colombia: Una crisis de los derechos humanos" (mimeo, London); Amnesty International (1989), "Colombia. El panorama de los derechos humanos: 'Escuadrones de la muerte' a la defensive?" (mimeo, London).

31. "Dirty war" is an ambiguous and unfortunate expression because of its diverse utilizations. It was used during the Argentine military regime of the late 1970s and early 1980s. Criticism of the expression's ideological imprecision has been formulated in D. Frontalini and M. Caiati (1984), *El mito de la guerra sucia* (CELS, Buenos Aires).

32. V. Moncayo and F. Rojas (1989), "Tendencias de reinstitucionalización del estado en Colombia," in *La reforma del estado,* Pedro Medellín, ed. (Fescol, Bogotá), pp. 285–87.

33. Americas Watch, *The Killings in Colombia;* Amnesty International, "Colombia: Una crisis" and "Colombia: El panorama."

34. Moncayo and Rojas, "Tendencias de reinstitucionalización"; E. Pizarro (1986), "100 años de la Constitución: Reforma política o catástrofe," *Revista Foro,* no. 1, and "Democracia restringida."

35. G. Murillo (1988), "Hacia la democracia participativa en Colombia: Restos y posibilidades," *Pensamiento iberoamericano* (Madrid), no. 13; H. Valencia (1989), "De las guerras constitucionales en Colombia: Un informe sobre la reforma Barco," *Boletín CAJ* (Lima).

36. Comisión de Estudios sobre Violencia, *Colombia: Violencia y democracia.*

37. S. Ramírez and L. A. Restrepo (1989), *Actores en conflicto por la paz* (Siglo XXI-CINEP, Bogotá).

38. Eduardo Farias (1989), *Direito e Justiça* (São Paulo: Atica).

39. G. Palacio (1989), "Servicios jurídicos populares y restructuración capitalista," in *El otro derecho,* no. 3 (ILSA, Bogotá); G. Palacio (1989), *Crisis institucional, jueces y alternativa* (ILSA, Bogotá); F. Rojas (1988–1989), "Comparaciones entre las tendencias de los servicios legales en Norteamérica, Europa y América Latina," in *El otro derecho,* no. 1–2 (ILSA, Bogotá).

40. *La Violencia,* a period of extreme violence that began as a confrontation between the Liberal and Conservative parties but quickly degenerated into generalized bloodshed throughout the country. Some estimates say that it took the lives of 180,000 Colombians. See Eduardo Galeano (1980), *Las venas abiertas de América Latina,* 29th ed. (Siglo XXI Editores, México, D. F.), pp. 163–68.

41. M. Maza (1988), *Justicia privada* (DAS, Bogotá).

42. Americas Watch, "The Killings in Colombia" (mimeo, 1989).

43. R. del Olmo (1989), "Quién mató a Galán?" (mimeo, Caracas).

44. V. Moncayo, F. Rojas, and G. Palacio (1989), "Tendencias reorgánicas del estado colombiano contemporáneo," in *Democratización, modernización y actores socio-políticos* (CLACSO, Buenos Aires); D. Restrepo (1988), "Política económica neoliberal y descentralización," in *La reforma de estado en América Latina* (Fescol, Bogotá).

45. Rojas, "Hacia la construcción de nuevos conceptos."

46. Arango and Child, *Los condenados.*

47. Americas Watch, "The Killings in Colombia."

48. *The New York Times,* (1991) "Drug Baron's Prison," 6/22.

III
THE DISCOURSE ABOUT VIOLENCE

INTRODUCTION

Darius Rejali

What is the relationship between language and the violent acts of governments? In this section, the writers examine how language supports what government officials do. But perhaps the proper place to begin is not with the languages that provide implicit support for vigilantism but with the languages that protect individuals from violence.

Today, the language of rights provides the universal vocabulary through which people struggle against oppression and articulate their diverse concerns. "Rights language" is universal in the sense that it is understandable by anyone from Chile to Liberia. Latin American countries, in particular, entrench this language by guaranteeing civil and religious liberties in their constitutions and by building up appropriate institutions, such as parliaments and independent judiciaries.

But anyone familiar with Latin America recognizes that constitutions provide a very poor blueprint for what is going on in the relevant governmental institutions, and the protection of civil and religious liberties is anything but guaranteed in practice. Echandía places this issue at the center of his analysis, examining the relationship between what governments say and what they do. He shows how government officials can justify, in their own minds, the gap between what they say and what they do. In particular, he shows how the concern for national security is legislated and how this in turn entrenches increasingly autocratic judicial practices. Rejali also picks up on this discussion of national security, but from a different angle. He examines how a community of social scientists tries to explain what is happening, showing how certain ways of reading violence make violence more tolerable.

Like Echandía, he focuses on how what social scientists say about violence does not always square with what people are doing.

For both writers, the important question is: How does the violent abuse of human rights, an extraordinary event within a constitutional state, become routinized through the ways people talk about security, violence, or justice? For Echandía, routinization occurs through legislation and legal judgments, which are enactments and interpretations from biased perspectives. For Rejali, routinization occurs through social scientific explanation; every explanation can function as a justification for why things ought to be as they are. Ideally, these two articles should be read alongside works that focus on how gossip and rumor function to routinize violence—for example, Michael Taussig's work on Colombia.

These writers, in this context, show particularly well the pervasiveness in modern times of a particular style of thinking, what has been called "national security" thinking, *raison d'état*, or *Staatsräson*. This is the view that whenever the vital interests of the state are threatened, rulers should be allowed great latitude in exercising power even when they violate legal and moral restraints that ordinarily are supposed to limit their actions.

What is important about this way of thinking is that it permeates all constitutional regimes, whether they are developed or developing states. To cite a particularly famous American example, in 1861 Abraham Lincoln, in a move reminiscent of many Latin American leaders, suspended habeas corpus and assumed extensive responsibilities traditionally exercised by Congress. Many of Lincoln's acts, which at best had very thin constitutional justification, fit Echandía's definition of national security legislation in Latin America.

Another important question is why national security legislation is more pervasive in some countries than in others. In this regard, both Rejali and Echandía lean toward endorsing what Rejali calls the "state terrorist hypothesis," although with significant qualifications. This is the view that most violence in Latin America is accounted for by the emergence of national security states that enforce the interests of multinational corporations. Whatever the readers may think about this particular explanation for the pervasiveness of violence, the articles in this section clearly articulate the different ways that language functions to support vigilantism.

8
HOW NOT TO TALK ABOUT TORTURE: VIOLENCE, THEORY, AND THE PROBLEMS OF EXPLANATION

Darius Rejali

What I would like to do in this chapter is to consider some common perspectives on modern torture and whether they are reliable guides for analysis. More specifically, I will set out to dislodge certain natural and tempting misconceptions about political violence by outlining what we now know about torture. In the case of torture, because these temptations are particularly inviting, a different perspective is much more difficult to appreciate. Insofar as I have a positive account of torture, its chief purpose is to act as an antidote to mistaken or misleading claims about modern political violence.

I will consider three approaches to torture in this chapter: The humanist, the developmental, and the state terrorist. I will briefly consider the strengths and weaknesses of these approaches, focusing first on the weaknesses and then returning to their strengths. Finally, I wish to consider how, in the broadest way, these approaches fail or fall short of serving as a guide to thinking about torture and how, by considering their strengths, we could turn our thoughts in a more promising direction.

THE HUMANIST APPROACH

Humanism involves the very strong claim that human beings are inherently worthy of respect. For many humanists, this claim cannot be separated from the creation of a vital public sphere in which individuals treat, and learn to treat, one another with dignity. Briefly stated, then, the humanist approach is the view that, as societies become civilized and establish vital public spheres, barbaric practices such as torture will eventually disappear.

In the nineteenth century many humanists believed that such a public life was firmly established in Europe, and the prospects for the rest of the world looked good. Pointing to the disappearance of many ceremonial spectacles of penal torture in the colonies, they could assert optimistically that torture would shortly disappear from the world through the impact of enlightened government.[1] Today, this seems wildly implausible even as a description of the nineteenth century. European and American police practices were notoriously brutal and set the standard for colonial interrogations, notably in India and the Philippines.[2] Since then many Western societies, including Germany, France, England, and the United States, have resorted to torture or, at the very least, have trained others in its use.

Humanists are hard pressed to explain these events. One can say that torture persists because modernizing societies have failed to adopt civilized norms. But this explanation simply sidesteps the main issue: that European societies themselves have practiced torture in the period since the late nineteenth century. A more interesting explanation was advanced by Hannah Arendt in *The Origins of Totalitarianism*.[3] Although she affirmed the importance of a public sphere, she argued that this sphere was under considerable pressure from the bureaucratic tendencies of modern societies. For Arendt, torture appears whenever bureaucratic life overwhelms the public, democratic life of modern societies. I shall focus on her work because it is so representative of radical humanist writers.[4]

Arendt's argument turns on a familiar thesis that there is an inevitable tension between bureaucracy and democracy in modern states. On the one hand, democrats needs capable bureaucrats to administer the law impartially and effectively. On the other hand, bureaucrats are specialists hostile to amateur politicians interfering with their work. Further, because bureaucratic work can be quite technical, democrats have a hard time regulating bureaucracies or making sure that work is being done properly. Bureaucracies, as a result, can expand in unregulated and sometimes antidemocratic ways. If democrats cannot do without bureaucrats, it is equally clear that democrats empower "a bureaucratically articulated group which in its turn may occupy a quite autocratic position, both in fact and in form."[5]

Arendt explored the tension between bureaucracy and democracy further. What would happen if, as in Nazi Germany and Stalinist Russia, the tension was resolved as a victory of bureaucratic life over public life? In such conditions, she observed, individuals no longer interact as equal subjects deliberating on a common good but as objects within a huge chain of command. To put it another way, men and women no longer act according to the rule of law (a substantive understanding of human dignity). Rather, they act according to administrative rules and quotas, what Arendt calls instrumentalist rationality.[6] Arendt illustrated this point forcefully in the case of Adolf Eichmann. By learning to submit to bureaucratic regulations, Eichmann learned to disregard any residual notions of dignity he possessed.[7] The disastrous results—repression, torture, and genocide—illustrated the workings of administrative terror. In the modern age, violence is no longer necessarily exercised by evil, cruel tyrants, as it had been in the past. Rather, it is exercised by bored yet dutiful bureaucrats, a situation pointing up the fact that, in the modern age, evil is banal. And what is most troublesome is that evil of this sort is embedded in beings who were indispensable for modern political systems: bureaucrats.

This sort of account is certainly a gripping one but, as an account of modern torture, it is quite misleading. The difficulty is that writers in this genre often simply denounce terror rather than explain it.[8] They do this despite their desire to clarify how torture works today. In fact, they are driven to do so by the way they talk about the world.

The humanist approach turns on a key distinction—one between the public realm and the realm of administration. Actually, this simple distinction hides a remarkable asymmetry. In the humanist view, the ideal of public life is set forth, and everything that is not part of this life is "administration." The notion of rule by bureaucracy is constructed not on the basis of observations but as a hypothetical opposite to rule of law. This fact is reflected in the problems that arise when we try to use the humanist distinction empirically.

Torture is, no doubt, administered by bureaucracies, but it is exercised in remarkably different ways. The manner in which torturers act on victims can vary according to the type of rationality that characterizes an administrative system. However, in the humanist approach, all these modes of governing individuals are thrown together in the same category, although they share little more than the label "administration." And to the extent that humanists ignore these differences, they have a harder time explaining what is going on in torture bureaucracies.

Let me illustrate this point by noting briefly the variety of different administrative rationalities and how these are related to torture. In some bureaucracies, human beings relate to one another solely as *objects* to be manipulated, that is, they act according to instrumentalist rationality. There are also bureaucracies in which people are treated as *subjects* to be transformed, converted, or healed. Examples of such bureaucracies might be church or psychiatric bureaucracies, which have had historical roles in the development of torture. In the 1950s one of the key ways that torture changed was with the introduction of psychological warfare and, with it, the participation of a new group of specialists in torture.

The purpose of these specialists was to treat their victims not as objects of punishment but as subjects whose perceptions had to be altered.[9]

Humanists, of course, are less concerned with these modes of administration than they are with the administrative modes that treat people as objects. But it is a mistake to think that because some bureaucrats treat persons as objects, there must be a single rationality that characterizes all their actions. There are at least three different types of instrumentalist rationality, that is, three ways in which people learn to treat other people as objects.[10] Each of these describes a particular type of administrative structure. One can, for instance, treat someone as a means to an end, as one does in a military organization or a post office. Or one can interact with another as part of a system, as people interact with one another in an information network. Or one can interact with people as opponents to be strategically defeated or won over, as one does within a policy institute.

Torture may be characterized by one or some combination of these instrumentalist rationalities. One may torture an individual for a confession, that is, use a person as a means to an end. Torturing people in this way seems to be particularly associated with judicial systems having rigid and severe standards of legal proof. This is because, in such systems, confessions are often the only sure way of obtaining a conviction.[11]

Or one may torture individuals simply to set an example to others. Thus, we have the spectacle in many countries today of tortured dissidents appearing on national television to praise the regime's policies. There is a semiotics of torture here that needs to be deciphered, one in which individuals and their torturers operate as part of a large media spectacle. This sort of media attention can raise the climate of fear and suspicion; sometimes governments that torture welcome independent coverage by journalists. Amnesty International reports that in Guatemala, newspapers are allowed to publish pictures of dead torture victims, although the accompanying articles are faithful to the government line.[12]

The main point is that in such a system, torture does not cease when individuals confess because, in most cases, individuals have little or no information to give. They are of no use except as parts of a system of media representations. And that is why they are tortured.

Finally, torture may be characterized by strategic rationality, especially when it occurs in the context of counterinsurgency warfare. For example, during the Huk campaigns in the Philippines, torture was part of a carrot-and-stick approach to win the support of the peasantry and to strategically undermine the rural support of Huk insurgents.[13] What is worth emphasizing here is that torture was not used primarily to gain confessions or to use individuals as part of a communications system but, rather, to strategically outmaneuver an opponent. Individuals could be tortured even when doing so served no intelligence or public relations purpose. The main point was simply to make the environment too hostile for political opposition to operate, and one way of doing this, it would seem, was to torture peasants.

Thus torture can be employed by different sorts of administrations characterized by specific forms of rationality. The torturer may act on the tortured as a priest seeking a conversion, a surgeon operating on a patient, a psychiatrist transforming a subject. The torturer may explain what is done in the same terms as a detective, a publicist, or a counterinsurgency expert. Each of these ways of acting describes a distinctive mode of government and casts an entirely different light on how torture operates in a society.

Can humanists integrate these insights into their explanatory scheme? Humanists can acknowledge that they conceived of administrative torture too unclearly, but in any case, torture does occur when administrative rationality overwhelms public, democratic life. The test of this, of course, would be to show that torture decreases as democrats gain more control of public life. But the record on this score is more than a little mixed. Torture has been practiced by many Western democratic states such as France, and continues today in others.[14] Perhaps humanists have in mind an ideal of public life other than contemporary democracies; but in that case they should not give the impression that they are trying to *explain* torture.

But even if we accept the humanist approach on these terms, I fear the normative ideal of public life serves as a poor guide to how to struggle against torture. On the humanist approach, the key problem is to establish the rule of law and basic democratic institutions; democrats will then solve the torture problem.[15] I am not persuaded that this argument is applicable to more than a handful of countries today, since it forgets that torture occurs in states with little prospect of becoming democratic. More than that, this argument is misleading; it asks us to struggle against torture in the wrong places. If torture is shaped by administrative rationalities, then human rights groups must struggle directly with the rationalities of modern administration—as, in fact, they do.[16] Finally, even if democracy is reestablished in repressive societies, this does not put politicians in a better position to confront administrative groups responsible for torture.[17] *At best*, the struggle for democracy may be related to the struggle against torture; but it is not identical with it for it cannot provide the tools for confronting modern administrative rationalities.

THE DEVELOPMENTALIST APPROACH

The developmentalist approach is concerned with the dynamics of economic modernization. Briefly, it is animated by the belief that as societies modernize, there is a decrease in the severity of punishments. This decrease does not necessarily occur because people become more enlightened. Rather, it is brought about by the rationalization of economic and political life. As individuals are introduced to civic and labor discipline, they learn to regulate themselves according to their conscience.[18] External sanctions, at least barbaric ones, are no longer necessary to maintain order.

This argument has had a tremendous influence on social scientists studying the process of modernization in developing countries. Nonetheless, these scholars disagree among themselves as to the kind of development that should be emphasized. Some believe that economic development allows for a decrease in the severity and extent of violence over time.[19] Others—notably Huntington, Pye, and Olson—argue that economic development has a destabilizing effect on societies and promotes violence.[20] In the latter view, the real cause of violence is the lack of *political*, not economic, development. Developing states are unable to broaden the scope of political participation fast enough to meet the new demands placed upon them. As a result, disaffected groups turn to violence and governments resort to harsh sanctions, including torture.

Since the second view is the one that eventually became orthodoxy, I shall be concerned mainly with the way its adherents deal with torture. For modernization theorists, the question is this: How can governments expand the scope of political participation while in a potentially violent and unstable situation? Huntington and Pye place particular emphasis on counterinsurgency warfare.[21] Counterinsurgency warfare not only contains the extent of random civil strife but also facilitates the process of political development. This is because, through the training of police and military to work effectively, individuals are created who regulate themselves internally rather than by threat of external sanction. Such self-regulating individuals are crucial for the development process: "The capacity for coordination and discipline are [*sic*] crucial to both war and politics and historically societies which have been skilled at organizing the one have always been adept at organizing the other."[22] State warfare, then, plays a role in the formation of disciplinary habits, habits that in turn facilitate political and economic development. "Discipline and development," Huntington says, "go hand in hand."[23]

From this perspective, the violence of the state can be characterized as an unfortunate, necessary, and (in the long run) beneficial response to high levels of civil violence in developing countries.[24] To be sure, counterinsurgency warfare is violent, but it is far preferable to government torture and civil strife. As Huntington puts it, "The civil violence which development produces is not the violence that produces development."[25] And if counterinsurgent troops do on occasion torture, this is clearly a technical problem of providing adequate resources and training to troops in the field: Good soldiers simply know better.

It is reassuring to know that torture is a temporary aberration, a dysfunction produced by the lack of political development. The trouble is that while economic modernization can lead to increased civil strife, there is no clear relationship between civil strife and the extent to which a government resorts to torture. In certain regions, notably Latin America, civil strife is strongly correlated with other factors. States that do torture are generally the states that receive the highest per capita foreign aid prior to repression, or military regimes that receive counterinsurgency training, or regimes with weak organized labor and high levels of direct foreign investment.[26] One can hope that military training can reduce random violence in the long run, but this seems to be a dim prospect.

Furthermore, development theorists suggest that when governments resort to torture, this is primarily reactive. The trouble is that, at least in Latin America and the Middle East, the proactive element is an important feature of government repression. Much of this is due to the impact of counterinsurgency training or, more recently, narcotics control training. For example, in Brazil the military had always played a role in maintaining internal order. However, counterinsurgency training intensified the military's interest in internal, rather than external, warfare. Once the military was shaped in this way, soldiers set about performing this task in a professional, disciplined way. And this meant that rather than waiting for a real incident of violence, paramilitary forces sought out social groups that they suspected *might* protest government actions.[27] Counterinsurgency training does teach better organizational skills, but this does not mean that it will reduce government violence against civilians.

And this leads to a third problem with the developmentalist approach. Development theorists suggest that torture occurs only in proportion to the extent of civil opposition, whereas, in many cases, torture continues long after there is no organized civil opposition to the state. In Argentina and Iran, for example, the intensity of government violence seems to bear no special relation to the extent of civil opposition. These states tortured systematically and intensely even when the opposition had been decimated.[28]

Why is the developmentalist approach so misleading about the world of torture? The reason has to do with the way in which development theorists think about the determinants of political stability. For them, political stability is based on the consensus of the political community. And this consensus grows to the extent that political systems allow for popular participation and effectively meet social demands.

Although political community may enhance political stability, it is not the only factor that conditions it. Take the example of South Africa. The lack of political consensus in this country may explain the high levels of civil strife, but it does not account for the continued stability of the South African regime. Its continued persistence raises an interesting theoretical point: that the lack of political community can be offset by the efforts of a determined minority as long as it is willing and able to repress a population.[29]

Most states today possess large and well-armed standing armies as well as efficient means of transport and communication. Many of these states, notably those in Africa, Asia, and Latin America, are led by determined elites who are quite willing to employ force to achieve their ends. The difficulty with the developmentalist approach is that one finds it hard to conceptualize such states within its framework. If such brutal states persist, it *must be* because they enjoy some measure of political community.[30] But of course this does not have to be the case. Development theorists draw the conditions for political stability too narrowly. They assume that only the consent of the governed is sufficient to ensure persistence of a regime. In this way, they turn a blind eye to the most common experience of this century, the creation of military–industrial states that have deliberately set about deporting, torturing, and exterminating their populations.

THE STATE TERRORIST APPROACH

Although death squads and terrorist groups may torture victims, only states have the resources to torture systematically. States possess the financial and human resources to sustain a torture complex. Further, they can rely on support from other sectors of society to provide technical support (hospitals and mental asylums) and information (universities, unions, the criminal underground). If state officials are responsible for most torture, then state terrorism, not civil strife, ought to be the focus of analysis.

Analysts who adopt this perspective work within what I call the state terrorist approach. Rather than survey this literature, I shall focus on the work of Noam Chomsky and Edward Herman, analysts who have done more than many others to provide a coherent picture of state terror in the late twentieth century.[31] Of course, Chomsky and Herman do not attempt to explain state terrorism everywhere, but only in states closely allied with the United States. But what is especially distinctive about their approach is that they put the focus firmly on the "economy of violence"[32] in these countries and not, as many others do, on the economy of exploitation.

Chomsky and Herman draw attention away from torture to what might be called a torture complex. Torture, they point out, is "a mode of governance"[33] characterized by "standard operating procedures in multiple detention centers, applicable to hundreds of detainees and used with the approval and intent of the highest authorities."[34] There is some dramatic evidence to support this claim. In 1978, the Vietnamese routed the Khmer Rouge from Kampuchea. The retreat was so sudden that the Khmer Rouge left behind an intact torture complex, the Tuol Sleng prison. Amnesty International researchers have uncovered remarkable material at Tuol Sleng including torture manuals; biographies of torturers; very thorough prison records; detailed accounts of interrogations, confessions, and medical examinations; and elaborate flow charts showing the interrelationship of enemy networks based on the forced confessions.[35] Similarly, in 1975 human rights investigators visited the Second Army Headquarters in São Paulo, a site of numerous human rights abuses. They found the headquarters to be "a huge torture complex which has at its disposal the most modern and sophisticated equipment, and which requires an increasing number of staff—jailers, drivers, executioners, typists, public relations officers, doctors and others—to run."[36]

Chomsky and Herman also point to the international side of torture, including the arms suppliers, the foreign governments that provide training, and the way torture complexes interact on a global scale. Again researchers have gathered evidence that gives qualified support to this thesis.[37]

Finally, Chomsky and Herman link torture complexes to the international economic system. In their account, torture appears to originate in the creation of national security states in developing countries. The task of these states is to crush class protests while maintaining economic growth on behalf of multinational interests. In short, torture exists in order to maintain labor discipline and to keep the cost of labor within a range acceptable to capitalist interests. Thus, Chomsky and Herman have no difficulty explaining why government violence is proactive or, for that matter, why this violence is disproportionate to the incidents of civil opposition.

Nevertheless, Chomsky and Herman do describe the operation of torture complexes in the language of economics, and it is here that difficulties arise. No doubt repression may be useful in maintaining exploitive economic relationships, but this does not clarify the character of repression. Why, for example, is torture employed in preference to a more intensive disciplinary system? And what accounts for changes and variations in a torture complex—for example, change from prison-based torture to the psychoprison?

Moreover, while economic rationality explains why businessmen support regimes that torture, it does not explain the behavior of those who torture. A torture complex is a very costly and inefficient system by economic standards. It is costly because it involves large expenditures of money, equipment, and training for torturers as well as for the maintenance of extensive detention facilities. Yet despite these expenditures, torture complexes are remarkably inefficient. Within them, discipline becomes lax. Bureaucrats and guards stop performing their duties and become more involved in the pursuit of personal profit and pleasure. These activities may range from sadism and blackmail to large-scale prostitution or drug-smuggling operations.

The Tuol Sleng "interrogator's manual" illustrates some of the problems that administrators confront in running a torture complex. At one point, the instructor tries to explain the ethics of torture to his students:

> The purpose of torturing is to get their responses. It's not something we do for fun. We must hurt them so that they respond quickly. Another purpose is to break them and make them lose their will. It's not something that's done out of individual anger, or for self-satisfaction. So we beat them to make them afraid, but absolutely not to kill them. When torturing, it is necessary to examine their state of health first, and then whip. Don't be so bloodthirsty that you cause their death quickly. You won't get the needed information.[38]

Here the instructor lays out a basic paradox of torture. Torture involves the destruction of human beings, but torturers fail if they allow victims to die. Torturers must have a particular discipline to keep their victims in pain and useful for political purposes. Yet torture encourages the loss of this self-control. As the instructor explains, "Our experience in the past has been that our interrogators for the most part tend to fall on the torture side. They emphasized torture over propaganda. This is the wrong way of doing it. We must teach interrogators how to do it."[39]

So torture complexes encourage indiscipline, which can pose tremendous difficulties for governments that torture. The Brazilian military government, for example, phased out torture in part because it needed to bring "those undisciplined military and police personnel under at least a degree of central government control even though there was little effort to punish them for their crimes."[40] But this is not all. It is not entirely clear whether torture produces documents that are particularly useful. Torturers do not seem to be more successful than regular policemen in securing confessions or reliable logistical information, and they have greater difficulty than police in keeping their victims alive long enough to provide such information. If Tuol Sleng is any indication, torturers use the confessions they gather simply to invent fanciful antigovernment plots, plots that help them justify their continued operation.

Finally, it is not clear how torture induces economic productivity. There are two separate issues here. First, does torture induce greater labor productivity? Well, if an economy relies primarily on unskilled manual labor, then one might agree with Marx that torture is rather directly related to economic productivity: Human beings might work harder in order to avoid torture, and thus produce more.[41] But torture seems out of place in an economy that relies on skilled labor and industrial discipline.[42] The problems associated with low labor productivity in Third World countries (lack of any real skill training and long work hours) do not seem to be problems that torture can address. In Iran, torture was so unhelpful that SAVAK not only tortured workers less but also tried to lobby to improve salaries and managed welfare programs so that workers would produce more.[43]

But perhaps states employ torture to destroy labor unions and thus keep wages in a range acceptable to industrialists, multinational corporations, or the IMF.[44] There is a great deal to be said for this account of why states repress labor unions; but it does not explain why states resort to torture. It is worth recalling that the most famous repression of labor agitation, during the French Revolution of 1848, was conducted *without torture* by an extremely vengeful and powerful police force—and this was certainly not because torture was unknown to French police and military officers.[45] Torture is not essential to such repression; more intensive discipline could be just as effective. Indeed, disciplinary punishments would seem to conform well with the demands of an industrial system—more so, at any rate, than torture.

In short, torture is difficult to explain solely in economic terms, although the temptation to do so is overwhelming since Marx. We can use economic motives to explain why businessmen and state officials support torture, but we are at a loss to use economic rationality to explain what goes on in torture complexes. To claim an economic rationality for all this is not simply misleading. It also seems to provide a rationale for the behavior of torturers, a rationale that makes their behavior a little more acceptable. No doubt, many torturers prefer to claim that they are fulfilling an essential function in the process of economic and political modernization.

STRENGTHS AND WEAKNESSES OF THE THREE APPROACHES

None of these criticisms are meant to detract from the stronger features of these three approaches to modern torture. In fact, I think researchers have grasped key features of torture despite their constant urge to misunderstand violence today. None of the problems we encountered using these approaches were empirical; rather, these problems were solved by looking to the workings of language and showing how the vocabulary of each approach drew our attention away from the world in which we live. I think that if we consider their strengths from the right perspective, we can gain a tentative way of understanding modern torture.

The strength of the state terrorist approach is that it is concerned with torture as a mode of government. It draws attention away from incidents of torture and to the systematic and international nature of torture today. But its chief difficulty remains moving beyond statistics and personal narratives of detainees to descriptions of this mode of government. This difficulty arises because it is hampered by an unduly narrow conception of torture as a form of economically rational behavior.

In this regard, the developmentalist approach is much stronger. It focuses on counterinsurgency practices. These practices describe some of the military, police, and bureaucratic conventions employed by those involved in torture. However, because developmentalist theorists regard torture as a premodern or accidental feature of politics, they remain peculiarly blind to the relationship between counterinsurgency practices and torture. All they can see is a technical failure in discipline, not the sociopolitical problem of the emergence of torture.

This sociopolitical problem is not lost on the humanists or the state terrorist theorists. Although they have a hard time explicating what goes on in torture complexes in detail, they make the point that torture complexes are part and parcel of modern political systems, that they are constituted out of the same sorts of rationality that characterize bureaucratic systems. They do not arise accidentally in the twentieth century. They are not aberrations of the modernization process or remnants of traditional society.

To put these insights more constructively, torture is a part of modern life in the sense that torture complexes can best be elucidated by means of ordinary features of modern life. Torture complexes are closely related to bureaucracies, prisons, hospitals, and to a certain extent, factories. Sometimes we can understand what people are doing when they torture by comparing their activities to these related institutions.

Indeed, sometimes the similarity between other practices and torture is so close that it poses tremendous difficulty for action against torture. Medicine, for example, has a particularly close relation to torture because interrogators use medical practices, hospital facilities, and doctors in their work.[46] Consequently, other doctors have to overcome major obstacles in order to help victims recover from the trauma of torture; too many of their techniques evoke memories of the tortures experienced by victims. This applies not only to actual physical techniques but also to the ways in which doctors examine and interrogate their patients. Doctors have to exercise tremendous care in the way they speak to and treat their patients, who can no longer effectively distinguish between what is torture and what is medicine.[47]

We can evade the deep interrelations between torture and modernity by invoking the term "developing societies" (logically, something belonging to the past of the "developed" world and, consequently, saying little to the present of the developed world), but we should be aware that, in this brave new language, "becoming modern" no longer functions as an empirical category but as a moral one. The humanists never tire of insisting on this point. But this means that we are left with a vocabulary through which we can reaffirm our confidence in the celebrated aspects of modernity, but only at the price of being unable to talk about torture except in the vaguest way.

If there is one difficulty that runs through all these approaches, it is that none provides a satisfactory *explanation* for modern torture. The causes they identify are too general to account for the details of torture complexes. Nevertheless, they have a tremendous hold on our imagination because they articulate visions of the kind of political community in which we aspire to live. And it is the power of these approaches to grasp our moral imagination that accounts for their persistence today, not their supposed ability to provide a detailed explanation of what is going on in the world of violence or how we got here. Our concern with the ideal turns our attention away from the present and thus defers a pressing question: In what ways and at what cost can we get from the world of torture to the ideal of political community? In particular, we should pay less attention to the question "Why is there torture today?"—a question that may be too tangled and deeply enshrouded in state secrecy—and much more attention to "How does torture work today?" For it is by increasing our scrutiny of how torture works that we can understand how we benefit (or do not benefit) from torture, as well as to what extent we can (and cannot) challenge this practice.

I have been arguing that torture does *not* work in any of the conventional ways theorists suppose. Torture does not increase labor productivity or produce any better intelligence results than ordinary police work, and it has a detrimental effect on social and bureaucratic discipline. I want to take a moment and spell out the implications of this thesis.

One implication is that if torture does not work, then there is little justification for its use. Torture's apologists always assume that torture works; for them, it is merely a matter of moral justification.[48] Now it appears that even this assumption can be questioned. However, if torture does not work, then what needs to be explained is why its practice persists today. The answer to this is clearly beyond the scope of this chapter, but I want to point out some ways in which this question could be answered. Perhaps it is because torturers are protecting their jobs.[49] Or perhaps intense fear mobilizes social elites to engage in "permanent counterrevolution"[50] in which torture may play a part. But I think a more promising explanation is suggested in Michel Foucault's work on the prison.[51] Foucault asks what purpose is served by the persistent failure of the prison. He replies that although the prison does not reform offenders, its failure serves to extend displinary power and to reinforce its legitimacy.

If this is a credible explanation of why torture persists, then we need to pay more attention to the relationship between torture and the process of rationalization. In part, this involves examining the relationship between torture and other social institutions. In his book on torture, Edward Peters argues that, historically, torture was not a primitive practice which survived into the medieval period. Rather, torture was introduced in Europe in opposition to tribal punishments, and its practice served to rationalize state power.[52] My own research on torture in modern Iran seems to suggest a similar point,[53] but it is worth investigating how the practice of torture today is related to different processes of rationalization.

At the same time, we need to pay careful attention to the process of linguistic rationalization. This means that we need to be careful how the use of increasingly specialized ways of talking can serve to mislead us about what is actually happening when torture occurs. Torture seems to thrive not so much on this or that ideology but on gossip, rumor, media sensationalism, and bureaucratic, social scientific, and legal jargon.[54]

Torture needs all the publicity it can get, but we have to be more careful about *how* we speak about torture. This does not mean that we should abandon the traditional ways we discuss torture, only that we should critically evaluate them at every opportunity.

NOTES

1. See, for example, Henry Charles Lea, *Superstition and Force* (Philadelphia: Henry C. Lea, 1870: repr. New York: Haskell, 1971); and W. E. H. Lecky, *History of the Rise and Influence of the Spirit of Rationalism in Europe*, rev. ed. (New York: Appleton, 1872).

2. The point of reference for Americans was the "third degree" treatment of prisoners by police and, for the British, the paramilitary tactics of the Royal Irish Constabulary. An excellent account of European police practice is in Edward Peters, *Torture* (New York: Basil Blackwell, 1985), pp. 103–14. For the use of torture in India and the Philippines, see Edmund Cox, *Police and Crime in India* (London: Hazell, Watson, and Viney, n.d.), pp. 170, 180–83; William Thaddeus Sexton, *Soldiers in the Sun: An Adventure in Imperialism* (Freeport, NY: Libraries Press, 1939), pp. 238–42; Daniel B. Schirmer, *Republic or Empire: American Resistance to the Philippine War* (Cambridge, MA: Schenkman, 1972), pp.225–40; and Richard E. Welch, Jr., *Response to Imperialism: The United States and the Philippine–American War 1899–1902* (Chapel Hill: University of North Carolina Press, 1979), pp. 133–49.

3. Hannah Arendt, *The Origins of Totalitarianism*, new ed. (New York: Harcourt, Brace & World, 1966), pp. 443–46.

4. Henri Alleg, *The Question*, with an introduction by Jean Paul Sartre, trans. John Calder (New York: George Braziller, 1958); George Orwell, *Nineteen Eighty Four* (Harmondsworth, UK: Penguin, 1954); and Arthur Koestler, *Arrival and Departure* (London: Hutchinson, 1966), pp. 104–13.

5. Max Weber, *From Max Weber: Essays in Sociology*, trans. and ed. by H. H. Gerth and C. Wright Mills (New York: Oxford University Press, 1958), p. 226.

6. Hannah Arendt, *On Violence* (New York: Harcourt, Brace & World, 1969), p. 46.

7. Hannah Arendt, *Eichmann in Jerusalem: A Report on the Banality of Evil* (Harmondsworth, UK: Penguin Books, 1963; rev. and enl. ed., 1965), pp. 135–50.

8. For some recent examples, see A. J. Polan, *Lenin and the End of Politics* (Berkeley: University of California Press, 1984); Peters, *Torture;* Michael Ignatieff, "Torture's Dead Simplicity," *New Statesman* (20 September 1985):24–26; and Richard Rubinstein, "The Bureaucratization of Torture," *Journal of Social Philosophy* 13 (1982):31–51.

9. See Frantz Fanon, *The Wretched of the Earth* (New York: Grove Press, 1968), pp. 283–88. Michel Foucault has characterized this exercise of power as "pastoral power" as opposed to the more familiar way in which persons are trained through "disciplinary power." See Michel Foucault, "Omnes et Singulatim: Towards a Criticism of Political Reason," in *The Tanner Lectures on Human Values*, ed. Sterling McMurrin (Salt Lake City: University of Utah Press, 1981).

10. I adopt and adapt these distinctions from Jürgen Habermas's work, particularly *The Theory of Communicative Action*, Vol. I: *Reason and the Rationalization of Society*; Vol. II: *Lifeworld and System: A Critique of Functionalist Reason*, trans. T. McCarthy (Boston: Beacon Press, 1981, 1987).

11. See John H. Langbein, *Torture and the Law of Proof: Europe and England in the Ancien Regime* (Chicago: University of Chicago Press, 1976). See also Gavan McCormack, "Crime, Confession, and Control in Contemporary Japan," and Igarashi Futaba, "Forced to Confess," both in *Democracy in Contemporary Japan*, ed. Gavan McCormack and Yoshio Sugimoto (Armonk, NY: M. E. Sharpe, 1986).

12. Amnesty International, *Guatemala* (London, 1976), pp. 5–6; 11–16.

13. See Franklin Mark Osanka, ed., *Modern Guerrilla Warfare: Fighting Communist Guerrilla Movements, 1941–1961* (New York: Free Press, 1962), pp. 175–212.

14. See Futaba, "Forced to Confess"; and Hylah M. Jacques, "Spain: Systematic Torture in a Democratic State," *Monthly Review* 37 (November 1985):57–62.

15. For the full argument, see James David Barber, "Rationalizing Torture: The Dance of the Intellectual Apologists," *The Washington Monthly* 17, (December 1985):17–18.

16. See Marjorie Agosin, "Notes on the Poetics of the Acevedo Movement Against Torture," *Human Rights Quarterly* 10 (1988):339–43; and Amnesty International, *Torture in the Eighties* (London: International Secretariat, 1984), pp. 71–72.

17. In 1989 the Uruguayans absolved military officers responsible for human rights violations by a 60 percent majority. This outcome reflects not a sense of

forgiveness but the fact that more democracy has not put Uruguayans in a better position to confront torturers.

18. Max Weber, *The Protestant Ethic and the Spirit of Capitalism*, trans. Talcott Parsons (New York: Scribner's, 1958), pp. 97, 128, 197. See also p. 167.

19. Seymour Martin Lipset, "Some Social Requisites of Democracy: Economic Development and Political Legitimacy," *American Political Science Review* 53 (March 1959):91.

20. Mancur Olson, "Rapid Growth as a Destabilizing Force," *Journal of Economic History* 23 (1983):529–52; Samuel P. Huntington, *Political Order in Changing Societies* (New Haven: Yale University Press, 1968); and Lucian W. Pye, *Aspects of Political Development* (Boston: Little, Brown, 1966).

21. See Pye, *Aspects of Political Development*, p. 127; and Samuel Huntington, "Civil Violence and the Process of Development," *Adelphi Papers* 83 (December 1971):6.

22. Huntington, "Civil Violence," p. 23.

23. Ibid., p. 24.

24. Lucian Pye, "The Roots of Insurgency and the Commencement of Rebellions," in *Internal War*, ed. H. Eckstein (New York: Free Press, 1964), pp. 157–79; and Samuel Huntington, "Guerrilla Warfare in Theory and Policy," in Osanka, ed., *Modern Guerrilla Warfare*, pp. xv–xxii. See also Barber, "Rationalizing Torture," pp. 12–13.

25. Huntington, "Civil Violence and the Process of Development," p. 15.

26. See Miles Wolpin, *Militarization, Internal Repression and Social Welfare in the Third World* (London: Croom Helm, 1986).

27. See Alfred Stepan, "The New Professionalism of Internal Warfare and Military Role Expansion," in *Armies and Politics in Latin America*, ed. Abraham F. Lowenthal(New York: Holmes and Meier, 1976), pp. 244–60.

28. David Pion-Berlin, "Political Repression and Economic Doctrines: The Case of Argentina," *Comparative Political Studies* 16, no. 1 (April 1983):37–66; Barry Rubin, *Paved with Good Intentions: The American Experience in Iran* (Harmondsworth, UK: Penguin, 1981), pp. 177–78; and Fred Halliday, *Iran: Dictatorship and Development* (Harmondsworth, UK: Penguin, 1979), p. 50.

29. In the case of South Africa, this point is made cogently in D. Russell, *Rebellion, Revolution and Armed Force* (New York: Academic Press, 1974). For more general criticism along the same lines, see Charles Tilly, "Does Modernization Breed Revolution?" *Comparative Politics* 5, no. 3 (April 1973):425–48.

30. Pye, "The Roots of Insurgency and the Commencement of Rebellions," pp. 159, 170, 178–79. See also Barber, "Rationalizing Torture," pp. 13–14. Huntington distinguishes between Western revolutions (in which the state has lost popular consensus) and Eastern revolutions (in which the state possesses some measure of popular consensus). But his examples of the latter sort of state (e.g., Chiang Kai-shek's China or South Vietnam) could be understood better as highly repressive military regimes led by determined minorities.

31. Noam Chomsky and Edward S. Herman, *The Political Economy of Human Rights*, Vol. I: *The Washington Connection and Third World Fascism* (Montreal: Black Rose, 1979); and Edward S. Herman, *The Real Terror Network* (Boston: South End Press, 1982). See also Michael Stohl and George A. Lopez, eds., *The State as*

Terrorist (Westport, CT: Greenwood Press, 1984); and Amnesty International, *Report on Torture* (London: Gerald Duckworth, 1973), pp. 18, 27.

32. I adapt this phrase from Sheldon Wolin's discussion of Machiavelli and the role of violence in politics. See Sheldon Wolin, *Politics and Vision: Continuity and Innovation in Western Political Thought* (Boston: Little, Brown, 1960), pp. 220–24.

33. Herman, *The Real Terror Network*, p. 113.

34. Ibid., pp. 112–13.

35. David Hawk, "Tuol Sleng Extermination Centre," *Index on Censorship* 15, no. 1 (January 1986):25–31.

36. Amnesty International, *Torture in the Eighties*, p. 66.

37. See Wolpin, *Militarization . . .*; Lars Schoultz, *Human Rights and United States Policy Towards Latin America* (Princeton, NJ: Princeton University Press, 1981); Michael Klare and Cynthia Arnson, *Supplying Repression*, with Delia Miller and Daniel Volman (Washington, DC: Institute for Policy Studies, 1977); Carol Ackroyd et al., *The Technology of Political Control* (London: Pluto, 1980); Suzanne Franks and Ivor Gaber, "The UK's Torture Trade Has Quietly Resumed," *New Statesman* 108, no. 4 (September 21, 1984):4; Amnesty International, *Torture in the Eighties*.

38. Hawk, "Tuol Sleng Extermination Centre," p. 27.

39. Ibid.

40. Amnesty International, *Torture in the Eighties*, p. 68.

41. Karl Marx, *Capital: A Critique of Political Economy*, trans. B. Fowkes (Harmondsworth, UK: Penguin, 1976), Vol. I, pp. 344–52.

42. See Georg Rusche and Otto Kirchheimer, *Punishment and Social Structure* (New York: Columbia University Press, 1939).

43. Halliday, *Iran*, pp. 193–97; 202–6. See also William H. Bartsch, "The Industrial Labor Force of Iran: Problems of Recruitment, Training, and Productivity," in *The Population of Iran: A Selection of Readings*, ed. Jamshid Momeni (Honolulu: East–West Center, 1977), pp. 322–26.

44. See Pion-Berlin, "Political Repression and Economic Doctrines."

45. See Thomas R. Forstenzer, *French Provincial Police and the Fall of the Second Republic: Social Fear and Counterrevolution* (Princeton, NJ: Princeton University Press, 1981); Jean Gottman, "Bugeaud, Gallieni, Lyautey: The Development of French Colonial Warfare," in *Makers of Modern Strategy: Military Thought from Machiavelli to Hitler*, ed. Edward Mead Earle, with the collaboration of Gordon Craig and Felix Gilbert (New York: Atheneum, 1966), pp. 234–56; Anthony Thrall Sullivan, *Thomas-Robert Bugeaud, France, and Algeria, 1784–1849. Politics, Power and the Good Society* (Hamden, CT: Archon Books, 1983); and Melvin Richter, "Tocqueville in Algeria," *The Review of Politics* 25, no. 3 (July 1963):362–98.

46. See Eric Stover and Elena O. Nightingale, *The Breaking of Bodies and Minds: Torture, Psychiatric Abuse, and the Health Professions* (New York: W. H. Freeman, 1985); and Richard H. Goldstein and Patrick Breslin, "Technicians of Torture: How Physicians Became Agents of State Terror," *The Sciences* 26 (March/April 1986):14–19.

47. See Peters, *Torture*, pp. 174–76; and Kevin Krajick, "Healing Broken Minds," *Psychology Today* (November 1986):66–69.

48. Theorists justifying torture draw on a variety of penal philosophies. Here

I am concerned especially with the utilitarian justifications of torture. See Michael Levin, "The Case for Torture," *Newsweek* (June 7, 1982):13; and the more cautious and thorough arguments in Gary E. Jones, "On the Permissibility of Torture," *Journal of Medical Ethics* 6 (March 1980):11–13. For retributivist justifications, see Edward G. Rozycki, "Pain and Anguish: The Need for Corporal Punishments," *Proceedings of the Philosophical Education Society of Australasia* 34 (1978):380–92; Graeme Newman, *Just and Painful: A Case for the Corporal Punishment of the Criminal* (London: Macmillan, 1983); Ernest Van den Haag, "Refuting Reiman and Nathanson," *Philosophy and Public Affairs* 14, no. 2 (Spring 1985):171. One of the earliest defenses of torture in the utilitarian vein was provided in Roger Trinquier, *Modern Warfare: A French View of Counter-Insurgency* (New York: Praeger, 1964).

49. Rubinstein, "The Bureaucratization of Torture," pp. 37–38.

50. Forstenzer, *French Provincial Police* . . . .

51. Michel Foucault, *Discipline and Punish: The Birth of the Prison* (New York: Random House, 1977).

52. Peters, *Torture*, pp. 40–73.

53. Darius Rejali, "Discipline and Torture, or How Iranians Became Moderns," Ph.D. dissertation, McGill University, 1987.

54. See Barber, "Rationalizing Torture," pp. 12–13; Agosin, "Notes on Poetics," p. 339; Peters, *Torture*, pp. 6–7; Michael Taussig, "Terror as Usual," paper delivered at the Conference "Talking Terrorism: Ideologies and Paradigms in a Postmodern World," Stanford University, February 4–6, 1988, and "Culture of Terror—Space of Death. Roger Casement's Putumayo Report and the Explanation of Torture," *Contemporary Studies in Society and History* 26 (1984):466–97.

9
LEGISLATION AND NATIONAL SECURITY IN LATIN AMERICA

Alfonso Reyes Echandía

NATIONAL SECURITY DOCTRINE

Politically and constitutionally the army's mission in Latin America has been to defend independence and national sovereignty. With the triumph of the Cuban Revolution in 1959, the thesis gained ground—obviously pushed by the U.S. government—that the enemy of national sovereignty was no longer external enemies, but enemies within the nation. The core of this thesis was national security ideology. According to Argentinian jurist and criminologist Raúl Zaffaroni, the ideology that supports Latin American national security states involves "taking as a given that the State is at war and, therefore, needs to strengthen the 'internal front' or, in other words, to achieve a maximum degree of homogeneity."[1]

According to national security ideology, internal political crimes—committed by those who aim to change the dominant structure of power—are a military concern. Police handling of this type of crime came to be seen as inadequate; intervention by the military was considered necessary to guarantee the survival of Western-style democracy. To achieve this end, national and international measures had to be taken.

Most Latin American governments subscribe to the Inter-American Treaty of Reciprocal Assistance (the Rio Treaty) and have received support from the U.S. Military Assistance Program. Through these agreements, the United States has offered military, financial, and technical aid to Latin American countries and their armies to strengthen the struggle against internal political enemies. In carrying out these accords, grants and loans have increased for acquiring military matériel; and Latin American military and police personnel have received training in "jungle warfare," "guerrilla warfare,"[2] "counterinsurgency," and "internal security" at special schools in the United States and the Panama Canal Zone. Increasing numbers of U.S. technicians and instructors have been sent to Latin American countries.[3] The United States has underwritten the installation of "strong governments," including military dictatorships. It has helped to create within Latin America legal instruments that guarantee harsh treatment for people accused of criminal or socially deviant acts, or who are suspected of jeopardizing the stability of a "system."

NATIONAL SECURITY LEGISLATION IN LATIN AMERICA

Since 1969 several Latin American legislatures have enacted legal instruments that build national security doctrine into existing legislation. For example, Argentina's Law on National Defense gave the military authority to try those accused of civil crimes; another Argentine law, of September 1974, established severe limitations on freedom of the press; a third law, enacted in June 1976, reestablished the death penalty. Bolivia issued its first national security law in September 1965, followed by others in 1967, 1969, and 1973. In 1971 Bolivia established the death penalty for terrorism, and in November 1974 it enacted two decree laws that suppressed the right of Bolivian workers to organize unions and to strike.

In January 1968, Brazil created its National Security Council; in December of that year the Brazilian military enacted Institutional Act No. 5, a sweeping piece of national security legislation. In 1969, the prosecution of civilians was turned over to military tribunals. In 1971, the president of Brazil was given the right to pass "secret and confidential" national security laws.

Chile turned the prosecution of civilians over to the military in 1974; in 1976, it established "national security" as a legitimate basis for all further legislation. Uruguay enacted national security legislation in 1972; in 1973 it created a National Internal Security Council. In 1978, Colombia enacted a "Security Statute" "to protect the life, honor, and property of persons and to guarantee security organizations."

These laws (some still in effect, others repealed) are aimed at guaranteeing the survival of strong governments and defending the socioeconomic and political structures on which such governments are based. In spite of the variety of issues with which these national security laws deal, and the diversity of countries in which they apply, they all share the following common elements:

1. Increased state intervention, often backed by military governments
2. Violation of the principle of "legal coherence"—they describe as punishable

behaviors that do not jeopardize the community's vital juridical interests; punishable behavior is identified through such vague and undefined language as "subversion" and "nonconformity"

3. The military is empowered to try civilians for civilian crimes, using procedures that violate a citizen's right to defense
4. Habeas corpus is totally suppressed by some laws and made difficult by others
5. They affect or suspend the exercise of such inalienable rights such as association, unionization, freedom of movement and expression.

NATIONAL SECURITY IN COLOMBIA

In Colombia, the electoral rite of renewing Executive and Legislative officers has been observed, although genuine power still benefits the same economic and political group and is enforced by the armed forces. This has been achieved by institutionalizing continued use of the "state of siege," allowed by the Colombian Constitution only temporarily—and then only to overcome difficulties of international war or serious internal upheavals. In spite of these restrictions, the state of siege has been in force in Colombia for more than twenty years since 1960.

Under the state of siege, the Colombian military has been given the right to mete out justice to civilians for political crimes, or for common crimes that directly or indirectly disrupt public order. Military justice has thus supplanted civil justice.

The state of siege has allowed the Colombian armed forces to absorb the National Police structurally and functionally, and to penetrate areas once reserved for ordinary criminal enforcement. The National Police director is subordinate to the minister of defense and, therefore, under the latter's control. Any operation related to public order must be coordinated by an army officer. When the military high command judges it to be appropriate, troops supplant the police in their traditional internal security activities. Military personnel simultaneously act as judicial police (and therefore make arrests, and conduct searches and interrogations), criminal investigators, judges, defense attorneys, and juries.

THE STATE OF SIEGE

In their political constitutions, Latin American states have exceptional measures for counteracting grave and extraordinary disruptions of public order. Such extraordinary measures usually escape the ordinary regulatory controls that guarantee institutional normality. Among the legitimate justifications for declaring a state of siege are international armed conflicts, internal guerrilla warfare, terrorist actions, and violent labor or student strikes. These extraordinary actions are labeled a "state of siege" in Chile, Argentina, Haiti, Paraguay, and the Dominican Republic; they are called a "state of emergency" in Venezuela; and a "state of suspension of guarantees" in Panama, Peru, Mexico, and Honduras.

In Colombia, a state of siege is permitted by Article 121 of the Constitution, under the following circumstances:

> In the case of external war or internal disorder, the President may, with the signature of all Ministers, declare public order disturbed and all or part of the republic under a State of Siege. By such declaration, the government will have, beyond normal legal authority, that which the Constitution authorizes for times of war or public disorder and that which, according to the accepted rules of international law, is applicable during war between nations.
>
> Decrees dictated by the President within those precise limits are mandatory, as long as they are signed by all Ministers.
>
> The government cannot repeal laws by means of such decrees. Their powers are limited to the suspension of those incompatible with the State of Siege.
>
> The existence of a State of Siege in no way impedes the normal activity by Congress. Consequently, Congress will meet under its own power during normal sessions and in any extraordinary sessions that it convenes.
>
> If Congress is in session at the time a disturbance of public order and a state of siege are declared, the President will immediately send an explanation supported by the reasons determining that declaration. If it is not in session, the explanation will be presented to Congress on the first day of normal sessions or immediately during extraordinary sessions.
>
> In the case of foreign war, in the decree declaring public order disturbed and the republic under state of siege, the government will convene Congress to meet within the following ten days, and if it is not so convened, Congress may meet under its own power.
>
> The government will declare public order reestablished as soon as the foreign war has ended or the internal disturbance has ceased, and extraordinary decrees that have been promulgated will no longer be in effect.
>
> The President and Ministers will be held responsible when declaring public order disturbed without a case of foreign war or internal disturbance having occurred, as will all other functionaries, for any abuse they commit in the exercise of the power referred to in the present article.
>
> The day after they are issued, the government will send the Supreme Court of Justice the legislative decrees it promulgates, using the authority to which this article refers, so the Court may definitively decide on their constitutionality. If the government does not comply with the order to send them, the Supreme Court of Justice will immediately determine the facts.
>
> The terms indicated in Article 214 will be reduced to a third, and noncompliance will bring about the dismissal of the responsible magistrates, which will be decreed by the Disciplinary Tribunal. (Legislative Act No. 1 of 1968, Art. 42)

In spite of the unequivocal exceptionality of Article 121, and its very limited time frame, in fact the state of siege has been converted by various Colombian governments into a normal mechanism of government administration. Effectively, from April 6, 1948, a state of siege has been decreed in Colombia fifteen times, for a total of twenty-five years and nine months. This means that during the thirty-six years from 1948 to 1984, Colombia had only ten years and three months of full juridical–institutional normality.

How has it been possible to transform this political–juridical mechanism, legitimate only during very brief periods, into a truly "normal" and nearly permanent system for regulating public order? It has been done by means of a curious legal interpretation. The Colombian government has the political power to decide, once a state of siege has been decreed, that new disturbances of public order justify taking additional official measures to counteract them. The government is no longer obliged to justify the original declaration of a state of siege.

Most jurists, of course, do not agree with this practice. In fact, the original justification for instituting a state of siege is its only legally relevant basis, which applies to any continued use of the state of siege. That is, an act or event unrelated to one that originally justified a state of siege cannot legitimize new legislative decrees, particularly when the reasons for subsequent decrees are far removed from the situations generating the original disruption of the social order. Such new decrees serve to prolong a societal condition that no longer has the status of exceptionality.

THE STATE OF SIEGE AND MILITARY CRIMINAL JUSTICE

Among the measures included in most states of siege is the investigation and prosecution of civilian common or political crimes by military tribunals. In Colombia, such action has always been considered unconstitutional, based on the argument that in peacetime the Colombian Constitution mandates that persons or institutions are prohibited from simultaneously exercising civil and military authority or civil functions with judicial ones. It follows that in peacetime a single person or corporation cannot simultaneously exercise political, civil, or judicial functions, or political, civil, and military functions. By inverse logic, in "nonpeacetime"—which could occur through civil or foreign war, and in a state of siege—the simultaneous exercising of political or civil authority with judicial authority, and both with military authority is juridically acceptable. In such periods, an army officer could fill the role of mayor, or a governor could discharge the functions of judge.

In fact, the Constitution suggests an unyielding semantic and grammatical opposition between the simultaneous functioning of judicial and military authority. Each has different and exclusive functions. At no time is it juridically possible for one and the same person or corporation simultaneously to exercise judicial and military functions. But the prohibition against the simultaneous exercise of judicial and military functions does not arise solely from cold, calculated abstractions. This prohibition grows also out of the differences between the civil and military branches of government. Judicial authority is assigned to the jurisprudential branch of public power; military authority is assigned to the administrative branch. A judge deliberates; the military is prohibited from exercising such deliberative activity because of its hierarchical subordination to civilian decision makers. Judicial activity is autonomous; military activity is dependent.

The Constitution's inflexibility about a single government branch simultaneously exercising military and judicial functions is so firm that the Colombian Constituent Assembly, in order to allow the military to try their own or to have judicial authority in times of war, established two exceptions to this constitutional prohibition. One declares that "the military commander may impose penalties *in continenti,* in order to contain insubordination or military mutiny or to maintain order in the face of the enemy." The other mandates that courts-martial or military tribunals try cases involving "those crimes committed by personnel in active military service and in relation to that same service."

While the first exception permits military judicial authority over civil or military personnel, the second peremptorily limits judicial authority to active-duty military personnel. It cannot be said that military jurisdiction involves little more than a simple transfer of power, through legal channels and procedures, from the judicial branch to the military. Such reasoning ignores the precise and uncompromising constitutional prohibition against one government branch's simultaneously holding both military and judicial functions. Besides the constitutional prohibition against such overlap, the Colombian Constitution declares that "the Supreme Court of Justice, the Superior District Tribunals, and other Tribunals and Courts established by the law [must] administer justice," and that "Congress, the government, and judges have separate functions, but harmoniously collaborate to achieve the State's objectives."

On October 4, 1971, the Colombian Supreme Court ruled:

> The Law of Military Justice cannot take the trying of common crimes committed by nonmilitary personnel from ordinary judges, because to do so opposes the principle conferred in Art. 170 of the Charter, according to which an exception is applicable only to those crimes committed by active duty military personnel, . . . which is conceived of only with respect to those personnel and in exclusive

relation to the activity and infractions committed in the development of the same. The trying of crimes involving persons other than those on active duty is equivalent to supplanting constitutional order.

The active-duty military personnel referred to above are officers, noncommissioned officers, and enlisted personnel of the Colombian army, air force, and navy. The police are not military; the Constitution clearly separates them from the armed forces. The army was constitutionally created to defend national sovereignty (Article 166) while protecting "the inhabitants of Colombian territory in their liberty and rights derived therein." The conservation of internal order is a police function. The army is an institution of war; the police, a civilian organization. Military personnel owe absolute obedience to their superiors; police obedience is reflective. Police voluntarily enter the police institution, they are public employees, and they can resign when they choose. Soldiers are conscripted into military service, and they are not public employees, though they receive a stipend. They cannot resign before they have completed the legally determined period of military service. Governors and mayors are "police chiefs" at their respective departmental and municipal levels; military conscripts recognize only their own military commander's superior rank.

The unfortunate decision to assign the Colombian National Police to the Ministry of Defense is merely an administrative formality; this assignment neither modifies, nor could it modify, the substantial structural and functional differences between the military and the police. This assignment represents, in the words of one Colombian magistrate, "one more symptom of our weak democratic structure."

THE PYRAMIDAL STRUCTURE OF THE MILITARY CRIMINAL PROCESS

Military criminal justice has been conceived and shaped to guarantee institutional trials for military personnel who commit crimes in the exercise of their duty—that is, a trial by judges selected from among military men. High-ranking military personnel investigate and pass sentence on crimes committed by members of their armed forces.

Colombia's Military Code of Criminal Justice provides for three types of trial: courts-martial, verbal courts-martial, and special courts-martial. The officers who generally participate in these trials are instructing judge, investigating judge, spokesmen or jurors, prosecutor, defender, and secretary. In verbal courts-martial, there is also a legal adviser. Except for the instructing judges, who tend to be lawyers, the remaining court functionaries are normally active-duty military personnel. The instructing judges, as well as magistrates of the Military Supreme Court, are named by the national government. The remaining members of the military's judicial apparatus (prosecutors, spokesmen, defenders, secretaries, judicial advisers) are named by the presiding military judge, who is also the military commander. One result of this structure is a rigid dependence of each level on the one above it; each judicial layer is appointed by the one above it, and each is hierarchically subordinated to the one above and to a presiding judge.

One characteristic of the civil criminal process is judicial autonomy. Such autonomy is guaranteed by jurisdictional boundaries, the judges' professional status, and their tenure of office. Another guarantee of judicial autonomy derives from procedural rules of debate: Both prosecution and defense have equal opportunities to present and challenge evidence. In Colombia, the Supreme Court of Justice—the highest level of the judiciary—is made up of magistrates elected by that same judicial entity. Supreme Court justices remain in their posts until they are 65, the age of mandatory retirement. The Supreme Court selects magistrates of lower courts for periods of four years; they in turn, name judges in their respective districts every two years.

When, during a state of siege, the Colombian government decides that certain civilian crimes should be tried by the military in a verbal court-martial, the government refers citizens to a presiding judge who is commanding officer of a military unit. All lower court officers under his jurisdiction have been named by him. This trial is entirely public; the evidence must be presented immediately. The defender is named—if he has not already been appointed—and an accusation against the defendant is made. The defender has only three hours to prepare the accused's defense. The constitutional principle of due process, including a genuine defense, is thus violated. It is impossible to hope for a fair and balanced trial.

During states of siege, among the crimes entrusted to military criminal courts are rebellions, sedition, and revolts. In addition, and in line with the military's political conception of national security, many Latin American countries have given the armed forces control over internal public order, including combat against rebellions that seek to overthrow governing regimes. The Left is most commonly the object of such military action.

When, in the course of internally located armed struggle, the army captures members of rebel units, it takes criminal action against them. From that moment, the soldier–rebel confrontation—in which each is pitted against the other as an armed enemy—gives way to a formal, juridical relationship in which the victorious military becomes judge and jury, and the defeated rebel is a criminal defendant. Can an impartial trial be expected when a judge is trying his archenemy? Definitely not. Especially when a guilty sentence is often based on a confession that has been dragged out of a defendant through physical and psychological torture.

CONCLUSIONS

The doctrine of national security is a political–military mechanism fostered by the United States to maintain strong governments in what superficially seem to be democratic countries. One of the instruments used by Latin American governments to secure strong control is the state of siege or state of national emergency. This period of state control, which most Latin American constitutions allow only for short periods, has tended to be prolonged beyond the narrow limits for which it was initially instituted.

In countries such as Colombia, Chile, and Brazil, these exceptional measures tend to be used indiscrimately, and function to give the prosecution of civilians to the military. The overlapping of military and civil functions infringes upon such constitutionally conferred personal guarantees as due process and the right to representation before the courts.

The state of siege must not become a normal mechanism of juridico-administrative control. We must develop a belief within the Latin American citizenry that such unconstitutional institutional mechanisms violate our sovereignty and retard our liberation from economic–political dependency. Latin Americans must demand self-determination, true democracy, and judicial systems that respect due process. We must demand an end to socioeconomic inequalities. We must struggle for these goals without regard to national borders. Our children and our children's children must have a world without exploiters or exploited, masters or slaves, devoid of the opulently wealthy or beggars, a world of freedom with equality of opportunity and harmonious coexistence.

NOTES

1. Raúl Zaffaroni (1982), *Política criminal latinoamericana* (Buenos Aires: Hamurabi), p. 108.

2. There are 142 schools of this type, in which a total of 4,269 Colombian officers were trained as of 1970. J. Saxe Fernández (1971), *Proyecciones hemisféricas de la paz americana* (Buenos Aires: Amarrotu Editores), p. 82.

3. In 1970, there were fifty members of the military mission in Colombia. Saxe Fernández, *Proyecciones hemisféricas*, p. 84.

IV
EXTRALEGAL POLICE VIOLENCE

10
"EXTRAORDINARY" POLICE OPERATIONS IN VENEZUELA

Tosca Hernández

In Venezuela since 1965, a period that includes the so-called democratic period, no government has failed to use "extraordinary" police operations. These have included police dragnets, and roundups and beatings, usually by Venezuela's Metropolitan Police. Increasingly, such police operations have included actions coordinated by the Metropolitan Police, the Intelligence Police (DISIP), the Judicial Police (PTJ), and the National Guard (FAC), with the ostensible objective of ending the "underworld's explosive growth."[1] These roundups have resulted in the detention of large numbers of suspected criminals. Such dragnets have created a feeling of personal insecurity in cities.

Initially extraordinary police operations had the facade of exceptionality. They were thought of as "extraordinary" because they were implemented only at specific times of the year—on weekends, Carnival, Holy Week, and Christmas. Today these operations have become part of the formal judicial apparatus, with official status and institutional labels. In effect, "extraordinary" police operations have become less exceptional; they are now used throughout the year.

The object of this chapter is to understand the social and political significance in Venezuela of "extraordinary" police operations. They have resulted in the detention of massive numbers of suspected criminals. A central premise of this analysis is that extraordinary police operations cannot be dissociated from perceptions about crime and the social problem of crime.

LEGISLATIVE FOUNDATIONS OF "EXTRAORDINARY" POLICE OPERATIONS

In Venezuela, mass arrests are made possible by the "Law Concerning Vagrants and Habitual Criminals."[2] Under this law a person can be arrested on a written order issued by an authorized official. Since such an arrest does not necessarily result from commission of a punishable act, no arrest report is available, and there are no grounds for defense at the time of arrest. This law is aimed not at punishing criminal acts but at conduct manifesting a "social danger."[3]

People arrested under the Vagrancy and Habitual Criminals Law and tried directly by the Executive (civil authorities, governors, and the Ministry of Justice) have three days to present witnesses, without the mandatory defense attorney (although Article 68 of the Venezuelan Constitution guarantees "that defense is an inviolate right in all levels and degrees of the criminal process"). These circumventions of the Constitution are possible because the suspect is not accused of a crime. The accused will be sentenced within fifty days of arrest, possibly up to 5 years in prison.

Extraordinary police operations are characterized by selectivity in terms of the "criminals" against whom they are directed. These operations are carried out primarily in the "marginal zones" of our cities, where they undoubtedly will net "socially dangerous characters." In these poor barrios the unemployed (vagrants) abound, not by choice but as a product of the social system. (Such unemployment exists in spite of the Venezuelan Constitution's guaranteeing every citizen the right to work.) It is in the poor barrios where police "roundups" are constantly carried out. Such roundups provide the raw material for police "rap sheets," which establish criminal histories and profiles. These can be used by the police during other normal or extraordinary police operations.

The Venezuelan police use extraordinary operations to pull in those convicted two or more times of crimes against property, or people accused two or more times of crimes against property who are in possession of false or altered keys. But such an arrest rationale is clearly unconstitutional: The Venezuelan Constitution does not allow police to target someone for arrest just because that person has a record of having committed a particular type of crime. That is, under Venezuelan law the police may not institute a street sweep against presumed criminals—usually defined as people who have committed a crime against property, often accompanied by crimes against persons—on the assumption that anyone with a past record of having committed such crimes or having been detained in past police roundups is fair game under the Vagrancy and Habitual Criminals Law.

The utility of this law for extraordinary police operations becomes evident when we contrast it with police action allowable under the Venezuelan Penal Code. The Law against Vagrants and Habitual Criminals is highly flexible and effective: It assures speed of arrest and trial, and ensures the arrested person's total lack of defense. When extraordinary police operations are carried out, the Law Concerning Vagrants and Habitual Criminals takes precedence over legally mandated repressive practices, in spite of the law's being an administrative expedient rooted in exceptional legal principles. In fact, police action in defense of the "social order" dominates during extraordinary police operations. Criminal law, which should normally inform the repressive apparatus, is relegated to second place, thus resulting in de facto suspension of constitutional guarantees for specific segments of the population.

CRIME, SOCIAL PERCEPTIONS, AND THE MEDIA

Extraordinary police operations are justified and legitimated by the perceived existence of a "crime wave" whose reality is usually confirmed by a dramatic crime that stirs public opinion through the victim's importance or the violence of the criminal act. The mass media play an important role in shaping public images about crime and criminals. The information given the public about a "crime problem," and the way such information is organized, are decisive factors in problematizing crime and creating a feeling of personal insecurity.

Here we are referring to public perceptions of a crime wave, not so much the reality of one. Police and court statistics, as reliable as they may be (which is not the case in Venezuela), are not a mirror of crime's objective reality. Police statistics can be considered an expression of official insecurity: They vary in accordance with selective and massive arrests, not with the commission of crimes. Judicial statistics reflect the action of social control institutions. Such statistics thus signify what the criminal justice system has designated as pernicious and reprehensible. Criminal statistics give insight into the operation of the police and larger criminal justice system. They selectively identify what is illegal (through criminalization) and designate the population considered criminal.

Whether a crime wave is real or not, it can be perceived as real. Perceptions about crime can justify the use of "extraordinary" police operations. Criminologists—as well as police and government institutions—know that extraordinary police operations do not stop crime, particularly not the common crimes against which they are directed. For as Nagel has concluded, "The massive use of jailing has not significantly contributed, nor will it contribute, to stopping crime or correcting imperfections within our social fabric."[4] In Venezuela, in recent years, the frequent use of extraordinary police operations lends credibility to Nagel's statement. In fact, it is possible that such operations actually instigate crime.

The Law Concerning Vagrants and Habitual Criminals has facilitated the arrest and jailing of many Venezuelan citizens, even though they have committed no crime. Such State action has the immediate effect of substantially increasing prison crowding. Convicts are eventually returned to a society that holds negative attitudes toward them. These attitudes make their reincorporation into society difficult. The "social rejects" may thus be pressured into committing new crimes.

Extraordinary police operations also involve the police in crime. Increasingly, and without always being clearly conscious of it, the police become involved in a tremendous amount of illegitimate violence against citizens. This violence is a "normal" reaction to the stress placed on police during extraordinary police operations. Demanding that police act within legal limits while insisting upon highly productive arrest action (e.g., mass arrests) places the police in a fundamental contradiction.[5] Practicing excesses against supposed criminals leads the police to lose sight of the legal limitations on their action. Citizen murders are carried out in the name of ending crime!

In earlier periods, extraordinary police operations were short-lived and the negative consequences resulting from them were more limited. In February 1981, the government of Venezuelan President Luis Herrera instituted the Union Plan, which has become the basis for ongoing police operations that are no longer "extraordinary." The Union Plan involves coordination between the police and National Guard. These ongoing police operations were baptized Security Act 84 by the Jaime Lusinchi government.

However, large-scale police street sweeps and arrests are ineffective against common crime. In contemporary Venezuela the most important "common crime" is organized and, therefore, cannot be effectively attacked through large-scale street sweeps—a fact constantly pointed out by many Venezuelan police specialists and criminologists. If street sweeps are ineffective against organized crime, why have such operations been utilized by various Venezuelan governments?

We can initially propose that such extraordinary police operations are in some sense "successful" precisely because they have been repeated so frequently. Their success seems to lie in the mass arrest of supposed criminals. The police obviously concur with this assessment. In an introductory preface to the Union Plan's 1981 statistical summary of crime, it was noted that in 1981 "The measures implemented [by the Union Plan] brought satisfactory results for the community in general, making 31,714 arrests, of which 19,973 were by the Metropolitan Police, 1,321 by the DISIP [Intelligence Police], 4,463 by the PTJ [Judiciary Police] and 5,957 by the FAC [National Guard]."[6]

The simplistic assumption that seems to lie behind and to sustain extraordinary police operations is that increases in crime call for increased arrests, which, in turn, will reduce the number of criminals. The assumption is also made that criminals are easily identifiable and detectable. Another associated assumption is that crime waves are quantifiable; they are statistical realities created solely by criminal action. Within this framework, the problem of crime ceases to be social and becomes technical: Criminal actors must be controlled.

But the real "success" of extraordinary police operations lies in their ability to satisfy illusorily the social desire to end crime. This logic is not held only by police officials; it is also ingrained in society's common sense: If more people (presumably criminals) are arrested and jailed, society will have greater personal security because fewer criminals will be on the street. The public establishes a logical relationship between the number of criminal acts and the number of criminals. Such an identification feeds the subjective construction of "criminal types" and "criminal acts," and objectifies the link between the two. We need to be clear that behaviors defined, represented, or appraised as crime are socially constructed; one of the elements in that construction is police action.

Criminals are people with socially constructed characteristics that *represent* them as "criminal types." These characteristics are stereotyped into social intersubjectivity. An important element in the social construction of criminality is selectively generated police action that, in the case of Venezuela, involves enforcement of the Law Concerning Vagrants and Habitual Criminals. In order to understand why extraordinary police operations are used, we need to examine (a) their social significance, which is indistinguishable from societal perceptions of crime, and (b) the connections between extraordinary police operations and the sociohistorical situations into which they are inserted.

SOCIAL PROBLEMS AND LEGITIMATION

Crime, social perceptions of it, and feelings of personal insecurity are intertwined. This represents the crime creation dimension. This interrelated and socially constructed configuration, in turn, becomes part of the justification for carrying out extraordinary police operations. This justification represents the social legitimation dimension. Let us draw this out further.

In the crime creation dimension we include perceptions of crime and feelings of personal insecurity. These create pressure to employ extraordinary police operations. In the process of carrying out extraordinary police operations, those operations come to be legitimated. This is the social legitimation dimension. While these two elements of criminological analysis can be separated analytically, they are connected in reality. Citizen perceptions about crime and their feelings of insecurity constitute elements in the legitimation and justification of extraordinary police operations. In fact, extraordinary police operations and the processes legitimizing them are two sides of the same coin.

The Italian criminologist Allesandro Baratta,[7] in a reference to Kitsuse and Spector,[8] pointed out that crime as a social problem exists both in social consciousness and in state organization. It results from a definition and an evaluation that are part of the process of communication and social interaction. Crime is not only socially constructed, it is also part of society's symbolic universe. The mass media play a fundamental role in creating and fostering social symbolization within this universe. The media are major producers and shapers of public opinion, and therefore play a role in the social construction of crime and in its problematization.[9]

Crime as a social phenomenon is ambiguous: It marks a point of convergence between subjective (cultural) and material (structural) realities. The judicial system classifies only certain behaviors as criminal. This classification represents the cultural component of crime. The system of objective social relations (the material sphere) includes the behavior of individuals defined as criminal. According to Baratta, an analysis of the material sphere of crime should be integrated into its subjective sphere.

In the social construction of crime, action by the mass media (the press in particular) is fundamental. The media can create social concerns, amplify them, and establish the relative location of an issue on the subjective scale of social problems. The media do this through propaganda strategies and techniques. They not only make crime public, they also publicize the action of social control agents. The mass media's discourse, therefore, mediates social interaction.

When extraordinary police operations are used, and become news, we learn something about the material foundations of crime. For example, according to Baratta, "law and order" campaigns are promoted by ruling political elites to distract the public from problems that threaten the foundations of elite privilege. We have seen this in Venezuela, where there appears to be a relationship between social and political crises and the use of extraordinary police operations. Such police operations usually have been carried out at times of economic or political crisis: spiraling food or gasoline prices, elevated unemployment, or political turmoil (government scandal, riots, strikes). The public is led to believe that extraordinary police operations will eliminate societal problems by doing away with common crime. These police operations serve the function of deflecting public consciousness from more pressing social and police problems. They place "common crime" in an elevated position within social consciousness.[10] Extraordinary police operations are part of the State's political arsenal for manipulating citizen perceptions about societal shortcomings. They represent moments in which a government confronts and neutralizes threats of state delegitimation.

Both extraordinary police operations and the media blitzes that publicize them push crises of state legitimacy into the background. They do so by thrusting safer (and well selected) socioeconomic and political problems into social perception. Extraordinary police operations, through the arrest of massive numbers of "criminals," illusorily satisfy (albeit provisionally) demands for the protection of life and property and neutralize the poor, marginalized, and exploited groups whose dissatisfaction with the system could seriously threaten the legitimacy of the existing order.

CRIME AND SOCIAL INEQUALITY

Crime serves a legitimizing function for the State by helping to mobilize consensus. In fact, according to Baratta, the making of crime into a social problem fulfills two State legitimation functions. First, criminal stereotypes are created. In most Latin American societies this involves the image of criminals as almost exclusively from the least favored social strata. This stereotype helps to reinforce social barriers; it reproduces social inequality.

Second, the social stigma provoked by criminalization reinforces a societal consensus in support of the existing power structure. That is, social stigma produces social distance that discourages solidarity with the "criminal," and fosters public disapproval of criminal acts and of the lower-class marginals who supposedly (exclusively) commit crime.

These processes isolate small segments of the population and hold them responsible for everything that is negative in society. The "silent majority's" fictitious cohesion is enhanced through exclusion of a socially distinct and marginalized minority. Those who honor the "social pact" have a community of common interest. This helps to legitimize the existing order of domination, which includes a social barrier between those whose rights are guaranteed and those whose rights are not.

Police action, based on the Law Concerning Vagrants and Habitual Criminals, plays an important role in social construction and legitimation. The carrying out of extraordinary police operations defines the social groups (always the least favored) who are "criminals," and who will be the object of future police action. This helps to reinforce forms of social marginalization and reproduces social relations of inequality. The media's reporting of such police action makes public the "criminal threats." By concentrating responsibility for all that is negative in society on the poor who are criminalized, extraordinary police operations hide the State's inability to satisfy basic needs guaranteed all citizens. Extraordinary police operations help to legitimize further repressive State action, thus reinforcing social consensus and avoiding questions that might delegitimize the existing structure of domination.

CONCLUSIONS

Certain conclusions can be drawn about the Venezuelan State's use of extraordinary police operations, the latter having a juridical base in the Law Concerning Vagrants and Habitual Criminals. A central conclusion is that extraordinary police operations are part of the social problem of crime, a short-run political solution to it, and a source of State legitimation. The social problem of crime is part of the symbolic sphere where a synthesis is formed between the material facts of crime and its symbolic side. According to Baratta, the material realities of crime should be integrated into analyses of its subjective sphere.

The mass media, particularly the press, play a fundamental role. They amplify social concerns and publicize law-and-order campaigns. Law-and-order campaigns become social facts in Venezuela through extraordinary police operations. News about such police operations is fundamental to the problematization of crime: Such operations make public the behavior considered negative and reinforce public perceptions about crime.

Extraordinary police operations highlight historically recognized social needs whose realization has been blocked or threatened. We can, therefore, propose that one of the functions of extraordinary police operations is to stave off crises of legitimacy by substituting one social problem—"crime"—for other, more serious ones.

NOTES

This chapter originally appeared as Tosca Hernández, "Los operativos policiales 'extraordinarios' en Venezuela: Dos acercamientos reflexivos al problema," *Anuario del Instituto de Ciencias Penales* y *Criminologicas*, no. 9, 1984–1985 (Caracas: Faculdad de Ciencias Juridicas y Politicas, Universidad Central de Venezuela, 1986). Reprinted by permission.

1. *Desbordamiento del hampa* in the original.
2. *Ley sobre vagos y maleantes*, in the original text.
3. For more information about this law and its consequences, see Tosca Hernández, *La ideologización del delito y de la pena* (Caracas: Instituto de Ciencias Penales y Criminológicas, UCV, 1977).
4. William Nagel, "On Behalf of a Moratorium on Prison Construction," *Crime and Delinquency*, 23, no. 2 (April 1977): 156.
5. See Maureen Cain, "Trends in the Sociology of Police Work," *International Journal of the Sociology of Law* 7, no. 2 (May 1979): 143–67.
6. Venezuela Policía Metropolitana, "Plan Unión Uno" (2–13081, 3–16–81) (Caracas, Departamento de Estadística, 1981), p. 1.

7. Allesandro Baratta, "Problemi sociali e percezione della criminalitá," *Dei delitti e delle pene*, no. 1 (1983).

8. J. Kitsuse and M. Spector, *Constructing Social Problems* (Menlo Park, Calif.: Cummings, 1977).

9. Rodríguez Ibáñez confirms this. He believes that the mass media do not merely "describe or paint reality a definite color, but . . . substantiate it . . . suggesting the same plan of daily action by means of [a given] emphasis and [with] silences." J. Rodríguez-Ibáñez, *El sueño de la razón* (Barcelona: Ediciones Taurus, 1982), pp. 133–34.

10. In Venezuela, several research projects have examined the media's role in creating criminal stereotypes. They include Xiomara de Valbuena and Marta Colomina de Rivera, "Los medios de comunicación de masa en una sociedad capitalista. El caso venezolano," in *Los rostros de la violencia*, Vol. I (Maracaibo: Instituto de Criminología LUZ, 1976); and, more recently, Audelina Tineo, "El estereotipo del delincuente en Venezuela" (Maracaibo: Instituto de Criminología LUZ, n.d.). (Mimeograph.)

11
POLICE AND POLITICAL CRISIS: THE CASE OF THE MILITARY POLICE

Paulo Sérgio Pinheiro

> The criminal is a savage beast whose death is sanctioned. If there were a plebiscite, the police's habit of opening fire upon the slightest protest would quickly be consecrated—with unqualified results.
>
> Hans Magnus Enzensberger, *Política e terrore* (1964)

The fragile line that in democratic regimes separates the repression of common crime from action against that which is recognizably political, completely collapses when the rule of law is suspended. Then the line between one form of crime and the other—common crime and political crime—is easily blurred, as are the motivations for repressing each type of crime and the repressive techniques considered appropriate to each.[1] When a slow process of political transition from dictatorship takes place in society, as was begun in Brazil in 1974, instead of the rule of law being restored immediately, there is a fusing of authoritarian and somewhat democratic police practices.

The military police in Brazil, a uniformed State police force, offer an excellent opportunity to examine the continuities and discontinuities in repressive forms and practices. In fact, in Brazil repressive authoritarian police practices have remained, even as the police's focus has shifted from repression of "subversion" to concerns about common crime.

THE MILITARY POLICE

The political role of Brazil's State military police was not created in 1969 by Institutional Act No. 5 (AI–5), a military government decree that suspended all constitutional guarantees, thus implanting martial law in Brazil. In fact, during their entire history, the State police have had the mission of assuring stability of power in each state of the Brazilian federation; they have supplemented the other civil police forces. In São Paulo and Rio de Janeiro, the cases examined here, the State police have always helped to maintain the order imposed by the ruling classes: the repression of strikes, workers, and popular protests.[2]

Especially after the arrival in São Paulo in 1906 of the French military mission, to train the State's *Força Pública,* this São Paulo Public Police Force was linked to the armed forces. The Força Pública was heavily armed; its members were called soldiers. It was used against urban rebellions—on the lookout for movements that subverted public order—frequently provoking the very violence that it had been appointed to eliminate.[3]

In 1906, the São Paulo press denounced the already exaggerated military structure of the State police, and also of the fire department, asking about "the government's intention, [in] wanting to militarize all of the State's forces"[4] under French training. This criticism of the Força Pública's progressive militarization foretold events in Brazil after 1969.

One of the arguments presented in Brazil in the early 1960s for disbanding the State police was that such dismantling would keep them from becoming the political instruments of local power figures. The government could thereby block such forces from becoming an arm of State government.[5] On July 2, 1969, the centralization and "politicization" of Brazil's police took the final leap with enactment of Decree-Law No. 667, which centralized the State police in Brazil under the army, as military police forces under supervision of an inspector, a post assigned to an army brigadier general on active duty. With Law 667, the State police, which had always been subject to manipulation by state governments, came under federal control. Thus, the implicit political content of the State police mission—to defend and protect the ruling classes from protest by the lower classes[6]—became much clearer through the subordination of the military police to the armed forces.

This new "politicization" of the military police was motivated by the Brazilian military government's assessment that they were unable to deal effectively with the task of implanting Brazil's authoritarian regime. Thus, after the promulgation of Decree Law 667, all the military police—besides confronting traditional forms of dissent—began functioning on a daily basis (in military form and practice) in the war against urban guerrillas. In so doing, these forces spared the Brazilian armed forces the inconvenience of a conspicuous and prolonged presence in urban centers.

After 1969, Brazil's military regime also created some specialized mobile shock units within the military police to facilitate the fight against

Brazil's "internal enemy." The military police shock units that operate in São Paulo City are called the *Rondas Ostensivas Tobias de Aguiar*, the ROTA. The ROTA, created in 1972, was considered necessary because of "the police's impotence in preventing and repressing terrorist actions, principally assaults on banking organizations. Thus, [a] handful of men were trained to combat this new order of public enemies."[7] After 1969, such shock troops as the ROTA, which is organized into groups of four heavily armed and mobile men in car patrols with excellent communications capability, became the vanguard of political repression by Brazil's military government.

After politically motivated armed dissent had been decimated in Brazil's "dirty war" (1968–1974), the ROTA shock troops lost their original reason for existence. But instead of being dismantled and abolished, the ROTA was turned against common crime. Thus, the military police's traditional "political" role was broadened, without abandoning the style and methods developed during the period when the "rule of law" had been suspended. In addition to ordinary police methods of mistreatment and torture, the military police, and particularly such special shock units as the ROTA, have retained the right to destroy the enemy without risking punishment. The enemy is no longer the guerrilla or "terrorist," it is the common criminal hidden among the masses, subsumed by the term *povão*,[8] as the military police "affectionately" call them.

In Brazil there has been an extraordinary expansion of the military police's role. During the military regime, the military police focused on "political crimes" and destruction of the "internal enemy"; during the slow transition to democracy it has come to focus on common crime. As was true in past action against armed urban guerrillas, the law is seen by the military police as an enormous obstacle. By itself, this is nothing new: The police always tend to make their own laws, as we shall see. Indeed, as Walter Benjamin stated in his "Critique of Violence": "The police intervene 'for security reasons' in countless cases where no clear legal situation exists, when they are not merely, without the slightest relation to legal ends, accompanying the citizen as a brutal encumbrance through a life regulated by ordinances, or simply supervising him."[9]

During Brazil's political transition from dictatorship, the de facto impunity enjoyed by the police during the military government's struggle against armed political dissent has continued. On April 13, 1977, the military police's de facto impunity was given legal status by an amendment to the 1969 Military Constitution, as part of the repressive "April Packet," and other executive decrees and (decidedly unconstitutional) Federal Supreme Court rulings. These guaranteed the military police *interna corporis* justice—the right to create and enact their own "law."

The Brazilian military government's "security reasons" for allowing arbitrary, unrestricted police powers were fortified during the dictatorship by a national security ideology. That ideology was increasingly transferred after 1974 to the struggle against common crime. But it is not this doctrine of national security alone that has changed the post-1974 character of Brazil's military police. After 1974 national security principles were transferred to civil policing; they have thus survived even during the period of tentative democratic construction.

At the same time that political repression was being extended in Brazil to the struggle against common crime, the military police were incorporating and broadening the "vigilante"[10] practices that have characterized civil policing throughout the history of the Brazilian Republic. However, mistreatment, torture, and "death squad" executions are now practiced as never before. And there is a new articulation between politicization and vigilantism in military police action. This cannot be analyzed simply from a juridical viewpoint. We need a new perspective for examining the interrelationship of police violence to politics.

Brazil's police institution is as it is because the police are rooted in tradition; they reflect the trajectory and resolution of conflicts over power—not only in the present but also in the past. The explanation of differences in policing between countries, as well as of differences in levels of police violence and other extralegal police activities, is historical. We must remember that police methods are dynamic and subject to change, in spite of what seem to be their apparent continuity.[11]

This analysis of Brazil's military police should cast aside the illusion that military police behavior could be altered only through revolutionary transformation. As E. P. Thompson has suggested, we need consciously to resist such structural reductionism, especially where law and justice are concerned. Postulating a mechanical relation—that law equals class power—is no longer satisfactory. We should restore the view that relations between social classes and the law, and between social classes and the police, are complex and contradictory.[12] It would be too simplistic to suggest that the arbitrariness and impunity of Brazil's military police serve the interests of all members of the dominant class. In fact, in order to mediate class relations, the law repeatedly imposes inhibitions on the rulers. Thus, the arbitrary power of the State is *not* equal to the rule of law, as so many Marxist readings have suggested. For, as E. P. Thompson has argued:

> The rule of law itself, the imposing of effective inhibitions upon power and the defense of the citizen from power's all-intrusive claims, seems to me to be an unqualified human good. To deny or belittle this good is, in this dangerous century when the resources and pretensions of power continue to enlarge, a desperate error of intellectual abstraction. More than this, it is a self-fulfilling

error, which encourages us to give up the struggle against bad laws and class-bound procedures, and to disarm ourselves before power.[13]

In order to understand both continuity and innovation in the practices of Brazil's military police, especially between 1969 and the present, we propose emphasizing three issues: (1) relations among the police, politics, and political crises; (2) the conditions under which military police become illegal armed groups—vigilante bands who follow a death squad model; and (3) specific acts of police violence, such as the 129 quasi-legal executions committed by São Paulo City's 720-man ROTA between January and September 1981, comparing such deaths with those caused by police in other countries and in different periods.

THE POLICE AND POLITICAL CRISIS

The development of the police in modern societies grew out of fears about threats to social order. The police were created to confront the "dangerous classes," to control lower-class protest, and to preserve the status quo, not merely to combat crime. This has been true since the enlightened despotisms of eighteenth-century Europe—the first to discover the enormous advantages of national and professional police forces.

Scholarship demonstrates that political crises have always been used as a pretext by those in power for implementing and broadening police power.[14] Any historical analysis that does not question the conditions under which the police emerge, function, and change is doomed to be trivial.

The Brazilian military police cannot be dealt with as an inexorably necessary institution whose practices demand no more than a few minor corrections or repairs. That way of thinking would limit this discussion to the parameters of the current police role.[15] By examining the relationship between political crises and changes in police institutions, we can take permanence and change into account; we can examine continuity, not stable equilibrium, and conflict, not revolution. This is an interpretation of crisis that lies between revolution and continuity.[16]

In this study, the political crisis on which we focus is Brazil's 1969 coup within the existing military junta. That crisis went beyond disputes between Brazil's ruling classes and sectors of the State over who would control the political process and institutions. At the time of the 1969 political crisis, the principal instrument of State control was direct coercion and repression, justified as necessary to defend "national security," economic development, and Brazilian geopolitical interests.[17] Within this context, it seemed natural for the military police to be rigidly subordinated to the national armed forces, which by 1964 had assumed control of the Brazilian government. But this subsuming of the police under the armed forces, through Decree Law 667 (June 2, 1969), did not create a new role for the Brazilian police. It highlighted their traditional political role and further amplified it.

Centralization of the military police was directly linked to the difficulties that the civil police were experiencing with political and social control. In the late 1960s, the Brazilian State had further to consolidate the authoritarian regime in order to confront armed struggle by opposition groups. Of course, confronting political and social dissent with police force preceded the outbreak in 1968 of armed struggle in Brazil. But it was post–1968 urban guerrilla warfare that, more than anything else, justified the expansion and greater visibility of government repression, including the incorporation of the military police into counterguerrilla warfare.

At the same time, the military police did not abandon their traditional role of controlling urban discontent—marches, strikes, mass rallies, protests. The novelty of the military police's role after 1974 was that it assumed the task of confronting conventional crime, in competition with the civil police, while remaining actually independent of the civil judiciary though formally subordinated to it. But this was not simply a new military police strategy for combating crime; it also represented the consolidation of a particular notion of state and society. The military police role combined into one functional entity what Brazil's Republican regime (1889–present) had traditionally sought to keep separate—political repression (the maintenance of political order) and the control of common crime. Within the military police's new role, the traditional distinction between civil and political policing was short-circuited.

This does not mean that Brazil's State police previously served no political purpose. However, in 1969 the military police became "hyperpoliticized," under control of the armed forces. This "hyperpoliticization" was justified by the cohesion considered necessary to confront Brazil's "permanent war" against urban guerrillas. Executive-level control eliminated the possibility of local political leaders using the military police to promote their own political interests. It also transformed the military police into a permanent political instrument of Executive intervention. Formally, the military police were subject to each state's Secretariat of Security.[18] After 1969, when all State secretaries of public security had to be selected from ranking members of the security apparatus and approved by the federal government, the police and Brazil's central state became stronger.

When confrontation with urban guerrillas ended in Brazil, the military police expanded the war on crime, using the same techniques they had employed against the guerrillas. The methods and equipment used in military police operations continue to erase the dividing line between the police and the military. For example, recent police sieges against urban squatters have absurdly reduced the separation of powers—in any case little more than a simple formality between the Executive and Judiciary branches.[19] Since solutions to crime could not be effected through civil police methods, crime came to be handled through military strategies, under control of the central Executive's military apparatus.

But civil police politicization did not result solely from the 1969 legislation that linked the military police to the Executive. The expansion of the military police's role was also legitimated by 1977 legislation, Amendment No. 7, known as the "April Packet," which created a privileged arena for the military police. After promulgation of that amendment, the police "war on crime" benefited from the same legal guarantees that it had enjoyed in its war against armed guerrillas. The military police were brought under the Military Penal Code, thus obliterating the boundaries between the "permanent war" against guerrillas and control of common crime. The same fusing of political and common crime that characterized Brazil's period of dictatorship (when the rule of law was suspended) has continued to hold sway during the transition to democracy. The formal distinction between crime control and repression of political violence has been completely cast aside. In today's war on crime, the military police behave as if they were confronting an "internal enemy" who must be liquidated.

In reality, no police action is strictly and totally apolitical; police action is always also political, stamped with an ideology rationalizing and justifying political action.[20] In Brazil, national security theory has provided such a rationalization. This theory sees armed confrontation as the only solution to social turmoil. Criminals are considered agents of evil who infiltrate a naturally peaceful and orderly population. According to national security ideology, any other explanation for crime—whether sociological, psychological, anthropological, economic, or religious—is illusory and false.[21] In the end, the only good criminal is a dead criminal.

In democratic societies open involvement of the police in politics is minimal or controlled. Beyond their implicit political function, the police are generally kept within the law. But the 1964 installation of Brazil's authoritarian regime subverted the traditional legal guarantees of a democratic society. In fact, such guarantees were never strictly observed in Brazil as far as common crime and the lower classes were concerned. However, these legal guarantees were totally abandoned by the authoritarian State; it suspended law and citizenship rights. These were considered obstacles in the military's war against subversion. This vision of repressive efficiency continues to prevail in today's "war on crime."

But what characterizes postdictatorship politicizing of the Brazilian police? Under normal circumstances police activities are defensive or preventive rather than offensive. The police are presented as nonpartisan defenders of public law, order, and justice—as "public guardians." But in Brazil's national security regime both the military and civil police moved from preventive and defensive action to an offensive role. Preventive policing was relegated to a secondary place; the police went into permanent combat. This readiness for permanent combat has carried over to the present. The police do not focus on crime prevention; increasingly physical repression has become the norm.

Today in Brazil there is an obsession with getting "more police into the streets." The São Paulo secretary of public security has proposed, as a panacea against crime, placing two policemen on every block in the city. In testimony before the São Paulo State Legislative Assembly's Special Inquiry Commission, a former commanding officer of the São Paulo military police, pointing to the absurdity of this proposal, estimated that "if we could employ an MP in each block [in] eight hour shifts, after 24 hours, [greater] São Paulo, with 48 thousand blocks, would [have] a frightening total of 144,000 men openly policing it, a completely impossible task for a currently authorized effective force of 60,123."[22] Moreover, recent research has shown no relationship, beyond a certain point, between increasing the number of police in the streets and decreasing crime. If the objective is to reduce crime, increased police presence does not seem to be a serious option.[23]

All police forces are concerned with maintaining order by upholding the law. But when a fundamental antagonism comes to exist between order and legality, police forces run the risk of pursuing order to the exclusion of legality—of going far beyond their legally mandated limits.[24] Brazil's national security regime (1968–1974) perverted the notion of order by equating it with unity, unanimity, and national cohesion. Any digression from such values was considered an evil to be vanquished. But this view of society is problematic—it does not reflect the reality of social order and change:

> All political systems oscillate between order and varying degrees of disorder; all political systems exist in an essentially unstable equilibrium; all political systems experience varying degrees of political violence and challenge to the rule of law and the authority of legitimately elected regimes.[25]

Brazil's authoritarian regime manifested a view of history as stable, according to which harmony, tranquillity, and social peace were to be imposed from above—from the State's overpowering authority. Consequently, the arbitrary use of discretionary authority—a potential of any police—became the rule. The police began to see the law as incompatible with maintaining social peace.

POLICE VIGILANTISM: WHEN DOES IT OCCUR?

In Brazil the self-confident belief that the police may act outside the law is an inheritance from the war against urban guerrillas. The police argued that in counterinsurgency situations, respect for the law represented an unacceptable limitation on their action. For guerrilla "outlaws," normal citizen guarantees were a luxury—a limitation that the State could not allow. Since today's criminal is also considered an "outlaw," the military police likewise would be handicapped if forced to adhere to the law. The roots of public officials' tolerance for vigilantism lie in those officials' expectations about order and about the proper means for controlling social turmoil. It is assumed that death squad violence and arbitrariness is functional: Death squads help to preserve existing property relations, and conservative economic, social, and moral values, as well as law and order.

Police vigilantism can occur when the police perceive that legal controls are lacking, or when the regime encourages abuses or ignores them as a way of maintaining the status quo, preserving an authoritarian regime, or overcoming a political crisis.[26] Whichever of these motivations prevail—and generally it is a combination of them all—the result is always a brutal enforcement that ignores self-control and moderation.

Death squads fit this description. Some civil police agents, wanting to maintain civil police prestige in the face of competition from the military police, decided to demonstrate civil police efficiency through the elimination of criminals. The police counted on support from upper police echelons and even State government officials.[27] In the late 1960s, death squad activity in Brazil moved to a new level: It came under the supervision of Brazilian intelligence agencies through an organization called Operation Bandeirantes (OBAN). OBAN, an integration of some cadres of the armed forces and police intelligence services,[28] was supported by national and multinational business funds. In its war against urban guerrillas, OBAN refined the traditional death squad practices of kidnapping, torture, and murder.

Death squad vigilantism clearly has a relationship to Brazil's political crisis: It began expanding during the 1968 crisis preceding the promulgation of Institutional Act No. 5. The death squads can be considered a response to perceived increases in guerrilla activity and crime. Such death squad activity was also associated with a surge in public accusations of police incompetence.

As the war against urban guerrillas drew to a close, the death squads became progressively involved in eradicating common criminals—drug traffickers, auto thieves, gambling bosses, and prostitutes. Of course, even during earlier and later constitutional periods in Brazil the police never abandoned vigilantism. In Brazil, rigorous and respected legal precepts regulating arrest, the right to counsel, interrogation, and imprisonment have never existed for the lower classes. Disrespect for civil rights is the rule in relations between police and the poor. And the rule of law has always been left to the discretion of each police officer.

Moreover, torture, especially the use of the infamous "parrot's perch"[29] during the interrogation of common criminals, is an established practice among Brazilian police. In all Brazilian police stations torture has been, and continues to be, used. Many policemen see it as the only effective punishment for thieves. Indeed, in police–criminal relations a code has been established: The criminal who is not beaten is thought to be collaborating with the police. By betraying his criminal associates, the criminal risks being killed by them.

After Brazil's 1964 coup d'état, and especially after the 1969 political crisis and resulting promulgation of AI–5, the tolerated vigilante practices of the police and the State's authoritarian designs came together. Authoritarian political arrangements allowed Brazil's military government a new impunity in its long tradition of violence against the "dangerous classes." Death squads and police vigilantism resulted from granting discretionary powers to the civil and military police. This granting of police discretionary power was one mechanism by which Brazil's bureaucratic military system sought to consolidate its power.

ROTA VIGILANTISM

It is worthwhile to compare "informal" death squad murders with citizen murders by the military police ROTA. Between January and September 1981, a 720-man ROTA unit in São Paulo City killed 129 people. Between 1968 and the very early 1970s, 1,000 deaths in Rio de Janeiro had been attributed to death squad activity. In 1968 alone there were 182 death squad murders.[30] Comparing the death squads' methods with those of the ROTA, and considering the high body count attributed to ROTA, it seems that there has been an institutionalization of death squad vigilantism on a broad and organized scale. Both the death squads and the military police, the latter being the parent body of the ROTA, take justice into their own hands; both claim to be compensating for "weaknesses" in Brazil's judiciary system.

To understand vigilantism in Brazil, we must identify the similarities and differences between the institutionalized and formal extralegal violence of the military police and the informal violence of death squads. First, the ROTA murders of "suspects" are often disguised by weakly supported claims of police self-defense. Such claims give the facade of legitimacy because of the perceived respectability of the military police. Indeed, in spite of some isolated cases of corruption by ROTA police (violators are frequently expelled from the force), ROTA involvement with organized common crime does not seem to be widespread. This allows ROTA vigilantism an aura of respectability. The death squads enjoy no such respectability.

In another difference between military police and death squad violence, the military police do not run the risk of having their violence examined by civil courts. The Brazilian Supreme Court, in a poor interpretation of earlier constitutional amendments, has allowed military courts to continue judging military police crimes. Military courts have not shown a willingness to act against their own—even the civil police. Thus, the ROTA is allowed to kill with impunity.[31] There have been some investigations into death squad activity.

In another comparison, military police vigilantism is not restricted to individual criminals or to identifiable groups. In contrast, death squads usually focus on individuals or small groups. The military police view the entire population as suspect. A popular population control technique of the military police is the "dragnet," "roundup," or "fine-tooth comb."[32] These illegal searches and seizures take place in a city's central districts and *bairros*. In one such brazen police operation in 1981, Rio de Janeiro's military police used a 3,600-man force to sweep from Rio's southern district through the city center to the suburbs. Scores of people were arrested.[33] Such raids are spectacular but absolutely ineffective. It is naive to assume that only criminals will be scooped up by police dragnets, as some military police seem to think. These street sweeps illustrate an important military police approach to crime: If they cannot prevent crime by occupying a city, they will do so by raids and street sweeps.

In early 1981, Rio's commander of military police asserted that police raids in Rio's central districts would continue, declaring, "The citizen has an obligation to identify himself when so commanded by the authorities."[34] He maintained that "the policeman not only works with good people, but also with criminals." When interviewed about the arrest criteria used by the military police, the commander explained that his police used "personal observation and the lack of documents, even though the latter creates legal controversies." Note the blithe use of the phrase "legal controversies" in the reference to "fine-tooth comb" street sweeps.[35] The commander must know that the "fine-tooth comb" operations performed under his direction are blatently illegal.

According to that same military police commander, his "police learn to recognize a bandit. The subject lowers his eyes, becomes tense. Mistakes are rarely made." A journalist remarked to the commander that the overwhelming majority of people arrested in "fine-tooth comb" operations were black and poor, and wondered if the street sweeps demonstrated discrimination. The commander responded, "There is no discrimination whatsoever. If there were, no white bandits would be arrested. Nor would foreigners be detained."[36]

Police dragnets have value beyond the insignificant numbers of criminals they turn up: They let the ruling classes know that the police are at their service, protecting their peace and tranquillity. (Unfortunately, these street sweeps are often so violent that they cause even the upper classes to doubt their efficiency.) Police dragnets also teach by example: The suspects who are scooped up, tortured, and threatened with death will carry the police's warning to their cohorts—alerting them to the risks of committing crime. In fact, these police methods—dragnets and street sweeps—are carbon copies of those used by police during Brazil's period of military rule, when the police employed such dragnets to root out "agents of international communism."

In spite of the obvious inefficiency of police dragnets, and the inability of such police operations to monitor an entire city, the military police still use them. This suggests that the implicit objective of police dragnets is population control and restraint, not combating common crime. For example, no one was arrested during a three-hour dragnet on Rio's Laranjeiras Street. That dragnet involved heavily armed teams from the military police's 13th Battalion—including three trucks, a van, three paddy wagons, and two patrol cars. But the 13th Battalion commander was not discouraged by his failure to net criminals: "To the extent [that] we occupy all locations, the enemy has no room to move." For that commander, the criminal is an enemy whose location is the entire city. The blitz's very generally stated objective is "to discourage any type of illicit activity";[37] its implicit function is to reduce crime by keeping the lower (and middle) classes terrorized.

Vigilantism in Brazil—the breakdown of legality—is explained by twenty-one years of authoritarian rule, compounded by a neglect of societal needs and the further loosening of judicial (albeit at times only theoretical) control over the police. Reports show that crime has never been discouraged by police raids and dragnets, in spite of Rio de Janeiro officials' claims for the positive effects of dragnets. For example, in Rio de Janeiro police dragnets have done little to stamp out such pervasive gambling operations as *jogo do bicho*.[38] But even more scandalous than the ineffectiveness of police dragnets is that these dragnets are totally illegal: The Brazilian Constitution states that arrest is permitted only when a person is caught in the act of committing a crime or when there is a judicial arrest order.

In fact, the military police have assumed the task of controlling labor market vagaries under the guise of combating vagrancy. The principal identity document demanded by police of the lower classes is the labor card.[39] In the face of high unemployment (and even higher disguised unemployment) in Brazil's large urban areas, the lower classes face a constant dose of police terror. The dragnets and the "war on crime" are, in fact, instruments for terrorizing the lower classes. They are an integral part of the military police's strategy for controlling society.

Military police vigilantism comes in several forms. Besides the large number of illegal arrests made during police dragnets, there is also the sheer number of arrests made at any time by the military police. For example, in 1977 Rio de Janeiro's military police arrested 160,000 people. In only 20,795 of these arrests were legal proceedings sent to the courts. This means that 139,205 of the 160,000 arrests were arbitrary. Thus, the principle of legal restraint was absent.[40] In another example of military police disregard for legal proceedings, from January to September 1981, according to official ROTA statistics, São Paulo City's 720-man ROTA force detained 5,327 people for "investigation"; only 71 of those detainees were actually convicted of a crime. And in São Paulo State during the first half of 1981, 40,264 people were detained in the capital for "investigation"; 21,956 were so detained in rural areas. In all, there were 62,220 detentions in the first half of 1981—just for investigation.[41]

The objectives of such arrests are similar to those of the dragnets: to demonstrate police performance of duty, to terrorize the population through example, and to ferret out "infiltrators." But such sweeping police arrests have had no lasting effect on common crime: It has never been reduced by force anywhere in the world, at any time. And here we are referring only to crimes of the poor. The military police are deeply concerned with crimes of the lower classes (theft, robbery, murder) while ignoring such organized and white-collar crimes as embezzlement, fraud, and illegal financial operations—these together constitute the sum of common crimes against national property.

Vigilantism by Brazil's military police is also manifested by illegal breaking and entering, torture, beatings, and deaths. With respect to military police beating of civilians, in July 1981, a married couple was taken to the 18th Military Police Battalion in Jacarepagua, São Paulo. Their neighbor was a military police officer who was suspected of assaulting an armored car. In an effort to get the couple to corroborate their neighbor's participation in the armored car assault, the police beat them.[42] In an example of kidnapping, in September 1981, a member of the Ademir Ferreira Feital Military Police Mounted Regiment, accompanied by seven members of the Special Activities Police,[43] invaded a private home and kidnapped three people. The arrest order had been issued by a military police colonel and transmitted to the mounted regiment by one of its sergeants.[44] Also in September 1981, a group of military police in São Paulo sought a car whose occupants had allegedly shot and killed a military police lieutenant. Upon locating the suspects, the military police kidnapped and tortured them— arguing among themselves who would kill these "miscreants" and avenge their colleague's death. It was later proven that a military policeman had accidentally shot the lieutenant.[45] And in another case of military police vigilantism, it was disclosed that a nearly six-foot-long boa constrictor had been used in a military police holding cell to coerce prisoners into signing confessions. According to former prisoners' accounts, the boa constrictor would coil around a suspect's body, squeezing the willingness to confess out of him.[46]

As has frequently happened to police in other countries, in Brazil police "constabularism" has given way to banditry.[47] Charges of assault and theft by military police abound; frequent dismissals serve to verify this.[48] In fact, there are many indications that in Brazil major thefts have been committed with the collaboration of former military and civil police.[49] Today in Brazil common criminal violence is often committed by those who once meted out repression against political dissidents. Former Public Prosecutor Hélio Bicudo pointed out:

> We need only to observe the sophistication of some of the major robberies carried out in São Paulo and Rio de Janeiro to confirm that they are not the product of the lower classes. They are committed by people highly trained in the *métier* of raiding homes in order to steal—once [it was for] documents or evidence against [alleged subversives]; today, [for] money and belongings.[50]

The continuity between vigilantism as practiced by death squads and that perpetrated by military police has been revealed by a commander of Rio's military police: He selected as the emblem for graduates of a "special operations" course a symbol gruesomely similar to the notes left pinned to death squad victims, and also similar to that of the Nazi SS—a skull pierced from top to bottom by a saber, with crossed pistols underneath, surrounded by a laurel garland.[51]

POLICE EXECUTIONS: "STRICTLY IN ACCORDANCE WITH THE LAW"

It would be interesting if, alongside graphs showing increases in crime (often manipulated by the Brazilian government and some media in order to frighten the population), the government also gave statistics on the number of people killed in confrontations with the police. As of November 1980, the São Paulo ROTA had killed 110 people. In no country under the rule of law, even where the death penalty exists (or has existed in the past), is there such a death toll. In fact, in no country where the police are subjected to democratic control would there be such a body count, if that country wished to continue claiming a strict adherence to the rule of law. The ROTA murders of citizens, which represent a deliberate police policy of exterminating suspected criminals, depend on protection by Executive-level authorities and on the impunity assured by the courts.

The military police ignore the Brazilian Constitution; it does not grant any State-level entity or its agents the right to decree and carry out death sentences without representation of the accused. The military police act as judge, jury, and executioner; they kill to create "law and order." But the law they apply does not respect legal dicta. As Bowden has pointed out, "Police vigilante law is handed out at the end of the night stick or through the barrel of a gun."[52]

São Paulo City's ROTA certainly fits this characterization. From January to September 1981, the ROTA killed 129 people, according to its own statistics. If we add to these deaths the deaths of all people resulting from confrontations with the military and other civil police, including those resulting from legitimate self-defense, unexplained "accidents," suicides in police stations, and murders in penitentiaries and jails, the number of citizen deaths in Brazil's criminal justice system is astronomical.

Having examined the explanations offered by the ROTA for the citizen deaths it has caused, we see that it almost always comes up with the same story—with extremely few variations: An arrest warrant was issued, the suspect either fired a shot or pulled a knife, the police were obliged to fire, the suspect was killed during this confrontation. There have been some witness testimonies suggesting that many citizen deaths in these police–citizen confrontations are nothing more than summary executions. What seems to verify this hypothesis is that between January and September 1981, in all of the police shootout deaths in São Paulo City, *not one* ROTA policeman was killed. The only death of a ROTA policeman, according to ROTA statistics, occurred in a traffic accident. Eighteen ROTA policemen were wounded in these police–citizen confrontations.[53]

These data suggest the hypothesis that we are facing fabricated rather than real armed resistance by citizens.[54] The only viable conclusion is that the police do not shoot to prevent crime or to respond to violence, but to assert the State's right to punish. These bloody results lead also to the conclusion that the death penalty has been reintroduced in Brazil through the back door and in violation of the Brazilian Constitution and the law.[55] The ROTA's disguised executions are not unfortunate accidents; they express a deliberate willingness of public authorities to support police abuses.

POLICE EXECUTIONS: COMPARATIVE DATA

ROTA's statistics demonstrate greater police violence than has been documented for other countries, even during riots or periods of terrorism. For example, in the United States during the entire decade of the 1960s, deaths resulting from *all* racial conflicts were slightly fewer than 250, with 15 police killed in police–citizen confrontations and riots.[56] In Italy, during the turbulent period between 1974 and 1980, seventeen terrorists were killed in confrontations with the police: two each in 1974, 1975, and 1976, one each in 1977 and 1978, two in 1979, and seven in 1980. And in all, between 1975 and 1981, fifty-six Italian civil police and carabinieri died in conflicts with terrorists or were victims of assassination.[57] To repeat the statistics on ROTA violence in Brazil: In 1981, during a nine-month period, the São Paulo military police ROTA killed 129 people; not one ROTA policeman was killed. The figures on police violence in other large Brazilian cities are as high as for São Paulo City.

The São Paulo military police ROTA also wins hands down in other comparisons of past and present police violence. If we examine court records from the Middle Ages or from Europe's early periods of modernity, comparable levels of police violence cannot be found. For example, during the period between 1389 and 1392, 100 people were executed by the Paris central criminal court. And in Brussels between 1404 and 1600, the hangman publicly executed 1,023 people (more than 5 a year) in a city of 40,000 people. Between 1451 and 1500, 519 people were executed (a little more than 10 per year) in Ferrara, Italy. In Milan, from 1625 to 1629, sixty-seven people were executed.[58] In the United States only three condemned prisoners were executed between 1965 and 1970.[59] And in South Africa during the 1970s, formal executions numbered between fifteen and seventy per year. In 1978, the number of formal death sentences in South Africa was considered enormous: 132.[60] This is compared with 129 citizen executions by the ROTA in *only* the first nine months of 1981 and in only *one* Brazilian city.

In Brazil it is easy to carry out violent police operations: There is *no* oversight on weapons used by military police. As a circular issued by a military police commander explained, weapons are checked out "in lots," thus eliminating the possibility of determining who used what weapon in which circumstances. It is virtually impossible to reconstruct how ROTA-caused citizen deaths have occurred. Thus, any police report is sufficient. These realities of police work in Brazil increase the police disposition to use firearms. The military police are certain they will not have to render any account if, indeed, an accusation is made against them.[61]

Between February and August 1981, one of São Paulo City's military police shock units, the *Tático Móvel,*[62] killed fifteen people, according to reports in the *Folha de São Paulo*. Between 1978 and 1980, 215 people were killed in São Paulo's prisons and police stations. Unofficial estimates are that no fewer than 350 people die annually in Brazil's prisons and jails: an average of one per day. This figure can be compared with prison deaths in Spain, where in 1981 there were 22,000 people incarcerated and 21 violent prison deaths.[63]

Inquests on violent deaths in Brazilian prisons are inconclusive. Many such deaths are attributed to convict violence, even though they are likely to have been caused by prison or police personnel.[64] For example, the military police execute prisoners during and after prison riots. They seem to have granted themselves the right to execute prison rioters, over and above the sentence that these prisoners are already serving, and beyond the punishments that they would receive for their involvement in a riot. The military police have thus set themselves above prison administrators and judicial authorities. Prisoners remain at the mercy of military police arbitrariness; this chills any protection of their rights.[65]

For the military police, preventive policing has been replaced by offensive military action. According to one São Paulo military police commander, the deaths of "suspects" in the custody of the São Paulo City ROTA demonstrate police efficiency: "If [the criminals] continued committing one assault a day, during any given six months, we would have an extremely high number of assaults." ROTA logic seems to be "the more bandits killed, the less crime." It is amazing that military police officials still consider deaths of "suspected criminals" low, in spite of their very high numbers. Indeed, one São Paulo military police colonel explained the violence of his police by means of a medical metaphor:

> There are various specialists within a hospital. It is evident that a general practitioner rarely operates. But the surgeon operates constantly. The *Rondas Ostensivas* [ROTA] were organized to act in areas where critical situations exist. Consequently, they always confront . . . situations from which critical problems result. If it is true that, in the conflicts with crime, ROTA eliminated 124 criminal subjects in the first half of the year, it carried out more than 6,000 arrests. Thus, the percentage [of deaths] is [actually] rather limited.[66]

The number of civilians killed in São Paulo, contrary to what that São Paulo military police commander claimed, is not only extremely high compared with other countries, it is also extremely high for São Paulo City: It amounts to 1 corpse for every 6 ROTA policemen, assuming that the ROTA's effective force is 720. And, graver still, the deaths caused by ROTA in the first eight months of 1981 exceeded the previous year's total.

Finally, the military police still retain the impunity that they were assured by the repressive "April Packet" and accompanying Constitutional Amendment No. 7. These laws brought the military police under the Military Penal Code, resulting in their impunity for many civil crimes. For example, in November 1979, a civil tribunal was to try five military police who four years earlier had machine-gunned and killed three young men. On the day before the trial, Brazil's Federal Supreme Court, ruling on a writ of habeas corpus presented by the police, decided that the ROTA case should be heard by a military court. Not surprisingly, the five policemen were acquitted: The thesis prevailed that "they [had] acted in strict performance of duty."

The military police believe that post–1977 Federal Supreme Court interpretations grant them the *interna corporis* justice, which guarantees full judicial legitimacy of citizen executions. Thus, in Brazil's period of political transition,[67] the military police, which theoretically fulfill eminently civilian roles, have continued to receive protection from military courts—as if Brazil were in a state of internal war.

CONCLUSION

One conclusion of this research is that in Brazil's process of democratic transition it is unsuitable for the military police to survive. If the myth of a permanent war and an internal enemy has been eliminated, and if political organization is moving away from an authoritarian model, why should police militarization be maintained? If the authoritarian ideology that once defined and shaped the military police organization has been superseded, militarization of the police is no longer acceptable.

The objective of abandoning police militarization is a long way from being revolutionary. In fact, the 1980 Report on Crime and Violence of the Work Group of Brazilian Jurists pointed out that "The military's unquestionable lack of preparation in police techniques, the absence of knowledge of the law or related questions, decreases efficiency and makes [military] solutions to problems difficult." The report proposes that the attributes of a judiciary police—investigating penal infractions and the perpetrators of such crimes, and presiding over legal proceedings, with review by competent police authorities—should constitute the civil police's role.[68]

But, in spite of a broad consensus in Brazil—ranging from jurists to critical criminologists and including some police authorities—the debate about the proper military police role and methods is not going anywhere. We find ourselves bogged down in extremely technical discussions when the real issue is political. The progressive autonomy that Brazilian police have enjoyed since AI–5 cannot be explained merely as a reaction to increases in crime or urban violence. The current status and organizational structure of Brazil's military police represents a survival of a particular conception of State and society. Within this conception militarized control of society is a dominant survivor. And, for this survival to be abolished, we must begin to discuss the nature and ends of political transition in Brazil. We need also to examine carefully the relationship of the military police to politics.

In Brazil, the struggle against common crime is seen as a war. It is possible that some Brazilian government officials and large segments of the Brazilian population—out of despair about police incompetence and corruption—believe that the armed forces' power and military methods are most effective in exterminating crime. This is an understandable but mistaken attitude: Crime is far too complex to be liquidated by absolute power and raw force. Ramsey Clark remarked about the inefficiency of military power in civil policing, particularly in the control of race riots:

> Military organization and techniques are the antithesis of the police's role in a free society. Those police departments whose dominant quality is paramilitary will never be effective, [not to mention the] expense and the inefficiency of placing more troops in the cities, giving our cities, perhaps . . . the air of occupied cities.[69]

The history of national and local "wars on crime" is a testimony to incompetence and failure. The war on crime has had unforeseen consequences, often in an opposite direction than intended.[70] The immediate consequence of those wars has been an increase in criminal violence, on the one hand, and state repression, on the other.[71] In Brazil this war on crime has aggravated tendencies toward vigilantism, authoritarian State forms, and violent citizen deaths.

NOTES

This chapter originally appeared as Paulo Sérgio Pinheiro, "Policia e crise política: O caso das policias militares," in *A violência brasileira*, ed. Maria Célia Paoli et al. (São Paulo: Brasiliense, 1982). Reprinted by permission.

1. Regarding this, see Paulo Sérgio Pinheiro, "Violência e cultura," in B. Lamounier, F. C. Weffort, and Maria-Victória Benevides, eds., *Direito, cidania e participação* (São Paulo: T. A. Queiroz, 1981), pp. 31–63.

2. For the history of the São Paulo public force, see Heloísa R. Fernandes, *Política e segurança* (São Paulo: Alfa-Omega, 1974); Dalmo de Abreu Dallari, *O pequeno exército paulista* (São Paulo: Perspectiva, 1977); Robert Shirley, "Legal Institutions and Early Industrial Growth: Manchester and São Paulo," in John Wirth, ed., *Manchester and São Paulo* (Stanford, CA: Stanford University Press, 1978). Concerning the training of Rio de Janeiro police until 1930, see Bernice Cavalcante Brandao et al., *A política e a força policial no Rio de Janeiro* (Rio de Janeiro: Department of History, PUC-RJ, 1981). For crime in São Paulo from a historical perspective, see Boris Fausto, *Urban Crime in Brazil: The Case of São Paulo, 1880–1924,*" Working Paper No. 87 (Washington, DC: Latin American Program, The Wilson Center, 1981), p. 19; Alberto Mota Moraes, "Polícia: Problemas e soluçoes," *Arquivos da polícia civil* 36 (1981), 97–155; "Sem formação e sem disciplina aumentam os crimes das PMs," *O Estado de São Paulo*, 1/17/83, p. 32.

3. For a description of the French police that inspired the mission, see Sir Leon Radzinowicz and Joan King, *The Growth of Crime* (New York: Basic Books, 1977), p. 32.

4. Dallari, *O pequeno exército*, p. 44.

5. Ibid., p. 80.

6. *Classes populares* in the original text, translated here as "lower classes" in order to avoid confusion over the meaning of "popular," which means "of or pertaining to the common people" in Portuguese.

7. *Batalhão Tobias de Aguiar em revista* (São Paulo, 1980), p. 10. In 1981, the military police in São Paulo State had 44,000 men (24,000 of them in the city of São Paulo). In Rio de Janeiro, there are 23,000 men.

8. *Povão* is a slang word for the masses, with a pejorative connotation.

9. Walter Benjamin, "Critique of Violence," in Peter Demetz, ed., *Reflections* (New York: Harcourt Brace Jovanovich, 1978), p. 298.

10. Here we incorporate the concept of vigilantism, which attempts to characterize some aspects of illegal police action, as elaborated in Tom Bowden, *Beyond the Limits of the Law* (Harmondsworth, UK: Penguin, 1978), pp. 93–112.

11. Daniel Singer, *Prelude to Revolution* (London: Secker and Warburg, 1955), p. 121; Bowden, *Beyond the Limits*, p. 141.

12. E. P. Thompson, *Whigs and Hunters* (Harmondsworth, UK: Penguin, 1977), p. 174. For an analysis of the Brazilian transition and of the state of law in Brazil, see Raymundo Faoro, *Assembléia Constituiente, a legitimidade recuperada* (São Paulo: Brasiliense, 1981), pp. 25–55.

13. Thompson, *Whigs and Hunters*, p. 266.

14. Bowden, *Beyond the Limits*, pp. 16–23.

15. Eric H. Monkkonen, *Police in Urban America, 1860–1920* (Cambridge: Cambridge University Press, 1981), p. 24.

16. Randolph Starn, "Metamorphoses d'une notion," *Communications* (Paris), 25 (1976), 14.

17. Peter Flynn, *Brazil, a Political Analysis* (London: Ernest Benn, 1978), pp. 519–20.

18. *Secretaria de Segurança*.

19. Sebastian Cobler, *Law, Order and Politics in West Germany* (Harmondsworth, UK: Penguin, 1978), p. 136.

20. Eurico de Lima Figueiredo, "A questão da violência policial e da hegomonia política," *Jornal do Brasil*, spec. ed., 5/25/81, p. 3.

21. "Cerqueira faz críticas à imprensa," *Jornal do Brasil*, 6/1/81, p. 12.

22. Testimony by Col. Arnaldo Braga, commander of the São Paulo military police, before the Special Inquiry Commission of the São Paulo State Legislative Assembly, 9/9/81.

23. Roy Carr-Hill and Nicholas Stern, "More Police, More Crime," *New Statesman*, 181 (1980), 85–86.

24. Bowden, *Beyond the Limits*, p. 13.

25. Ibid., p. 14.

26. Ibid., p. 95.

27. Hélio Bicudo, *Meu depoimento sobre o esquadrão da morte* (São Paulo: Pontífica Commisão de Justiça e Paz, 1976), pp. 24–25.

28. P. S. Pinheiro, "Expedições punitivas," *Folha de São Paulo*, 1/6/81, p. 3.

29. *Pau de arara*, literally "the parrot's perch," is an iron bar wedged behind the victim's knees; his wrists are then tied to it. The bar is placed between two tables, leaving the prisoner hanging in an extremely painful position. See Archdiocese of São Paulo, *Torture in Brazil* (New York: Vintage Books, 1978), pp. 16–17.

30. *Jornal do Brasil*, 4/20/79; Flynn, *Brazil*, p. 469; and Bowden, *Beyond the Limits*, p. 104.

31. Helio Bicudo, "Hoje a ROTA mata impunemente," *Folha de São Paulo*, 8/25/81, p. 25.

32. *Arrastão, rondão* and *pente-fino*, respectively, in the original text.

33. "Batida com 3 mil 600 PMs occupa a Zona Sul," *Jornal do Brasil*, 2/14/81, p. 1.

34. *Jornal do Brasil*, 2/22/81.

35. "O duro xerife do Rio," *Vêja*, 4/29/81.

36. *Vêja*, 4/18/81.

37. "Arrastão occupa 4 equipes da PM durante três horas mãs não prende ninguém," *Jornal do Brasil*, 1/23/81.

38. *Jogo do bicho*, a type of numbers game.

39. The labor card (*carteira de trabalho*) is a type of identity card issued by the Ministry of Labor in which a person's employment status is registered.

40. Virgílio Luiz Donnici, "A política de repressão e a crise do sistema social," *Seminário sobre criminalidade violenta* (Rio de Janeiro: OAB, 1989), pp. 230–31.

41. Special Commission of Investigation, Legislative Assembly of São Paulo, Interview of Cel. Arnaldo Braga PMSP, 9/9/81.

42. "Tortura na PM," *Veja*, 7/22/71, p. 24.

43. *Polícia de Atividades Especiais.*

44. "Soldado da PM diz que um coronel ordenara a invasão e prisão sem ordem judicial," *Jornal do Brasil*, 9/4/81, p. 20.

45. "Para vingar tenente PMs ameaçam matar inocentes," *Folha de São Paulo*, 9/4/81.

46. "Polícia mantém em Jaula Jiboia para intimidar presos," *Jornal do Brasil*, 8/15/81, p. 5.

47. Antonio Gramsci, *Maquiavel, a política e o estado moderno*, trans. Mario Gazzaneo (Rio de Janeiro: Civilização Brasileira, 1978), p. 43.

48. "Mecânico acusa PM por agressão e furto," *O estado de Sâo Paulo*, 8/9/81, p. 37; "Porteiro é agredido por PMs," *Folha do São Paulo*, 8/9/81, p. 28; "Tenente da PM é autuado por tentar matar detetive," *Jornal do Brasil*, 6/6/81, p. 20.

49. "Delgado admite que ex-tenente da PM assaltou a Brinks," *Jornal do Brasil*, 6/13/81, p. 7.

50. Hélio Bicudo, "Debate: Violência não é privilêgio das classes populares," *Folha de São Paulo, Folhetim*, 2/1/81, p. 5.

51. "Polícia terà que estudar novo distintivo," *Folha de São Paulo*, 8/13/81, p. 14.

52. Bowden, *Beyond the Limits*, p. 99.

53. In three years, sixty-seven military police have been killed. Special Commission of Investigation Interview of Braga.

54. Bicudo, "Hoje a ROTA mata impunemente."

55. See Cobler, *Law, Order and Politics*, p. 137.

56. Ramsey Clark, *Crime in America* (New York: Simon and Schuster, 1970), p. 174.

57. Figures furnished by the Italian Ministry of the Interior and *Isto É*.

58. V. A. C. Gantrell et al., eds., *Crime and the Law* (London: Europa, 1980), pp. 12–14.

59. Clark, *Crime in America*, p. 174.

60. John D. Jackson, *Justice in South Africa* (Harmondsworth, UK: Penguin, 1980), p. 228.

61. See Cobler, *Law, Order and Politics*, p. 134.

62. Mobile Tactical Unit.

63. *El País*, 10/7/81.

64. Carlos Alberto Luppi, "215 presos de SP Morrem em 3 anos" and "No pais média é 1 por dia," *Folha de São Paulo*, 4/26/81, p. 20.

65. Pinheiro, "Expedições punitivas."

66. Special Commission of Investigation Interview of Braga. See also Percival de Souza, "Os caça-bandidos," *Jornal de tarde*, 9/25/81, p. 15.

67. Eurico L. Figueiredo, "Nas crises das PMs, inflação e indefinição," *Folha de São Paulo*, 3/22/81.

68. *Criminalidade e violência* (Brasília: Ministerio da Justiça, 1980), pp. 59–60.

69. Cited in Charles Silberman, *Criminal Violence, Criminal Justice* (New York: Random House, 1978), p. 173.

70. See Odon Pereira, "Violência urbano," *Folha de São Paulo* 1/17/81, p. 2.

71. Ibid.

12
POLICE DEADLY FORCE AS SOCIAL CONTROL: JAMAICA, BRAZIL, AND ARGENTINA

Paul G. Chevigny

This chapter compares the police use of deadly force in three culturally diverse urban settings—the island of Jamaica (chiefly in Kingston), the urban states of Rio de Janeiro and São Paulo in Brazil, and the City and Province of Buenos Aires in Argentina. Although they differ in size, in language, and in political traditions, they have a few notable characteristics in common. Under continuing conditions of debt and underdevelopment, their cities are swollen with poor people[1] in relation to the countryside.

They also share some political characteristics with the United States and Canada. They are also now liberal-democratic polities, with popularly elected officials and an aggressive free press, in which the police bear a roughly similar relation to the executive power. In each case the police bodies are protomilitary bureaucracies formally answerable to civilian law-enforcement officials, but with a large amount of customary discretion.

In the United States, furthermore, the study of the use of force in common street confrontations is very familiar; it is often what we talk about when we talk about police "due process" problems. So much work has been done on deadly force in the United States that it is useful to try to apply some of the insights from that work to the problem in the Caribbean and Latin America.

One of the most salient trends concerning deadly force in U.S. cities, according to a study by Lawrence Sherman and Ellen Cohn,[2] is that the number of civilians killed by police officers dropped drastically in the years from 1971 to 1984, by about 50 percent. To give a dramatic instance, in New York City, killings of civilians dropped from a high of eighty-seven in 1971 to twelve in 1985.[3] The trend appears to be the result of a policy decision made by police officials generally throughout the country since the 1970s. It was notoriously the case that the urban rebellions of the 1960s were frequently precipitated by police actions (not always of deadly force, to be sure) and that they were exacerbated by indiscriminate gunfire.[4] The rebellious were not cowed but enraged by the excessive use of force. Furthermore, some police officials thought that there was no sufficient reason to shoot a person who was not a threat to the life of another. Each of these factors—societal interests combined with humane principle—have led not only to the abolition of the substantive rule justifying the shooting of any unarmed fleeing felon (*Tennessee* v. *Garner,* 471U.S.1 [1985]) but also to the radical reduction in the use of deadly force.

This narrative tells us much about the use of deadly force in nonmilitary situations. When such force is broadly used, it reflects a policy of social control by violence. It is, moreover, in the last analysis a conscious policy; the senior officials have enough command over their subordinates to change the way they use their weapons. And the policy fails, finally, when it systematically provokes a violent response. It has ceased to be legitimate when it is perceived as begetting an endless round of violence.

Studies of police deadly force were conducted in Jamaica in 1986 and in São Paulo and Rio de Janeiro in 1987 by the human rights monitoring group Americas Watch,[5] through missions in which the author participated, and by the Centro de Estudios Legales y Sociales in Buenos Aires in 1987 and 1988.[6] The initial reports for Jamaica and Brazil were based on statistics and cases collected through direct complaints and newspaper tallies made by local human rights groups; they have been buttressed in this article by official figures collected later by the Núcleo de Estudos da Violência at the University of São Paulo.[7] In Buenos Aires, the Centro de Estudios Legales y Sociales (CELS) had official statistics in addition to its own. These investigations show that there are proportionately more police homicides on the island of Jamaica, in São Paulo and Rio de Janeiro, and in Buenos Aires than there are in the United States. The contrast with the United States raises the question of whether the more frequent use of deadly force is minimally legitimate in those societies and, if so, how the justification occurs. Moreover, insofar as the patterns of violence seem to be repeated from place to place, the similarity raises the question of whether they reflect common cultural and socioeconomic patterns.

Blocking the way to this or any other comparison, either among the three countries or with the United States, is the explanation customarily given by all such governments for the use of deadly force. In liberal–democratic states such as these, it appears not to be politically acceptable for the police to admit killing a large number of people arbitrarily; they must act under the cloak of the rule of law. In all but a small fraction of cases, then, each of the governments claims that shootings of civilians were justified because the civilians were armed, and often because they shot first. Fortunately, studies conducted in the United States since 1975 in the course of the effort by police officials to reduce the number of shootings, whether justified or not, imply some methods for seeing roughly what is going on behind the statistics and the justifications.

Yet these methods, even if they can rend the veil of rationalizations, only make it more difficult to understand why police violence prevails in these societies, as well as why both elites and the victim class find the level of violence acceptable or even tolerable. In this connection, I have tried to construct a comparative index (also very rough) of the "perceived threat of unrest," based on earlier studies of Latin America. Finally, I have looked at public attitudes reflected directly in opinion as well as at indirect indicators such as incidences of vigilantism.

PROBLEMS OF METHOD

The justifications given by governments for the use of violence raise the question of how anyone could decide, without a detailed investigation of individual cases, that a given level of the use of deadly force is "excessive." There may be many shootings by the police, but every one of them may turn out to be justified as being in response to some life-threatening situation, as officials in Jamaica and Brazil always claimed about the shootings in their countries. There emerge from the studies in the United States, however, several ratios that suggest persuasively when the police are using a relatively extraordinary level of deadly force. When the number of civilians killed exceeds those wounded by the police, when the number of homicides by police becomes a large fraction of all homicides, and when the number of police killed by civilians is only a small fraction of the civilians killed by police, there is an inference that deadly force is being abused.[8] Taken by themselves, these ratios cannot explain in detail what has happened in a case, or even a range of cases; read together with the details of exemplary cases, however, they can give us a way of evaluating claims by police that all the homicides in many hundreds of instances are justified.

Let us first consider the relation between the number of shootings and the number of deaths. The real indicator of how much deadly force is being used is not the number of deaths but the number of shootings (possibly even the number of occasions shots are fired), because every police shooting is a potential killing. In the normal situation, there are many more persons wounded than killed.[9] If the police kill more than they wound, or if their apparent accuracy suddenly starts to rise, it suggests that the shootings may be deliberate.

Second, there is the relation between deadly force by and against police. If police are constantly in life-threatening situations, we expect them to use deadly force more frequently; thus the ratio between shootings of police and shootings by police is always significant. The relation between the number of police killed by citizens and the number of civilians killed by police is a much more rough estimate, but it is still useful; in some Third World situations it is the only ratio that can even be approximated. It has been suggested to me by the criminologist Mark Blumberg that a ratio of about seven to one is expected in the United States overall.[10] When ten or fifteen times as many civilians as police are killed, then that suggests deadly force may be in use for purposes other than the protection of life in emergencies.

Finally, we should examine the relation between homicides by police and the overall homicide rate. Police use their weapons within a more or less violent society, and sometimes use them to protect other people. Nevertheless, we commonly see most violence occurring between private people. We expect that homicides by police should be some small fraction of the total homicide rate; Sherman and Langworthy estimated that 3.6 percent of all homicides in the United States in the years 1971–1975 were by policemen.[11] I do not mean to suggest that the ratio in other countries need be that low; I do suggest that when the number killed becomes a very large percentage of the overall homicide rate, there is an inference that the police are not so much reacting to incidents within a violent society as they are using violence for purposes of social control.

Although these "disproportionate violence ratios," as I call them, taken together with the details of particular cases, can help us to understand a pattern of violence, they can tell little about what causes a police body, or the city or state of which it is a function, to persist in a policy that emphasizes deadly force. Some studies focusing on this issue in the United States have assumed that a high rate of the use of deadly force is correlated with a rising rate of violent crime and specifically with a rising homicide rate.[12] For the reasons given above in connection with the three disproportionate violence ratios, however, the equation of deadly force with violent crime is misleading. It implies that the use of deadly force is "justifiable" or even "natural," that it rises in response to the threat of deadly violence. But the recent United States experience shows that the causation is not automatic; police commanders have the ability to control the amount of deadly force, even when the crime rate is perceived to be rising.

More interestingly, some studies[13] have argued that police use of deadly force is correlated with the degree of economic inequality in the locale where it occurs, on the theory that the latter is an indicator of social conflict. This correlation may have some power when income inequality can be compared from city to city within a country, as Jacobs and Britt have done. The comparative economic statistics from country to country, however, are too often undetermined or a well-kept secret.[14]

The causal relation implied by the assumption of a correlation between official violence and economic inequality is, moreover, quite ambiguous. At least two related scenarios are possible: (1) The relative poverty of the place results in a rise of life-threatening crime, and thus increases the incidence of the police use of deadly force; and (2) when economic inequality is extreme, elites and the polity as a whole may see a need for a show of violent force to discourage civil disturbances. Although these two may, and often will, prevail at the same time, it is the second that is more significant for us. Among the things we are after, then, is an index of the perceived threat of social unrest among the poor.

Since at least the beginning of the 1960s, students of social conflict have been trying to create indices that will correlate social conditions, or changes in conditions, with social turmoil or rebellion.[15] Duff and McCamant[16] constructed an index that collected factors of "social mobilization" (including urbanization and means of mass communication), discounted by factors of social welfare (including literacy, nutrition, medical services, and gross national product), on the hypothesis that the difference would be an indicator of social dissatisfaction and conflict. They did find the difference to be correlated with violence and repression in Latin America, using figures that are now out of date. The index has been updated for this chapter, using recent statistics for South America and the Caribbean, and arranging the countries in the order of the greatest differential between the social mobilization and social welfare factors (Tables 12.1–12.6).[17]

Correlations of the sort produced by Duff and McCamant, insofar as they are offered as indices of rebellion or revolt against the established order, have come under increasing and successful attack since 1970.[18] The argument of the critics has been that social conflict is so endemic in modern society that merely charting the reasons for conflict would not approach the reasons for social upheaval; the real indicators are thought to be the conditions that mobilize resources to supply organization for underlying dissatisfaction.

Because such indices cannot explain rebellion, however, does not mean that they have no explanatory power for underlying, unmobilized conflict. Quite the contrary; Duff and McCamant[19] found that their index was correlated with civil violence, and for explaining that sort of conflict, their methods have been found useful.[20]

In the cases discussed in this article, the index is thus being offered to show that there is at least some reason to expect or fear unrest as a result of dissatisfaction. It points to a *risk* of social unrest from the point of view of the political elite; for that reason, I call this the "perceived

Table 12.1
Social Mobilization in South America

	Newsprint	Radios	TVs	Urban	Total
Argentina	.04	.45	.38	.55	1.42
Bolivia	-.21	-.15	-.10	-.50	-.96
Brazil	-.14	-.08	.12	-.30	.20
Chile	.10	-.07	.07	.55	.65
Colombia	-.06	-.11	.01	.06	-.10
Ecuador	-.05	.01	-.10	-.36	-.50
Guyana	-.16	.07	--	-.95	-1.04
Paraguay	-.20	-.15	-.25	-.65	-1.25
Peru	.25	-.10	-.15	.09	.09
Surinam	-.03	0	.11	-.24	-.16
Uruguay	.21	.18	.11	.55	1.05
Venezuela	.26	-.07	.11	.50	.80

Sources: (Tables 12.1-12.6): Newsprint per capita: Statistical Yearbook for Latin America and the Caribbean (1987). Radios per thousand persons: World Bank Social Indicators (1987); United Nations Statistical Yearbook (1983-84). Televisions per thousand persons: SYLAC; UN. Urban population as a percentage of total population: Economic and Social Progress in Latin America (1987); SI. Literacy rate: SI; ESPLA. Calories per diem: SI. Doctors per capita: SI. GNP per capita: SYLAC; World Bank World Development Report (1986).

Note: (Tables 12.1-12.6):
All scores are standardized. The factors in the social mobilization and social welfare indexes are as follow: In the social mobilization index, urban = 1/2 and the remaining factors = 1/6 each; in the social welfare index, GNP = 1/2 and the remaining factors = 1/6 each.

Table 12.2
Social Welfare in South America

	Literacy	Calories	Doctors	GNP	Total
Argentina	.18	.36	.12	.32	.98
Bolivia	-.25	-.21	.01	-.65	-1.10
Brazil	-.35	.06	.003	.43	.57
Chile	.15	.06	.04	.28	.53
Colombia	-.09	.02	.04	-.39	-.42
Ecuador	-.09	-.26	.07	-.40	-.68
Guyana	.17	-.05	-.17	-.80	-.85
Paraguay	.09	.15	.02	-.05	.21
Peru	-.04	-.07	.05	-.45	-.51
Surinam	.06	-.06	-.003	.60	.60
Uraguay	.17	.08	.10	.55	.90
Venezuela	-.02	.06	.08	.60	.72

Sources and notes: See Table 12.1.

Table 12.3
Social Mobilization and Social Welfare Rankings in South America

Mobilization Ranking		Welfare-Mobilization Differential		Welfare Ranking	
Argentina	1.42	Peru	-.60	Argentina	.98
Uruguay	1.05	Argentina	-.44	Uruguay	.90
Venezuela	.80	Colombia	-.32	Venezuela	.72
Chile	.65	Ecuador	-.18	Surinam	.60
Brazil	.20	Uruguay	-.15	Brazil	.57
Peru	.09	Bolivia	-.14	Chile	.53
Colombia	-.10	Chile	-.12	Paraguay	.21
Surinam	-.16	Venezuela	-.08	Colombia	-.42
Ecuador	-.50	Guyana	.19	Peru	-.51
Bolivia	-.96	Brazil	.37	Ecuador	-.68
Guyana	-1.04	Surinam	.76	Guyana	-.85
Paraguay	-1.25	Paraguay	1.46	Bolovia	-1.10

Sources and notes: See Table 12.1.

Table 12.4
Social Mobilization in the Caribbean

	Newsprint	Radios	TVs	Urban	Total
Antigua/Barbuda	--	-.08	.06	-.62	-.64
Bahamas	--	.09	-.05	.41	.45
Barbados	.26	.16	.06	-.26	.22
Bermuda	--	.40	.55	--	.95
Cuba	.03	-.05	-.01	.47	.44
Dominican Repub.	-.06	-.19	-.10	.12	-.23
Grenada	--	-.04	-.08	-.03	-.15
Guadeloupe	--	-.15	-.07	.27	.05
Haiti	-.26	-.20	-.18	-.74	-1.38
Jamaica	-.07	-.14	-.10	.03	-.18
Martinique	--	-.13	-.06	.30	.11
Neth. Antilles	--	.68	-.01	.83	1.50
St. Lucia	--	.18	-.18	--	0
St. Vincent	--	--	--	--	--
Trinidad	.10	-.08	.11	-.88	-.75

Sources and notes: See Table 12.1.

Table 12.5
Social Welfare in the Caribbean

	Literacy	Calories	Doctors	GNP	Total
Antigua/Barbuda	--	-.26	0	--	-.51
Bahamas	.07	.06	.09	.62	.84
Barbados	.13	.30	.10	.20	.73
Bermuda	.13	--	--	.87	1.00
Cuba	.12	.14	.17	-.22	.21
Dominican Repub.	-.08	-.02	.05	-.41	-.46
Grenada	.12	-.09	-.02	-.43	-.42
Guadeloupe	--	--	.12	.11	.23
Haiti	-.46	-.32	-.45	-.52	-1.75
Jamaica	-.12	.003	-.04	-.38	-.54
Martinique	--	--	.13	.34	.47
Neth. Antilles	--	--	.05	.17	.22
St. Lucia	-.03	-.08	-.03	-.38	-.52
St. Vincent	--	.07	-.29	-.43	-.65
Trinidad	.11	.16	.12	.70	1.09

Sources and notes: See Table 12.1.

Table 12.6
Social Mobilization and Social Welfare Rankings in the Caribbean

Mobilization Ranking		Welfare-Mobilization Differential		Welfare Ranking	
Neth. Antilles	1.50	Neth. Antilles	-1.28	Trinidad	1.09
Bermuda	.95	Haiti	-.37	Bermuda	1.00
Bahamas	.45	Jamaica	-.36	Bahamas	.84
Cuba	.44	Grenada	-.27	Barbados	.73
Barbados	.22	Cuba	-.23	Martinique	.47
Martinique	.11	Dominican Repub.	-.23	Guadeloupe	.23
Guadeloupe	.05	Bermuda	.05	Neth. Antilles	.22
Grenada	-.15	Antigua/Barbuda	.13	Cuba	.21
Jamaica	-.18	Guadeloupe	.18	Grenada	-.42
Dom. Repub.	-.23	Martinique	.36	Dom. Repub.	-.46
Antigua/Barbuda	-.64	Bahamas	.39	Antigua/Barbuda	-.51
Trinidad	-.75	Barbados	.51	St. Lucia	-.52
Haiti	-1.38	Trinidad	1.84	Jamaica	-.54
St. Lucia	NA	St. Lucia	NA	St. Vincent	-.65
St. Vincent	NA	St. Vincent	NA	Haiti	-1.75

Sources and notes: See Table 12.1.

threat of unrest" scale. The theory is that the consciousness of the risk may make an increase in official violence more likely, at least where the climate of opinion would favor it. On the other hand, as common experience tells us, and as the Feierabends[21] have formalized it, official violence can provoke as well as quell social unrest. When there is little protest against prevalent police violence, that passivity requires some explanation.

When the use of deadly force seems prevalent in law enforcement, then, I propose to examine it in the light of three factors:

1. A likelihood of social unrest. In this connection the indices in Tables 12.1–12.6 are meant only to be suggestive. Placement on the scale points to problems that might create enough apprehension to give rise to police action.
2. Elite opinion concerning the use of coercive social control and deadly force.
3. Mass attitudes toward coercive social control and deadly force.

JAMAICA

Judging from cases and statistics collected by the Jamaica Council for Human Rights, supplemented by official figures that became available later, the use of deadly force by the Jamaica Constabulary presents an extraordinary pattern (Table 12.7).

The ten-year average of 208 killings, drawn from newspaper and official figures, may be somewhat undercounted. On their face, however, whether undercounted or not, these figures are large and puzzling on an island that has fewer than 3 million people—about as many as, say, Brooklyn, New York—with a constabulary of some 6,000 officers and 2,000 auxiliaries, a force proportionately somewhat smaller than that of New York City.

Jamaica has one large, poor city, Kingston, where many of the social problems are concentrated, and is otherwise farm country and small towns through which the police are thinly distributed. The official explanation for all but a tiny handful of the police homicides, in which an error is admitted, is that Jamaica is an extraordinarily violent society, and that in each case the police are responding to an "ambush" or a "shoot-out" in order to protect their lives. If this claim were true, it might indicate a dire social situation, but it at least it would make the figures less puzzling.

The three disproportionate violence ratios outlined in connection with the U.S. studies afford a way to start evaluating the official scenario. Jamaica's statistics for homicides, apart from killings by police, in the five years 1984–1988 yield an average of 445 per year.[22] The average for homicides by police in the same period (Table 12.7) is 212, not quite half

Table 12.7
Homicides in Jamaica, 1979–1988

Homicides by Jamaica Constabulary (Police), 1979-1988

1979	1980	1981	1982	1983	1984	1985	1986	1987	1988	Yearly Average
199	206	319	101	196	288	210	178	205	181	208

Homicides Other Than by Police, 1984-1988

1984	1985	1986	1987	1988	Yearly Average
484	433	449	442	414	445

Police Killed in the Line of Duty, 1980-1985

	1980	1981	1982	1983	1984	1985	Yearly Average
Regulars	22	4	7	13	13	4	10.5

	1979-1983	1984	1985
Auxiliaries	31*	7	5

*In the period 1979-1983, thirty-one auxiliary police were killed in the line of duty, but no annual breakdown is available. Figures for regulars killed before 1980 are not available.

Source: Homicides by Constabulary, *The Gleaner* (Kingston); other figures, official Jamaican government statistics.

the civilian homicide rate. In other words, the police account for about one-third of all homicides in the island.

The official figures for the number of civilians killed and the number wounded were made available only for 1988. Only 98 persons were wounded, according to police figures, during the same period that 188 were killed.[23]

The relation between deadly force used by and against the police is also revealing (Table 12.7). In 1985, for example, over twenty times as many civilians were killed by police as police were killed in the line of duty. For that year, furthermore, we received an extraordinary bit of official data concerning the low risk of injury run by officers in shooting incidents: In 1982, in 372 reported shooting incidents involving police, 22 police were injured.[24] This argues against the "ambush" scenario.

The Jamaica Council for Human Rights has a dossier of a dozen officers who have repeatedly been involved in alleged abuses of deadly force. We linked one of the officers in the dossier, Det. Cpl. Alfred Laing, to thirteen shootings in a three-year period; there may well be more. One of Laing's cases will serve as the paradigm. In April 1985, Laing arrested a suspect and had him arraigned on a charge of possessing a gun, a serious charge in Jamaica. When Laing failed to produce some documentation required by the court, the suspect was released on bail, whereupon Laing threatened, "Tell your mother to get your burial suit ready." Three weeks later, Laing showed up at the suspect's house with a heavily armed squad and killed him. The police took the other young men in the house into custody and beat them in an attempt to find where the supposed gun was hidden.[25]

On the basis of records of cases like this one, together with interviews of witnesses and lawyers on the island, we in the Americas Watch mission concluded, in light of the disproportionate violence ratios, that many of the police homicides are summary executions of suspects, usually in routine cases, whom the police have killed in lieu of taking the cases to the courts. In connection with such cases, the police often use semiautomatic weapons, so that in crowded neighborhoods other individuals are shot through either indiscriminate firing or mistaken identity.

Social and economic relations prevailing in Jamaica are, from the point of view of the propertied, menacing. Unequal distribution of land and income, while traditional in Jamaica, has increased in the last generation.[26] Land distribution has resulted in increasing urbanization of the poor. On the "threat of unrest" scale (discounting social mobilization by social welfare factors) for the Caribbean (Table 12.6), Jamaica has one of the largest negative differentials, even though the island is not among the poorest in resources. It is interesting to note that in Trinidad, which has somewhat less than half the population of Jamaica and has one of the most favorable "threat of unrest" ratios, it is reported that there were 200 police homicides in the years between 1970 and 1986.[27]

Under these socioeconomic conditions, we were afforded a window into the attitudes of elite opinion makers concerning police violence through their reactions to the Americas Watch report on human rights in Jamaica. The island's main newspaper, *The Gleaner*, serialized the report in the fall of 1986, spawning an avalanche of commentary.

The columnists for *The Gleaner* took a curious middle course; they did not so much deny the conclusion as seek to explain the practice. The noted social scientist Carl Stone, a regular contributor, produced at least four columns about the report.[28] In one of them he wrote:

> The average policeman in uniform cannot shoot straight enough to handle the tough criminals with M–16 rifles and to protect you and me against serious criminals. . . .
>
> The much criticised Eradication Squad which wiped out many such criminals was designed for that purpose. Sharp-shooting CIB [Criminal Investigation Bureau] men at various Police stations have earned the support of citizens by demonstrating a capability to shake down criminals and send them in flight from sheer fear of their awesome reputations and their daring deeds of violence. . . .
>
> . . . Even if this macho type police strategy really does not work, it gives citizens a deep sense of confidence that there are tough cops who they think drive fear into the hearts of criminals. . . .
>
> Some way has to be found to reduce the incidence of killing of innocent citizens and to prosecute policemen who kill outside of circumstances when their lives are threatened. But tough macho cops the country needs to maintain a "balance of terror" in the streets.
>
> The excesses must be curbed but there must be no removal of the frontline cops who strike fear in the hearts of the violent criminals and have the courage to confront them on the battlefield of violence.
>
> To do that is to ensure that many citizens would have to fill the vacuum and become frontline men fighting crime in highly organised vigilante squads along the South American pattern.[29]

Gleaner columnist Morris Cargill claimed that Jamaica is a "violent and anarchic society" with a crime rate "in excess of any other country with even a vestigial claim to be civilized." He expressed despair about the quality of prosecutors and court personnel in Jamaica, adding that the island is too poor to afford proper law enforcement. ". . .[W]e have not got the police capacity to track down and arrest our criminals in a nice, orderly, civilized manner." Toward the end he wrote: "The police do shoot down known murderers and armed gangsters when they catch them, sometimes in cold blood. This is not the best way of justice, but in our present circumstances my only complaint is that they don't shoot enough of them."[30] For opinion makers on the island, then, police use of deadly force is seen as an inescapable consequence of underdevelopment, crime, and poverty. Through a curious reversal of loyalties, they justify a system of repression because of a supposed lack of access to a more "civilized" system, painting a picture of their society as so "anarchic," so filled with terrorists, as to have no alternative to police violence.[31] They rely on factors that are often correlated with police violence. Jamaica does have the highest homicide and robbery rate in the Caribbean; more important, perhaps, the rate of crime has risen rapidly. There were more than ten times as many homicides on the island in 1983 as in 1953.[32] But those factors taken alone, as we have seen, do not serve to explain why police violence is acceptable to the opinion makers; the threat of unrest may give them an extra reason to fear possible violence from the poor.

Their views, moreover, are reflected in more general public attitudes. Those toward the police are ambivalent. Carl Stone tells us that he found in one poll 66 percent of the public throughout Jamaica felt that the police did not respect citizens' rights, whereas in another he found that 68 percent in Kingston did not believe the police used excessive force. Indeed, 41 percent felt that not enough force was used, and 10 percent said that "certain types . . . should not be brought in alive."[33] The public thus seems to share the opinion makers' sense that the police, like the criminal justice system as a whole, are not competent enough, and that reliance on desperate violence is the only way.

Class relations in Jamaica have tended to support a system of summary punishment. Commentators have remarked repeatedly how postcolonial social relations replicate colonial ones. Those who are "educated," who have "manners," often have a contempt for those without; this is close to the contempt of white colonial administrators for black Jamaicans generally.[34] Under the unstable economic conditions prevailing on the island, moreover, those who are not in the underclass run a risk of being thrust into it. Their fear of social unrest and of the underclass associated with it, is so strong that they deny any common social bond.

Vigilante violence has been increasing for several years. The parliamentary ombudsman, condemning both official and nonofficial violence, counted thirty-five instances of vigilante killings in 1984,[35] and now such instances of summary justice, in which suspects are summarily killed, seem to be at least as frequent. One was reported while I was in Jamaica in July 1986: The vendors in a local market disarmed a robber and beat him to death.[36] Lynch law and police violence are two aspects of the same problem; police use of deadly force can be seen, in many cases, as official vigilantism, and it is notable that, so far as I can tell, arrests are never made for private vigilantism. In the column quoted earlier, Carl Stone wrote:

Vigilante killings are popular and supported by a majority of Jamaicans because they feel that the Police are not able to control crime effectively due to inadequate manpower, guns and motor vehicles and because they fear that the courts system does not work for them. To protect themselves, they take the law in their own hands and seek to establish their own "balance of terror."[37]

As we shall see more vividly in Brazil, society presents a particularly terrifying prospect to those just above the underclass when it says that the state is too poor and the authorities too incompetent to protect them, and their only salvation is self-help. It creates a grim world of vengefulness in which those accused of crime are literally "outlaws," subject to execution by everyone, official or private.[38]

Apart from the public opinion studies of Carl Stone, which sometimes do not distinguish with respect to class, the attitudes of the poorest people, who are the chief victims both of police violence and of crime, is hard to determine. No doubt many ghetto dwellers share the view that those who are criminals deserve no more consideration than a lynch mob would give them. They sometimes also accept the hegemonic values of those who are a little better off than they are. Some have relied traditionally on patron–client relations, formed not only with politicians but also with policemen. A Jamaican defense lawyer told us that many people in Det. Cpl. Alfred Laing's precinct do not consider him a bad fellow, despite the number he has killed, because he has the reputation of not killing the innocent. He has financed local dances, which are said to be well attended, out of his own pocket. People in the neighborhood have been known to bring him gifts from their friends and relatives abroad, apparently to keep on his good side.

The fact remains that there has been little protest, organized or otherwise, from any sector of society. There does not seem to be any substantial political advantage to either of the major parties in making police abuse into an issue, because it has not seemed to be a matter of general public concern. There are a handful of superior officers in the Jamaican police, we learned, who would like to change the level of deadly force, but can find little political leverage for reform. Florizelle O'Connor of the Jamaica Council on Human Rights suggested to me that those among the poor who might protest against abuse are surrounded by those who are ambivalent about it and, from their position of isolation, they are intimidated by the possibility of retaliation. From a certain point of view, then, the policy of social control by the use of deadly force could be said to be working passably well.

BUENOS AIRES

For generations, Buenos Aires, which by itself is more populous than the island of Jamaica, has been the center of trade and culture for Argentina, and a magnet for immigrants. Since the collapse of the military dictatorship and the election of Raúl Alfonsín in 1983, the Center for Legal and Social Studies (CELS), a human rights organization in the city, has been monitoring police violence in cases that do not involve overt "political" repression and are apparently "routine." Based on official figures and news reports, the CELS studies show a pattern in the city and surrounding province of Buenos Aires similar to that of Jamaica. According to police figures, 304 civilians were killed by the police while 26 police were killed (a ratio of not quite 12 to 1) during the period December 1983 to July 1985. Most indicative of the deliberateness of the shootings are the figures on woundings; the police report that in the same period, 172 "public servants" were injured and 199 "criminals" were injured. In other words, while only about one-eighth of shootings of police resulted in death, three-fifths of all police shootings of civilians resulted in death. During 1984 alone, it appears that the police accounted for over a quarter of all homicides.

Interestingly, CELS found that officials at some level seemed to have a considerable amount of control over the number of homicides by police; when there was a demand by an opposition deputy in the legislature for an explanation of the violence, and after a scandal about a kidnapping masterminded by a police inspector, the killings dropped precipitately for a short period. Like the history of the decline of deadly force in the United States, this suggests that superiors can limit the violence if they choose to do so.[39]

In a pattern common to Jamaica and Brazil, the victims were not powerful or socially important criminals but the most petty of wrong-doers, if they can be described as criminals at all. In one case reported at length by CELS, the victim was chased by police and eventually shot because he was dead drunk, fell heavily over a car, and ran away. In another case, the victim was an addict accused of petty thievery.

The history of Argentina does not at first make it seem a likely candidate for such police violence. It has had a relatively high standard of living, has not suffered from overpopulation, and has attracted hundreds of thousands of European immigrants. Under the surface, however, the socioeconomic indicators point in a rather different direction.

The negative spread between social mobilization and social welfare is one of the highest in Latin America, not because welfare is low in relation to other nations but because the elements of mobilization are so much more developed (see Table 12.3). The situation of the poor, moreover, has worsened over the last generation, with increasing external debt and unemployment. Argentina is a nation of blasted hopes.

The ruling groups of Argentina have been haunted by the fear of rebellion among the poor since the 1930s. The political arrangements from the Great Depression up to the last military government that collapsed in 1983 were established, at least in part, for the purpose of forestalling revolution. Juan Perón played upon that fear and justified his policies, and later his power, on the basis of the danger of a revolution.[40]

Despite the success of the elite in containing the working class, there is a long tradition of elite fear of and contempt for the lower classes in Argentina. While outright political repression and military rule form one aspect of these attitudes, a tradition of repressive police action outside the arena of partisan politics may be seen as another. The police violence that CELS identifies in the Alfonsín years is nothing new. The journalist Rodolfo Walsh, who "disappeared" in the 1970s, complained about it. And the father of one of the recent victims is quoted as shouting at the police who informed him of his son's death, "I get it. I know this kind of shoot-out with the police all too well. My father was a policeman and I have relatives in the police, so you'll see if I know! . . . First you shoot him and then you fire a gun for him. It's an old story."[41]

There is some liberal agitation against police violence in Buenos Aires because the level of social mobilization is high. CELS has campaigned together with opposition politicians, newspapers, and lawyers. There have been some demonstrations over particular incidents, but the matter has not become an issue against the Alfonsín regime. Eugenio Raúl Zaffaroni, a noted criminologist and judge in Buenos Aires who is among those most critical of the police, comments:

> The deaths are published in the daily papers and are taken by the population as a "natural" phenomenon. Death by violence on the part of the criminal justice system is "naturalized" with the phrase "he who acts bad, ends badly." It is not seen as a social phenomenon; from the point of view of newspaper reporting, the deaths are considered as a problem of the individual, as something produced by the victim himself. . . .
>
> It is a matter of a sort of intimidation exerted on a whole social sector, carried out by persons drawn from that sector, which shows the clear purpose of exacerbating the contradictions in that sector. . . . These deaths have the object of generating or deepening the antagonism, fragmentation and of dissolving the bonds of solidarity within the poor sectors.[42]

BRAZIL: SÃO PAULO AND RIO DE JANEIRO

The city of São Paulo is roughly five times as populous as the entire island of Jamaica or the city of Buenos Aires. The state, moreover, is an industrial giant, producing half of all of Brazil's manufactured goods; more than half the people live in the slums around the city. Rio de Janeiro is somewhat smaller, although still larger than New York, with a smaller percentage of its people living in the slums.[43] The Baixada Fluminense ("Rio lowland"), a slum outside Rio, houses some 3 million people. These are enormously more complex societies than Jamaica, with a much more complex police situation.

The state governments in Brazil use two police forces, the civil police, which do mostly investigative work and run the police stations, and the military police (PM), which do most of the patrol.[44] It is the PM, numbering approximately 60,000 officers in the state of São Paulo, which is responsible for most of the use of deadly force.

In São Paulo and Rio, as in Buenos Aires, there is an implied question of how much the years of military repression have increased the use of violence against the population in day-to-day encounters, leaving a residue now that the partisan political repression has passed. Liberal reformers, however, are as clear as the Argentines that the abuse of ordinary suspects is not a result of the authoritarian repression. They say that the police have always violated the rights of suspects; interest in human rights burgeoned during the military dictatorship, because in those years police abuses involved members of the middle and upper classes. Now that the repression has passed, abusive police practices, having reverted to their usual victims among the poor, have again become invisible.[45]

There is some evidence, nevertheless, that violence became more systematic against all sorts of suspects during the years of the dictatorship, and that some of that system has been carried forward. The PM in São Paulo continued an elite extermination patrol, called the ROTA, numbering some 700, which during one nine-month period in 1981, just as the country was emerging from the military dictatorship, shot 136 civilians, killing 129 of them, while suffering 1 officer dead and 18 injured.[46]

In 1982, the administrations of André Franco Montoro in São Paulo and Leonel Brizola in Rio de Janeiro swept in, dedicated to the reform of the police as well as other service institutions. The Montoro administration particularly aimed to abolish the ROTA, as well as to dismiss individual police officers who had been brutal. It succeeded in dismissing some 1,500 officers in 4 years, but the support for the ROTA, both inside and outside the police, has been so strong that it continues, although its officers have received some retraining.

The disproportionate violence ratios for São Paulo are revealing. Comparing civilian deaths at the hands of the police, which may be undercounted because they are drawn from newspaper or official counts, with deaths of military police "in service," which are overcounted for our purposes, including as they do accidental deaths (Table 12.8), the ratio of civilians to officers killed is still very high. More indicative, perhaps, is the ratio of civilians killed to civilians wounded by police; at least twice as many are killed as are wounded, and in some years the proportion is much higher.[47]

Table 12.8

Homicides and Wounded, Military Police (PM) and Civilians, in the State of Saõ Paulo, 1982–1987

	Civilians Killed by PM	Civilians Wounded by PM	PM Killed in Service	PM Injured in Service
1982	286	74	26	897
1983	328	109	47	819
1984	481	190	45	654
1985	585	291	34	605
1986	399	197	45	599
1987	305	147	40	559
Total	2384	1008	237	4133
Average	397	168	39	689

Source: Núcleo de Estudos da Violência, *Violência do estado e militarização* (São Paulo: Núcleo de Estudos de Violência, 1989).

Some of the homicides by police, as in Jamaica, are summary executions of suspects. The PM tend to dispose of criminals this way not in major cases but in fairly routine ones involving drugs or theft, in which the victims are anonymous. The circumstances sometimes are revealed when the victim turns out not to be anonymous, as in the case of Fernando Ramos da Silva, killed on August 25, 1987. He was apparently a petty criminal who eight years before had been the star of the film *Pixote*. Although the PM claimed that he had been killed in a shoot-out when he was being chased after an attempted robbery, it is tolerably clear that Ramos da Silva was executed; he was shot eight times while crouching or lying down, and after a witness heard him say, "Don't kill me. I have a daughter to support."[48]

Cases like this of killings on duty are probably less common than they used to be; the reformers in São Paulo have worked very hard, and there are many criminal charges pending against PMs in the courts. Nevertheless, public support for reform is spotty, and that for summary violence is very strong. A "security group" has been elected as representatives to the state legislature, including a spectacular captain from the ROTA, who had been cashiered after killing more than 100 suspects by his own count, and Afanasio Jazadji, a commentator on a call-in radio program famous for stories about violence, who is a staunch supporter of the ROTA. Afanasio paints a picture of a criminal class ever stronger against a police force inadequately trained and equipped and weakened still further by the policies of the reformers.[49]

The social indicators that might imply a threat from the have-nots against the haves in Brazil are not simple. At first glance (Table 12.3), the social mobilization–social welfare disparity seems rather favorable to social peace in Brazil. But the scale is distorted by the enormous GNP of Brazil; if we look instead only at the other factors in the social welfare index (literacy, caloric intake, and the population of doctors), it is apparent that the GNP masks an enormous disparity. Inequality in income is extreme and is increasing.[50]

The ruling class, as well as the bureaucratic elite, has reason, then, to fear the effects of unrest. It has traditionally mistrusted the political participation of the masses, and has contrived to limit it through a hierarchical structure likened to Weber's patrimonial state.[51]

There is a large amount of vigilante violence in both Rio and São Paulo. Some of it takes the form of spontaneous lynchings of suspected thieves; Brazilian sociologists counted eighty-two such incidents reported in the press in the two states during the thirty months from September 1979 to February 1982; thirty-eight resulted in death.[52] Arrests are occasionally made for lynchings, but not often; the police sometimes encourage such actions.[53] Waldemar de Castro, later an under secretary for police in Rio, said in 1980: "Lynchings make the bandits see that they do not own the streets. It is not a matter of doing justice with hatred for criminals, but with love for their victims."[54]

An even more common form of vigilantism is the work of death squads or individual gunmen. How many death squad killings there are each year can only be estimated; the figure often given of "hundreds" is surely not wrong. The death squads are often staffed and organized by off-duty policemen. "Cabo Bruno," a São Paulo PM who moonlighted as a gunman, claimed to have killed more than fifty people before being convicted of murder in 1983. When the head of homicide investigations in the Paulo Montoro administration sought in 1984 to solve the murders of more than eighty youths found shot "death-squad style" in the slums of São Paulo, he found that several PMs were involved. Similarly, in Rio de Janeiro, a commission has found that between 1983 and 1986, in 189 investigations of crimes in a huge slum of Baixada Fluminense, mostly of such homicides, a majority turned out to involve policemen.[55] Much of the death squad activity thus involves police vigilantism. This involvement makes the figures on the numbers of killings by police, of the sort set out above, still more suspect because they never include the vigilante killings by off-duty police.

Much of the obvious support of vigilantism and police violence is traceable to small businesspeople who employ death squads and individual gunmen to kill thieves. In 1986, when there was yet another shake-up in the ROTA after some scandalous killings, the São Paulo taxi drivers, who are often the victims of crime and constitute a law-and-order pressure group, protested by tying up traffic outside PM headquarters. Merchants demonstrated against the investigation in the Ramos da Silva killing, driving a truck decorated with a sign saying, "Society ought to thank the police."[56]

Yet the support is not combined with much confidence in the police; Benevides and Fischer found that more than half of those in Rio and São Paulo who claim to be been victims of crime do not complain to the police.[57] Afanasio himself speaks of the relative ineffectiveness of the police. The constant threat of violence, combined with the sense that the police not only will not control it but also actually participate in it, and the burden on citizens to use self-help to solve their problems, increase anxiety to a level that one of the reformers called "a psychosis of fear." It is a curious state of mind in which a lack of confidence in the power of the government to keep order is combined with vocal support of police violence.

The attitude of the very poor, the victim class, toward deadly force is not easy to gauge. On the one hand, they seem passive. Observers of Brazilian politics have commonly remarked that the urban poor have remained immobilized; populist leaders, while calling on the people for their support, have avoided organizing them.[58] In the early 1970s Janice

Perlman, interviewing slum dwellers in Rio, found that they thought they had "important rights," among them the "right to respect the authorities" and the "right to obey the laws."[59] Almost twenty years later, the journalist and political scientist Paulo Sérgio Pinheiro remarked that most people still do not perceive their rights against authority.[60]

The poor are just as frightened of crime as any other sector of the population; they supported Afanasio by the thousands in his election campaign in São Paulo. Many poor people seem to take it for granted that a person who commits a crime does not deserve any better than a retaliatory death. The words from the father of a boy killed by the PM after some late-night pranks with other boys are perhaps typical: "If my son had been robbing, then he could have been killed. No one likes a thief. But he was not that. They [the five boys] were having a party and threw some stones at a house."[61] In another case from 1983, a mother expressed approval when, after she had called the police to deal with her violent son, the ROTA killed him.[62] The PMs, who are largely recruited from the poor, seem to share these views and bring them to bear on other poor people.

In their study of lynchings, Benevides and Fischer found that 44 percent of those interviewed in Rio in 1980 supported this practice, chiefly because of the shortcomings of the police. In the cities, they detect a desperation in the lynching violence, which is itself an expression of anger against the conditions of life. They describe an intricate relation between support for private and official violence.[63]

But, it is an oversimplification to view the reactions of the Brazilian poor as mere "passivity." Certainly the mass movement of squatters onto unoccupied urban land in the last two generations cannot easily be perceived as "passive." While many of the poor do not seem to conceive of citizenship and rights in relation to the state as a chief arena for conflict, they have perhaps made a practical judgment to bargain with the elites for more immediate goals. In the Baixada Fluminense, local leaders told us they were much more concerned with getting the train to run into Rio more frequently than with police violence.

CONCLUSION

When we consider some indicators of the disproportionate use of deadly force by police—the number of civilians killed, the ratio of those killed to those wounded, the ratio to the number of police killed, and the ratio to the general homicide rate—the statistics, both official and unofficial, for Jamaica, São Paulo, Rio de Janeiro, and Buenos Aires all point to the conclusion that the police are summarily executing suspects in routine, nonpartisan cases. Used almost exclusively against anonymous, poor people, this abuse of deadly force appears as an extreme form of coercive social control. When the threat of social unrest seems high, because of increased social mobilization together with increased economic misery, the police may summarily execute a group of suspects, providing that both elite and lower-class opinion will tolerate the executions as legitimate. In all these cases, while opinion is split, the violence is minimally acceptable; the prevalence of lynching is an indicator of its acceptability to the mass of people.

On the other hand, because these are all liberal states, it is difficult to view police homicides as legitimate except as part of "crime control" and under the rubric of a rule of law. Accordingly, they are virtually all justified to the public as acts of self-defense, typically in response to "shoot-outs." This justification appears to be essential for organizing public opinion even though, for some people in the elite as well as the middle and lower classes, summary executions are acceptable as punishments. Experience in other countries suggests that it is possible for the authorities to control and prevent these killings; that is not done in Jamaica, Buenos Aires, São Paulo, or Rio de Janeiro, however, so long as they constitute means of social control that are acceptable to elite and mass opinion.

NOTES

Thanks are due to Bell Chevigny, Russell Karp, and Lois Whitman, and to Americas Watch for sponsoring human rights investigations in Brazil and Jamaica, to El Centro de Estudios Legales y Sociales in Buenos Aires, to Paulo Sérgio Pinheiro, and to Frances Piven for reseach advice, and to Anne Buckborough for essential research assistance. Thanks to my colleagues in the Law and Society Colloquium at NYU for helpful comments. I am grateful for the generous support of the Filomen D'Agostino and Max E. Greenberg Research Fund of the New York University Law School. A different version of this chapter appeared in *Criminal Law Forum*, Vol. I (1990), pp. 389–425.

1. Alejandro Portes and John Walton (1976), *Urban Latin America: The Political Condition from Above and Below* (Austin: University of Texas Press).
2. Lawrence Sherman and Ellen Cohn (1986), *Citizens Killed by Big City Police* (Washington, D.C.: Crime Control Institute).
3. Ibid.; New York City Firearms Discharge Review Board (1985), *Report*.
4. National Advisory Commission on Civil Disorders (Kerner Commission) (1986), *Report* (New York: New York Times/Bantam); Robert Fogelson (1968), "From Resentment to Confrontation," *Political Science Quarterly* 83, p. 217.
5. Americas Watch (1986), *Human Rights in Jamaica* (New York: Americas Watch); Americas Watch (1987), *Police Abuse in Brazil: Summary Executions and Torture in São Paulo and Rio de Janeiro* (1987) (New York: Americas Watch).
6. Centro de Estudios Legales y Sociales (CELS) (1987), "Muertos por violencia policial" (Buenos Aires). (Unpublished report.)
7. A tabulation of newspaper accounts was made at first because the gov-

ernments declined to give an official count. After the publication of the Americas Watch reports, governments have started to give official figures. Both unofficial and official figures appear in Tables 12.7 and 12.8. Until recently, municipal police departments in the United States did not give official counts. See Lawrence Sherman and Robert Langworthy (1979), "Measuring Homicide by Police Officers," *Journal of Criminal Law and Criminology*, 70, p. 546.

8. There is a fourth possible statistical relationship, suggested by James Fyfe (1982) in "Blind Justice: Police Shootings in Memphis," *Journal of Criminal Law and Criminology* 72, which uses figures for shootings per officer in relation to the total number of arrests for violent felonies to compare police killings in Memphis, Tennessee, with those in New York City. This gives a very suggestive picture of the relation of police use of deadly force to the danger to police. I have not used the statistic in this work because I do not have figures on "shootings," as distinguished from homicides, and it is not clear that reliable figures on arrests for "violent felonies" could be assembled.

9. See William Geller and Kevin Karales (1981/1982), "Shootings of and by Chicago Police: Uncommon Crises, Part I," *Journal of Criminology* 72; statistics supplied to author by New York City Police Department (1986).

10. As quoted in Geller and Karales, "Shootings."

11. Sherman and Langworthy, "Measuring Homicide." See also Sherman and Cohn, *Citizens Killed by Big City Police*.

12. Kenneth Matulia (1982), *A Balance of Forces* (Gaithersburg, Md.: International Association of Chiefs of Police), p. 39.

13. Mark Blumberg (1985), "Research of Police Use of Deadly Force: The State of the Art," in A. Blumberg and E. Niederhoffer, eds., *The Ambivalent Force* (New York: Holt, Rinehart and Winston); David Jacobs and David Britt (1979), "Inequality and Police Use of Deadly Force: An Empirical Assessment of a Conflict Hypothesis," *Social Problems*, 26, p. 403.

14. Ernest Duff and John McCamant (1976), *Violence and Repression in Latin America* (New York: Free Press), p. 80; Michael Ward (1978), *Political Economy of Distribution* (New York: Elsevier), p. 165.

15. Ekkart Zimmerman (1983), *Political Violence, Crises and Revolutions* (Boston: G. K. Hall).

16. Duff and McCamant, *Violence and Repression*, Ch. 3.

17. The placement on the scale is only suggestive and should always be evaluated in terms of all the component factors. In the case of Brazil, for example, its large GNP has moved it down the index, although the GNP does not greatly affect the lives of common people.

18. J. Craig Jenkins (1983), "Resource Mobilization Theory and the Study of Social Movements," *Annual Review of Sociology*, 9; Anthony Obwerschall (1973), *Social Conflict and Social Movements* (Englewood Cliffs, N.J.: Prentice Hall); Charles Tilly (1978), *From Mobilization to Revolution* (Reading, Mass.: Addison-Wesley).

19. Duff and McCamant, *Violence and Repression*.

20. Zimmermann, *Political Violence*, p. 115; Ekkart Zimmermann (1980), "Macro-Comparative Research on Political Protest," in Ted R. Gurr, ed., *Handbook of Political Conflict* (New York: Free Press), pp. 178–85.

21. Ivo Feierabend, Rosalind Feierabend, and Betty Nesvold (1969), "Social Change and Political Violence: Cross-National Patterns," in Ted R. Gurr and

Hugh Graham, eds., *Violence in America*, Vol. 11 (Washington, D.C.: U.S. Government Printing Office).

22. Lois Whitman (1989), Letter from Americas Watch to Michael Manley, March 30, 1989. The data in the letter were obtained from Jamaican officials and given to the prime minister in connection with inquiries.

23. Ibid.

24. Americas Watch, *Human Rights in Jamaica*.

25. Ibid.

26. Carl Stone and Aggrey Brown (1977), *Essays on Power and Change in Jamaica* (Kingston: Jamaica Printing House); Sidney Chernick (1978), *The Commonwealth Caribbean: The Integration Experience* (Baltimore: Johns Hopkins University Press).

27. In 1986 H. Delroy Murray, then the legal officer of the Jamaica Council for Human Rights, at a conference of the Trinidad and Tobago Bar Association, "Law and Civil Liberties in the Caribbean," said, "So rightly alarmed at the fact that 200 or so persons had been killed by the police since 1970 in Trinidad, I had to chuckle—not because the situation he describes isn't serious, but because compared to the Jamaican statistics, you are still, comparatively speaking, living in, for want of a better term, a fairy tale world." H. Delroy Murray (1986), "Police Excesses, the Courts and Human Rights in Jamaica," paper presented to the Bar Association of Trinidad and Tobago Conference "The Law and Civil Liberties in the Caribbean."

28. *Gleaner*, Oct. 1, 13, and 15, and Nov. 10, 1986.

29. C. Stone, *Gleaner*, Oct. 15, 1986.

30. *Gleaner*, Oct. 19, 1986.

31. While not wanting to clutter the text with data on relative crime rates, the argument that Jamaica has a crime rate so bad as to put it in a moral class by itself—a point made explicitly by *Gleaner* columnist Morris Cargill and less vigorously by Carl Stone (See fn. 29, 30)—should not pass unchallenged. The overall homicide rate in Jamaica is about the same as that in large American cities. Stone tells us (*Gleaner*, Oct. 13, 1986) that the homicide rate in the Kingston area is 43.5 per 100,000. This rate in Detroit, Michigan, is higher (Superintendant of Documents, *Uniform Crime Reports*, 1984 [Washington, D.C.: U.S. Government Printing Office]). The point is not to show that some places in the United States are "as bad as Jamaica," because conditions are bound not to be comparable, but to suggest that people manage to live with high crime rates.

32. Klaus de Albuquerque (1984), "A Comparative Analysis of Violent Crime in the Caribbean," *Social and Economic Studies* (University of the West Indies), 33, pp. 3, 93; A. Lewin (1978) "Social Control in Jamaica" (Ph.D. diss., City University of New York).

33. C. Stone, *Gleaner*, Oct. 1, 1986.

34. Diane Austin (1984), *Urban Life in Kingston, Jamaica* (London: Gordon & Breach); Gordon Lewis (1968), *Growth of the Modern West Indies* (New York: Monthly Review Press), pp. 187–91.

35. Americas Watch, *Human Rights in Jamaica*.

36. *Gleaner*, July 3, 1986.

37. *Gleaner*, Oct. 15, 1986, p. 8.

38. One example of lynch law exercised by the police with a citizen is illustrative. The victim had hired a driver and a car to help him transport some work

materials. As they were driving along, the police drew up beside the car and fired shots. The car, it later turned out, had been stolen; the driver, who was probably aware of the fact, pulled over to the curb and ran away. The owner of the car, who was riding with the police, urged them to kill the victim. When he ran away, the police shot and wounded him, then shot again as he was begging for his life, putting a gun in his open mouth. The victim lived to collect damages from the government; he was able to corroborate the last, most grisly aspect of the story by introducing medical evidence that there was an exit wound in the back of his neck, but no entry wound. This case was reported by Richard Small, the lawyer who represented the claimant. Americas Watch, *Human Rights in Jamaica.*

39. Centro de Estudios Legales y Sociales, "Muertos por violencia."

40. Juan Corradi (1985), *The Fitful Republic* (Boulder, Colo.: Westview); Carlos Waisman (1987), *Reversal of Development in Argentina* (Princeton, N.J.: Princeton University Press).

41. Centro de Estudios Legales y Sociales, "Muertos por violencia."

42. Ibid.

43. Richard Nyrop, ed. (1983), *Brazil: A Country Study* (Washington, D.C.: U.S. Government Printing Office).

44. The name "military police" is somewhat misleading in the Brazilian context. It is not, except in times of military repression, under the jurisdiction of the armed forces. The name is meant to designate a body similar to the French gendarmerie, upon which it is modeled.

45. Núcleo de Estudos da Violência (1989), *Violência do estado e militarização: Mortes em conflitos policiais em São Paulo nos anos 1980* (São Paulo: Núcleo de Estudos da Violência, Universidade de São Paulo), p. 5; Americas Watch, *Police Abuse in Brazil.*

46. Paulo Sérgio Pinheiro (1982), "Policia e a crise política," in Maria Paoli et al., eds., *Violência brasileira* (São Paulo: Brasiliense).

47. It is possible to construct a ratio between the homicide rate as a whole and the police homicide rate. I have not done so because, as clarified in the text, the general homicide rate includes an unknown number of killings by off-duty police.

48. Americas Watch, *Police Abuse in Brazil.*

49. Ibid.

50. James Lang (1988), *Inside Development in Latin America* (Chapel Hill: University of North Carolina Press), p. 151.

51. Riordan Roett (1984), *Brazil: Politics in a Patrimonial Society* (New York: Praeger), pp. 18–19.

52. Maria Benevides and Rosa Fischer Ferreira (1983), "Respostas populares e violência urbana: O caso de linchamento no Brasil (1979–82)," in Paulo S. Pinheiro, ed., *Crime, violência e poder* (São Paulo: Brasiliense).

53. In April 1986, when military policemen captured three youths accused of kidnapping, they turned the three over to the victim. He killed two and wounded the third, who survived to be interviewed by the newspapers. Americas Watch, *Police Abuse in Brazil.*

54. Benevides and Fischer, "Respostas populares," p. 237.

55. Americas Watch, *Police Abuse in Brazil.*

56. Ibid.

57. Benevides and Fischer, "Respostas populares."

58. Anthony Leeds and Elizabeth Leeds (1976), "Accounting for Behavioral Differences: Three Political Systems and the Responses of Squatters in Brazil, Peru and Chile," in John Walton and Louis Masotti, eds., *The City in Comparative Perspective* (New York: John Wiley); Roett, *Brazil*.

59. Janice Pearlman (1976), *The Myth of Marginality* (Berkeley and Los Angeles: University of California Press), p. 188.

60. See also Núcleo de Estudos da Violência, *Violência do estado*, p. 10.

61. Americas Watch, *Police Abuse in Brazil*, p. 52.

62. "Mae chama a ROTA para mater o proprio filho," *Noticias populares* (São Paulo), March 2, 1983, pp. 1, 6. The mother, who had nine other children, was quoted: "I did not want his life to end this way, but it was he who brought on this end. My son has tried many things in life and now he has suffered the consequences. It was better for him and better for us."

63. Benevides and Fischer "Respostas populares," p. 242.

13
U.S.-SUPPORTED STATE TERROR: A HISTORY OF POLICE TRAINING IN LATIN AMERICA

Martha K. Huggins

There is nothing new about the U.S. government's training Latin American police. The United States has been training and equipping such police for over ninety years. For more than forty years this training has been a coordinated and integral part of U.S. international security policy. But, in 1974, when mounting evidence of torture, disappearances, and killings by U.S.-trained and -equipped foreign police could no longer be ignored in the United States, Congress finally banned the training and equipping of foreign police.

This did not put an end to U.S. foreign police training, however. The 1974 congressional ban exempted U.S. police and military assistance for narcotics control. In 1985 the administration was allowed to reinstitute foreign police training to counter what President Reagan labeled Nicaraguan and Cuban "terrorism." In particular, CIA and U.S. military advisers resumed training police "counterterrorism" units in El Salvador, Guatemala, and Honduras; Costa Rican civil police also receive such instruction.[1] The U.S. Regional Security System for the Eastern Caribbean includes police "counterterrorism" training.[2] In 1986, the CIA began recruiting U.S. police for temporary duty in its "war against terrorism" abroad.[3]

There is no evidence that almost a century of U.S. assistance to foreign police has improved either the security of the people in recipient countries or the democratic practices of their police and security forces. Consider, for example, El Salvador, where the United States has had police training programs since the late 1940s. Today, El Salvador's police have one of the worst human rights records in the Western Hemisphere. During the first nine months of 1988 there was a 33 percent increase in deaths of civilian noncombatants caused by the police, army, and other forces.[4] And Guatemala, the country where in the 1960s the expression "to be disappeared" originated, has had U.S. police training programs since the 1954 U.S.-orchestrated overthrow of President Jacobo Arbenz Guzmán. The Guatemalan police and army have continued to torture and kill thousands of civilians. In late 1989, while the United States was training Honduran police to combat terrorism, "there were at least 78 [civilian] killings by the police and security forces; torture and beatings by Honduran security forces more than tripled between 1988 and 1989."[5] In early 1988 reports surfaced that a U.S.-trained Honduran Special Investigations Directorate, notorious as "Battalion 316," had been operating as a death squad, responsible for the murder of at least 120 Hondurans.[6]

U.S. training of Latin American police seems to have backfired.[7] "Professionalizing" them and providing them with more sophisticated arms and equipment has had none of the effects proposed by the stated U.S. objectives of democratizing and humanizing their practices. It may be necessary to pursue the hypothesis that U.S. training of Latin American police was never meant to make them more democratic or more responsive to civilian government. The outcome of such training may suggest that the training of Latin American police has deliberately been used to increase U.S. control over recipient countries and those governments' undemocratic control over their populations. It is necessary to examine the amount of attention given by U.S. government policymakers and field officers to human rights, and the consideration that such officials give to human rights in the day-to-day execution of foreign policy.

POLITICAL POLICING

While all policing is political, the quintessential example of politicized policing is the training by one country of another country's police and security forces. There are several ways in which such training is highly political. In the first place, the training of one country's police by another is carried out within an unequal international distribution of power: The recipient country always holds a subordinate position relative to the training nation. Given such inequality, police training by another nation reduces the international and internal autonomy of the country in which it is being carried out. Second, the training of foreign police not only increases the involvement of a recipient country's police in its own national politics but, at the same time, transforms such police into actors in global politics through their relations with the donor country. Third, wherever such training has taken place, sectors within both the receiving nation and the training country have used it to achieve their own political ends. Finally, the training of one country's police forces by another almost inevitably leads to resistance to the process in both the donor and the recipient nation. Thus police training is inevitably political in its consequences, as well as its origins.

POLICE TRAINING: A DEFINITION

In theory, civil police or constabulary training involves civilian police professionals providing knowledge and skills about policing to people who either are already in police work or aspire to be. The mission of civil police trainers presumably is to improve the administration and practice of routine civil police work.

Instead, what has been billed as "training" of foreign police by the United States has deviated markedly from the theoretical model. In the first place, U.S. police trainers have frequently come from the military, not civil police agencies. Second, the techniques taught and the equipment provided have most frequently been oriented toward a military and not a civil model of social control. Furthermore, a central objective of such civil police training has been intelligence gathering for the United States; this has included improving not only the intelligence-gathering opportunities of the United States but also the ability of the indigenous security forces to gather intelligence. One of the primary uses of such intelligence gathering has been to monitor internal political threats to U.S. interests or to a political regime or faction allied with the United States, and more generally to shore up unpopular but pro-U.S. governments. In short, the emphasis of foreign police training by the United States has not been on improving the policing skills of the officer walking the beat.

SOURCES

This chapter examines U.S. training of Latin American police. The primary sources come from the U.S. presidential libraries and the U.S. National Archives. Information also was gathered from the records of the International Association of Chiefs of Police, the U.S. Agency for International Development, and the U.S. foreign police training program at Michigan State University. The Freedom of Information Act has made it possible to obtain many previously classified U.S. government documents. The documentary sources have been supplemented by interviews.

PHASE ONE: POLICE TRAINING AND GUNBOAT DIPLOMACY

Cuba was the first country in the Caribbean/Central America to receive U.S. constabulary training. The Cuban constabulary, which was established at the time of the U.S. occupation in 1898, was trained, equipped, and directed by U.S. Marines. Retired New York City police officers helped to organize the Havana municipal police system.[8]

Within two decades after setting up a constabulary in Cuba, the U.S. War Department had established constabularies in Haiti (1915), the Dominican Republic (1916), and Panama (1918). Most interesting were the U.S. attempts to establish a constabulary in Nicaragua in the 1920s, before finally succeeding in 1927.[9]

In 1925, the United States used a private citizen, Major Calvin B. Carter, formerly an officer in the Philippine constabulary, to organize the Nicaraguan constabulary. This was done through a private contract with the Nicaraguan government facilitated by the U.S. State Department. Major Carter and his four U.S. assistants remained in Nicaragua for almost two years. But Carter had a difficult time organizing a constabulary. In the first place, he could not recruit enough Nicaraguans; in the second place, Nicaraguan President Carlos Solórzano failed to give Carter sufficient financial and material support. In retrospect, Solórzano's withholding of support for a U.S.-backed constabulary was prescient: In October 1925, Carter "actively . . . comforted and aided" General Emiliano Chamorro, President Solórzano's political rival, during a successful revolt against the Solórzano government.[10]

In 1927, the United States attempted direct establishment of a "nonpartisan" constabulary in Nicaragua. This time the constabulary had a better chance of living up to Washington's expectations: U.S. Marines disarmed the Nicaraguan army and set up a national constabulary officered by the Marines themselves.

The United States was not the only country to train police in Latin America during the first decades of the twentieth century. In the early 1900s, France sent military missions to train and equip the police of Uruguay, Peru, and the Brazilian state of São Paulo. In fact, French police trainers in Brazilian states predated such training for the Brazilian military.[11]

Germany, which in the early twentieth century competed with France to provide police training in Latin America, reorganized the Argentine, Chilean, and Bolivian police.[12] In 1927, Italy sent a military mission to train the Ecuadorian police, and dispatched another mission in 1936 to reorganize the Bolivian constabulary.[13] Even Latin American countries were active in police training in the region. Chile was especially involved, and in the 1930s organized the Colombian national police.[14]

Nonetheless, early U.S. police training efforts were much more ambitious than those of the Europeans or Latin Americans. In the early twentieth century, Washington reasoned that one way to secure U.S. interests in a country with a weak, highly politicized, or nonexistent military was to increase internal security by disarming the country's army and establishing a police force with primary loyalty to the United States. The constabularies, while initially designed for civil police functions, were almost always transformed through domestic political developments and U.S. encouragement into military units to become their countries' national guard.

"GOOD NEIGHBOR" POLICE TRAINING: THE ROOSEVELT PRESIDENCY

The second period of U.S. police training in Latin America stretches through the 1930s to World War II. U.S. training of Latin American police during the 1930s involved primarily ad hoc arrangements between the United States and countries requesting police assistance. It was common for a police assistance request to go from a local police or government official in Latin America or the Caribbean to the U.S. State Department. Sometimes the State Department forwarded the request to the police commissioner or mayor of New York, Chicago, or Los Angeles. Funding for such training was usually the responsibility of the Latin American country, with financial assistance sometimes given by the host U.S. police department.

During the Roosevelt presidency, the most dramatic international-level cooperation between U.S. and foreign police occurred between 1935 and 1937, a time when many countries' concerns about communism were on the rise. In 1935, the agencies of several foreign governments, including the British Secret Service and the German Gestapo, began working with the United States to track down and capture "communists" in countries considered vulnerable to such movements. The Gestapo had arrangements with thirteen nations of Europe and Latin America, among them Brazil and Argentina, to combat communism and "movements dangerous to the State."[15]

The U.S. government in particular, through its embassy in Rio de Janiero, in 1935 entered into a close partnership with the Brazilian police, who were cooperating with the Gestapo by exchanging information for the purpose of eradicating "communists." There is every reason to believe that both Hugh Gibson, the U.S. ambassador in Rio, and the U.S. State Department were fully aware of the agreement between the Brazilian police and the Gestapo, since Gibson worked closely at the time with Rio's political and security police [the DOPS].[16]

Two Brazilian police officers with whom Ambassador Gibson was in especially close contact were Captains Affonso Henrique de Miranda Corrêia and Francisco Jullien of Rio's political police, which was headed at the time by a pro-Nazi chief, Felinto Mueller. According to Gibson, Miranda Corrêia, throughout 1935 and 1936, cooperated "wholeheartedly with the Embassy," including opening "his secret files to us in a way that I have never seen in any other country."[17] Gibson described Miranda Corrêia and Jullien as "two extremely able young men who are so convinced of the essential nature of their efforts to track communist activities here, that when officials [*sic*] funds have not been forthcoming they have reportedly hung up their belongings with a pawnbroker in order to carry on."[18]

Police officers such as Miranda Corrêia and Jullien were rewarded by the United States and Brazil for their services. Ambassador Gibson recommended to the State Department that it help the two officers; as he explained, if the Brazilian police "are not successful at securing guidance from us, they will turn to the British or the French, who are fully aware of the able opportunity."[19] Gibson argued that "Brazil will probably continue for many years to be an important center of radical activities, and we ought to begin laying plans now for making sure of the fullest possible volume of information." He explained to the State Department that helping interested Brazilian police secure training in the United States was "something like giving the goose a correspondence course in laying golden eggs."[20]

There is no evidence that Miranda Corrêia ever came to the United States to study police work. The State Department did, however, arrange for Jullien to visit the police departments of Chicago and New York City, and to pay a call at the FBI Academy in Washington, D.C.

THE ROLE OF THE FBI

U.S. efforts to combat communism in Latin America were displaced at the end of the 1930s by increased concerns about Axis influence in the Western Hemisphere. At this time the FBI began working more actively with the police and security forces of Latin America. One of the first Latin American requests for an FBI agent to set up a "secret service" came from Brazilian Foreign Minister Oswaldo Aranha. Brazilian authorities had turned up a Nazi plot to foment rebellion in Brazil, Argentina, and Uruguay.[21]

Aranha wanted the new Brazilian secret service to be separate from, and perhaps even unknown to, the undercover section (S–2) of the Federal District's political police, headed by Filinto Mueller. One benefit of a separate secret police would be to bring the new organization under federal control: Mueller's security police, while technically under the minister of justice, were virtually independent of federal authority; his S–2 surveillance network even spied on Cabinet members and diplomats.[22] The proposed secret service would be able to monitor Axis activities in Brazil and also keep an eye on Mueller's secret police.

The man recommended by J. Edgar Hoover to establish the new Brazilian secret service was Edgar K. Thompson, a young bachelor previously employed by the FBI in Puerto Rico who "had a thorough knowledge of Spanish" (the Bureau had no one who spoke Portuguese). Thompson was sent to work with the Federal Police in Rio for five months.[23]

As for the other parts of Latin America, in March 1939, Colombian Foreign Minister Lonzano y Lonzano attempted to sign a contract directly with the New York City Police Department to establish and train a Colombian secret service. Spruille Braden, U.S. ambassador to Colombia, agreed at the time that Colombia needed a secret service, but he argued against the U.S. government's encouraging Colombia to sign a contract with New York City. Braden thought that the State Department should have control over such training, because "If a secret police force is organized in Colombia, it probably will be employed, in some degree, in watching the political as well as civilian activities of certain aliens (Germans, Italians, Japanese, and Nationalist Spaniards). Hence its finds might be of distinct interest to the U.S. government."[24]

After some stalling by Hoover, the State Department (with the backing of President Roosevelt) forced Hoover to transfer agent Thompson from Brazil to Bogotá.[25] With war imminent in Europe, the State Department thought that Colombia, with its proximity to the Panama Canal, should have a strong and efficient security police. However, Thompson remained in Colombia only three months: Hoover argued that he was needed to direct the FBI's Puerto Rico office.

The relatively overt assignments of Thompson in Brazil and Colombia stand in sharp contrast with the covert intelligence work with indigenous police and security forces, and with the use of covert informants subsequently carried out in Latin America (1940–1947) by the FBI Special Intelligence Service (SIS). President Roosevelt established the SIS on June 24, 1940, by a "telephonic directive." The only signature that appeared on the document establishing it was that of A. A. Berle, an assistant secretary of state. This would allow the president to disavow public knowledge of the SIS in the event that it encountered political difficulties.[26]

Once the SIS had been established, Hoover quickly moved to consolidate an FBI monopoly over intelligence gathering in the Western Hemisphere. By October 1940, the FBI had placed SIS undercover agents in Argentina, Brazil, Colombia, Chile, Cuba, and Mexico.[27] Not until 1942 did Roosevelt officially recognize the SIS, which by then had been operating for two years throughout the Western Hemisphere without formal approval of either the U.S. Congress or the recipient governments.

SIS undercover agents "maintained an extensive program of counterintelligence, utilizing the services of American business firms."[28] But the FBI provided little training for the first SIS agents sent to Latin America, and almost no formal training for the Latin American police and security agencies with which they worked. In fact, some high-ranking FBI officials mistrusted such training, fearing that a government might succumb to an enemy of the United States and use what had been learned from the FBI against the United States.[29]

The SIS operatives, usually inexperienced at working outside the United States, were relatively untrained in intelligence gathering and counterespionage, and had almost no language training. One SIS operative had studied Spanish for only two weeks before being sent to Portuguese-speaking Brazil.[30] Rolf Larson, who went to Brazil in November 1941 on an undercover SIS assignment, was somewhat of an exception among new SIS operatives: He had lived in Latin America before entering SIS service. Between 1937 and 1940, Larson had been a Mormon missionary in Buenos Aires.[31]

Shortly after arriving in Brazil, Larson began assembling his covert network of informants, which was to include Mormon missionaries living in Brazil. He proposed to the FBI that the missionaries would make excellent FBI informants; those in Brazil were frequently transferred from one place to another, giving them an opportunity to interact with people in all parts of the country. Moreover, they would be particularly useful in ferreting out Nazi activities because the Mormons had proselytized among "Teuto-Brazilians," Brazilians of German ancestry. Larson reasoned that the Mormon missionaries and their Brazilian converts could provide "an excellent source of information were it coordinated properly" on Nazi activities in Brazil.[32]

A U.S. foreign intelligence program both operating outside the U.S. diplomatic community and frequently unknown to key leaders within the host government created considerable inefficiency. In 1942, the American consul in Natal, Brazil, wrote to the U.S. secretary of state: "There is every evidence that William Bradley . . . is some type of secret agent, with all indications pointing to the FBI."[33] The consul went on to explain that one of his "most trusted police informants" had told him that Bradley had been collecting Axis information and keeping "a weather eye trimmed on the American personnel with . . . Pan American Airways, Ltd." He asserted that Bradley's efforts in behalf of the *American Exporter Magazine* (probably Bradley's SIS cover) looked "decidedly silly . . . as does his export trade knowledge, which is pitifully faltering."[34] Such assessments by U.S. diplomatic personnel probably reflected their resentment at being kept in the dark and even, at times, becoming the object of FBI intelligence gathering. They also deplored SIS operatives' lack of preparation for intelligence work abroad.

But there was an even more problematic side to SIS work. In Brazil, for example, SIS agents worked with the Federal District's Political and Security Police (DOPS) in the interrogation of suspected spies. It is clear that the SIS knew torture was used by DOPS, because information about "the torture of some prisoners was forwarded [by the SIS] to Washington."[35] SIS agents explained to Washington that it was necessary to "look the other way" when DOPS became too heavy-handed with a prisoner: If SIS agents intervened to protect prisoners too frequently, the DOPS might become less cooperative. Rout and Bratzel argue that if J. Edgar Hoover, Secretary of State Sumner Welles, and Assistant Secretary of State Adolf Berle "were ignorant of what was transpiring in the Brazilian jails, it was essentially because they preferred not to know."[36]

FORTIFYING THE NATIONAL SECURITY STATE: THE TRUMAN PRESIDENCY

The third phase of U.S. involvement with police and security forces in Latin America and the Caribbean began after World War II. It was then that Washington's international security planners elaborated and expanded the U.S. national security state. This included administrative machinery to coordinate the U.S. security apparatus and extend it into the Third World.

The administration of Harry Truman adds an important chapter to the history of U.S. training of Latin American and Caribbean police. Truman neither broadened the scope of police training nor placed a significant number of U.S. trainers in the field, yet his administration did establish the ideological justifications and bureaucratic machinery for future police training programs.

Two developments during Truman's first term indirectly but profoundly influenced the future of U.S. training of foreign police:

1. The formation in 1947 of the National Security Council (NSC), with jurisdiction over the international security of the United States
2. The creation, in that same year, of the Central Intelligence Agency (CIA) out of the Office of Strategic Services.

With the creation of the NSC and the CIA, Truman improved Washington's capacity to monitor and take action against perceived international threats to U.S. security, and to coordinate these efforts.

The Truman administration's Cold War posture indirectly influenced the future of U.S. foreign police training. Cold War rhetoric helped to mold public consciousness in the United States and abroad, and to lay the foundation for future congressional funding for police training. The ideological centerpiece for the Cold War, and a legitimizing ideology for later U.S. police training efforts abroad, was the philosophy of "containment," which argued that U.S. interests would be served best by a patient, firm, and vigilant long-term containment of the Soviet Union, looking less toward the eventual overthrow of its communist government than to a gradual lessening of Soviet power. With the end of the war, the ideological transformation of the Soviet Union from a respected wartime ally to a postwar competitor and potential military menace was accomplished; the antifascist component of police work was dropped in favor of the prewar anticommunist emphasis.

During the Truman administration, the biggest U.S. police training programs were military projects. The most ambitious efforts by the U.S. military to reorganize foreign police were carried out in occupied Germany and Japan, the reoccupied Philippines, and in Greece and Turkey, where Truman's aid program provided funding for the training of police. Truman's subsequent Point Four Program, which became law in 1950, offered technical assistance to all developing countries (although it concentrated on Latin America), to fortify them against communism. One form of "technical assistance" funded by Point Four was earmarked for improvements in public administration, which included assistance to foreign police. A direct beneficiary was Iran in the years around the U.S.-backed overthrow of Prime Minister Mossadegh in 1953.

During the Truman administration, neither police training nor Latin America were high priorities. From 1950 on, Truman focused primarily on the war in Korea. Military solutions to containing communist countries took priority over the use of indigenous civil police to protect or guarantee a country's internal security. Under Truman defense spending grew to almost 70 percent of the federal budget.[37]

POLICE TRAINING FOR COUNTERINSURGENCY: THE EISENHOWER PRESIDENCY

Dwight D. Eisenhower, in his 1952 presidential campaign, promised to cut Truman's heavy military spending by letting "Asians fight Asian wars." Such a policy would mean preparing foreign military forces to stand up to attacks by an aggressor. Within the context of the containment doctrine, plugging the dikes against the initial stages of expansionism aimed against the free world would now increasingly fall on the shoulders of the vulnerable allies of the United States.

What emerged over the next few years was an approach to containment that saw the U.S. allies' military as only one element in a combined U.S.–indigenous defense system. An aspect of Eisenhower's containment policy clearly different from that of Truman was his proposal to make foreign police and security forces into the first line of defense in the "war against communism." The United States presumably could reduce its own military spending by limiting the deployment of U.S. forces to more serious confrontations with the Soviets. The indigenous military and police forces of Third World countries were to become U.S.

partners in the combined "weapons system." These forces were to be trained by the United States for gathering intelligence and resisting limited military probes by anti-U.S. forces. The United States would be able to cut its own military spending by shifting the cost of defense to the developing countries themselves.[38]

It was not by chance that the National Security Council and its planning arm, the Operations Coordinating Board (OCB), began planning a worldwide program of civil police training in 1954.[39] In that year, the French faced defeat at Dien Bien Phu, and Washington completed plans for the CIA-orchestrated overthrow of President Jacobo Arbenz in Guatemala. Washington reasoned that the French defeat in Indochina was due in part to its lack of effective control over Vietnamese security forces; such control might have kept all of Vietnam in the "Free World."

A complementary argument, in the case of Guatemala, was that if the United States had exercised greater control much earlier over the Guatemalan police and security forces, Washington might have been able to control President Arbenz before he could move to reduce U.S. influence in Guatemala. In other words, the United States might be able to prevent the loss of other "free" countries to "communism" if Washington could ensure their loyalty by bringing their police and security forces into the U.S. orbit. Police training, Washington argued, would prevent subversion before it could develop.

Civil police training under Eisenhower was called the 1290-d Program. But such training was not the only component in Eisenhower's international security program. In fact, civil police training was just one part of a larger U.S. international security policy that Washington implemented through its Overseas Internal Security Program (OISP). A primary objective of the OISP was to help vulnerable countries develop the capabilities of their national security agencies to "counter communist subversion." In the mid–1950s, this involved assisting such countries as Brazil and Guatemala to establish or improve their intelligence organizations. The OISP also helped vulnerable countries to make legislative and judicial procedures "more sensitive" to internal subversion. In the case of Guatemala in 1955, this meant "recommending" that Guatemala's new pro-U.S., anticommunist Castillo Armas government draft a constitution that would "discourage the formation of political splinter parties"; this, in effect, amounted to outlawing the Communist Party.[40]

The newly established United States Information Agency (USIA) played an important role in the OISP. Indeed, the information aspect of the OISP was the key to the success of U.S. internal security programs abroad, since many of the countries targeted for OISP programs were reluctant to accept Washington's Cold War view of international relations. In 1958, U.S. international security planners complained that the OISP had "not gained the support it should from Latin American governments who . . . did not feel sufficiently threatened by communism to overcome local political problems inherent in establishing new security organizations."[41]

Therefore, many countries first had to be convinced that there was a "communist threat," and then persuaded (or coerced) to accept the OISP. The work of the USIA in getting Latin Americans to see the need for increased internal security included the publication in Mexico, for distribution throughout Central America, of anticommunist posters and pamphlets, and 90,000 copies of an anticommunist cartoon book. In the mid–1950s, the USIA placed two anticommunist, pro-U.S. cartoon strips in over 300 Latin American newspapers.[42] U.S. support was also given to USIA in Brazil "before and during" the November 1954 elections. Such support included, but was not limited to, "the production of a study of the ties . . . between the Brazilian communist party and Soviet Russia."[43]

When more gentle methods of anticommunist persuasion failed to generate foreign government support for the United States and for its internal security programs, Washington's ultimate weapon was to threaten to cut off aid. In the early 1950s, Washington made ongoing aid to Cambodia contingent on that country's acceptance of an internal security program.[44] The United States was a little more subtle with Indonesia: In 1955, the State Department let "the word get around quietly" that the extent of aid to that country would be "influenced by how cooperative that government is toward the United States." The OCB suggested using similar forms of what it called "gentle persuasion" with Ceylon, Burma, and all other "neutral countries" in South and Southeast Asia.[45]

Such resistance to the OISP slowed this program's implementation but did not block deployment. At the end of 1955, there were only three civil police training programs in operation. By 1957, the United States expected to have twenty-nine civil police advisers working in eight countries.[46] During that year, 620 foreign police were to receive training in the United States or in Third World countries. By 1958, there were 115 U.S. police advisers working in 24 countries, with a budget of $14.2 million.[47]

Most civil police training during the Eisenhower administration went to Asia: By the mid–1950s, Washington's biggest programs were in Laos and Vietnam; U.S. funds supported the entire Laotian police force. After several years of assistance to Laos, the United States was able to double the size of the Laotian police and security forces.

The first countries in Latin America to receive a civil police program were Guatemala and Bolivia; Guatemala got its 1290-d program soon after the U.S.-orchestrated overthrow of Arbenz, although the United

States had been working with elements of the Guatemalan military, police, and security forces before the coup.

Bolivia received its civil police training program in the wake of increased labor strife in the tin mines. But some elements of Bolivia's 1290-d program were short-lived. From the inception of U.S. training of foreign police, Washington was very clear that the United States should not assist police who did not support Washington's view of international and internal political relations. The Bolivian peasant-controlled militia, which was included in the 1290-d program, had political objectives conflicting with those of Washington. In 1957 the United States suspended assistance to Bolivia's worker/peasant militia. According to the U.S. embassy in La Paz, the militia portion of Bolivia's 1290-d program was "politically counterproductive."[48]

Most civil police training during the Eisenhower presidency was at least formally carried out by non-U.S. government organizations. The principal organization with which the International Cooperation Administration (ICA), predecessor of the Agency for International Development (AID), signed training contracts was the International Association of Chiefs of Police (IACP). The IACP placed foreign police officers in police departments across the United States and at the FBI in Washington, D.C. Working closely with the IACP in the training of foreign police was International Police Services, Inc. (INPOLSE), described by former CIA agent Philip Agee as a Washington-based "CIA training school for police . . . under commercial cover."[49]

Indeed, behind all the organizations more overtly involved in foreign police training during the Eisenhower presidency, and all later administrations as well, was the CIA. Robert Amory, deputy director of intelligence for the CIA under John F. Kennedy, maintains that the CIA worked closely with the ICA and AID to develop police-training programs. According to Amory, CIA officials reasoned that since "the brains [for police training] are in the CIA . . . we'll just move those brains over to the Agency for International Development." The training moved "back and forth" between AID and CIA, according to Amory.[50]

Public recognition of the problems associated with CIA involvement in U.S. foreign police training did not materialize until the late 1960s. Before that, most of the dissatisfaction with such training centered on other issues. A 1957 OCB Progress Report, "U.S. Policy Toward Latin America," warned that there was

> a danger that U.S. programs to strengthen the internal security forces [of Latin America], which are often used as political instruments, may provide grounds for a belief that the U.S. has abandoned the principle of nonintervention and

has committed itself to the preservation of the status quo through repression of the political opposition, including noncommunist groups.[51]

In fact, in 1955 the OCB had specifically recommended against establishing U.S. civil police programs in Honduras and El Salvador because such programs would "identify the U.S. government with . . . regimes [that are] repressive of a noncommunist opposition."[52] But in spite of such warnings, the ICA established civil police training programs in both countries.

There were also concerns in the 1950s that U.S. training of foreign police exacerbated political problems within recipient nations. One OCB report to the National Security Council explained that in some recipient countries, the

> legally constituted law enforcement and military bodies, as well as the noncommunist opposition, resented and feared the introduction of new security agencies designed to combat communist subversion, fearing they would be used (as they have in some cases) as political weapons under the control of the existing governments, primarily directed at the political opposition . . . and function[ing] to the detriment of existing security organs.[53]

But neither the evidence that foreign police training was politically costly to the United States nor the frequent warnings of possible abuse of citizens' civil liberties by U.S.-trained police impeded the growth of foreign police training during the Eisenhower administration. What finally called such training into question was the mounting evidence that the OISP was not reducing U.S. military expenditures. A 1958 OCB report conceded that technical programs "probably [had] provided an increased measure of internal security in several countries," but maintained the OISP programs "had not been responsible for any significant diminution in military assistance costs."[54] In light of the poor showing in reducing military expenditures, the OCB at that time recommended a reassessment of the costs, consequences, and benefits of continuing U.S. internal security programs abroad.

Another argument of those advocating a reassessment of the OISP in the late 1950s centered on the suspicion that the increased economic burden on developing countries was itself destabilizing. U.S. international security planners had advanced the notion that "security and order [were] preconditions of independence," and that political and social turmoil slowed the flow of domestic and foreign private capital into productive enterprise. But by 1959, international security planners had growing evidence that their strategies for ensuring the internal security of the Third World were undermining those countries' development. It was becoming clear that such expenditures drained scarce resources from economically productive, income-generating activities.

INTENSIFICATION OF GLOBAL COUNTERINSURGENCY: THE KENNEDY PRESIDENCY

Such doubts about the future of U.S. training of foreign police were quickly set aside, however, by the administration of John F. Kennedy. In fact, the greatest expansion of U.S. training of foreign police came during the presidency of the Democrat Kennedy. Perhaps the failure at the Bay of Pigs led John Kennedy and his brother, Attorney General Robert Kennedy, to prepare the United States to mount major counterinsurgency operations abroad.[55]

Out of the concerns of the Kennedys and their close advisers, Walt W. Rostow, U. Alexis Johnson, and McGeorge Bundy, grew the "Counter-Insurgency Group" (C–1 Group), to institutionalize the teamwork needed to cope with counterinsurgency.[56] Most of the recommendations of the C–1 Group for combating insurgency abroad had been implemented on a smaller scale under Eisenhower. Yet the Eisenhower OISP was modest compared with the counterinsurgency program developed by Kennedy's C–1 Group.

An important administrative change in the U.S. international security machinery, aimed at challenging insurgency abroad, was the establishment by the White House in April 1962 of an Inter-Departmental Police Advisory Committee consisting of representatives from the CIA, FBI, Defense Department, and other concerned agencies.[57] One of its recommendations was that the United States redirect and expand its police programs. Indeed, the committee advised doubling existing programs within one year. One rationale for such rapid expansion was that "the cost of equipping and maintaining the average policeman [is] one-fifth that of the average soldier, yet the police [are] often more central to internal defense."[58] In Alexis Johnson's mind, the police in developing countries could serve as "preventive medicine" by rooting out and eliminating insurgency before it reached the crisis stage.

In late 1962, within the AID, President Kennedy established the Office of Public Safety (OPS), to develop and administer U.S. training of foreign police.[59] His executive order gave OPS greater power "than any other technical office or division within AID"; OPS was to have "all the capabilities for independent action and judgment that are consistent with the status of that office as a competent office within AID."[60] At the head of OPS was Byron Engle, a man described by former CIA Deputy Director of Intelligence Robert Amory as "from the CIA."[61]

Under John Kennedy civil police training expanded greatly over previous efforts. Southeast Asia (Vietnam and Thailand) received the biggest portion of the public safety budget, but Latin America had the largest number of police training programs.[62] The number of police advisers sent to Latin America in 1962 was almost double the 1961 level, and the number of Latin American police trained in the United States increased by 100 over 1961.[63]

Other changes in U.S. overseas police training programs also signaled an expansion of such training. In July 1962, the Inter-American Police Academy at Fort Davis in the Panama Canal Zone began training middle-level police officials from Latin America. In 1963, it was transferred to Washington, D.C., and renamed the International Police Academy (IPA). Both academies had close connections with the CIA. According to Philip Agee, the first academy was founded by the CIA's Panama station;[64] the second was a "CIA-controlled police training school under AID cover."[65] But the CIA did not have to twist many arms to get these police training facilities: Both John and Robert Kennedy were enthusiastic about a facility that would provide counterinsurgency training for foreign police.[66]

The biggest portion of the training curriculum for foreign police, whether at one of the academies, or in the host country, dealt with counterinsurgency, which included surveillance techniques, interrogation procedures, methods of conducting raids, riot and crowd control, and intelligence.[67] One of the "visual aids" in the IPA course on "methods of extracting information" was Gillo Pontecorvo's *Battle of Algiers*, which portrayed policemen loyal to France going out at night in secret patrols to hunt and kill Algerian nationalists. An IPA official, who admitted that the film dealt with "questionable techniques of extracting information" in its graphic scenes of police torture, maintained that such material had been shown to create abhorrence for inhumane methods of interrogation.[68]

Police education in the field included both a training and an operational component. For example, the 1963 Public Safety Program in Venezuela "provided the impetus for the Venezuelan government's successful maintenance of law and order," which helped to ensure the election of President Raúl Leoni, according to David Bell, AID administrator at the time.[69]

A *Los Angeles Times* article, introduced by Bell into the 1964 foreign assistance hearings of the House Foreign Affairs Committee, explained how U.S. public safety advisers had helped to ensure Leoni's election. According to the article, "Red terrorists in Caracas were trying . . . to kill a policeman a day . . . [while] very few Caracas policemen were killing terrorists."[70] U.S. police advisers argued that this pattern could not be reversed until three conditions had been corrected.

In the first place, the Venezuelan legal system had to be changed. Venezuelan law required the arrest of a police officer who killed a suspect; this, according to the *Los Angeles Times* reporter, frequently meant three months in jail while awaiting trial. But "under American tutelage, a policeman who killed a terrorist would be examined in one day by a civilian board of lawyers, and would be quickly restored to duty."[71]

Another factor that U.S. public safety advisers felt was keeping the Venezuelan police from establishing law and order was their policy of regarding a sawed-off shotgun as merely another type of "fowling piece." U.S. police had to make their Venezuelan counterparts realize that "a sawed-off shotgun is also deadly against lawbreakers."[72] Finally, the Venezuelans had to be encouraged to use more "roving patrols" to hunt suspects.

These changes on the part of the U.S. public safety team in Venezuela turned "the tide of battle . . . [so that] the cops were outkilling the communists." As the *Los Angeles Times* explained, "enemy casualties included a number of red students who hitherto had roamed the city in sports cars and carried on their marauding almost without hindrance."[73]

CONTINUED BUILDUP AND EVENTUAL DISMANTLING: THE JOHNSON AND NIXON PRESIDENCIES

The final period of U.S. training of foreign police covered in this chapter begins with the continued buildup of Third World police and security forces under Lyndon Johnson. It ends with the dismantling of the U.S. Office of Public Safety in 1974 at the end of the Nixon presidency, when Congress could no longer ignore evidence of systematic violations of human rights by U.S.-trained and -equipped police forces. But such recognition was slow to come.

In spite of mounting evidence through the 1960s of such practices, AID continued to deny that its police advisers had been associated with undemocratic regimes. AID Administrator Bell did concede in 1964 to the House Appropriations Committee that "the popularity of the heads of state in all countries that we are working with . . . varies. We are working with a lot of countries where the governments are controlled by people who have shortcomings. We have to work with the situation we find."[74]

Indeed, the U.S. government had worked very well with what it found. The International Cooperation Administration, AID's predecessor, had provided police assistance to the repressive, virulently anticommunist Castillo Armas government of Guatemala, even going as far as to make Castillo Armas an honorary police chief "for his unselfish labor for the good of democratic law enforcement in . . . Guatemala."[75] In spite of Guatemala's abysmal human rights record, public safety assistance to that country continued. Looking back over the history of public safety assistance to Guatemala, a 1971 Senate minority report complained that such assistance had been given even though "the Guatemalan police operate without any effective and juridical restraints. How they use the equipment and techniques which are given them through the public safety program is quite beyond U.S. control."[76]

The U.S. Office of Public Safety also worked with the Brazilian police and security forces, whose brutality rose abruptly in 1968, when the military government's Fifth Institutional Act (A1–5) closed Congress, imposed widespread press censorship, eliminated habeas corpus, and provided a mechanism for stripping individual noncriminal citizens of their civil rights for ten years for political activities. Over the decade that A1–5 remained in force, 4,683 Brazilians lost their right to vote, many of them were forcibly retired from government jobs, and censorship suppressed some 500 films, 450 plays, 200 books, 100 magazines, 500 musical scores, and numerous radio programs.[77]

Brazil's system of repression tightened even further in 1969 when a military decree placed all police forces under the army. In that year, the number of Brazilian police trained in the United States almost tripled over the previous year.[78] Ted Brown, chief AID public safety adviser to Brazil at the time, did express "some concern that the top management of both federal and state levels of police organization . . . are Brazilian Army rather than career police." However, his concern was that such military commands were likely to suffer rapid turnover as the officers made their career moves. Brown felt that he could work with the army, "barring development of a political disorientation of the government of Brazil from a pro-West, pro-U.S. stance." According to Brown, "project accomplishments do and will continue to justify the input of [U.S. AID] resources."[79]

What Brown seemed able to overlook, as long as Brazil retained its pro-U.S. orientation, was that between the military coup of 1964 and his 1971 assessment of Brazil's political climate, 3,000 Brazilians had been killed or had "disappeared;"[80] by 1971, Brazil's prisons and jails housed 12,000 political prisoners.[81] Furthermore, Brown seemed untroubled by the fact that deaths in Brazil from torture had increased markedly after 1969. According to official records, which understated such violence, seven people died from torture in 1969, eleven in 1970, and twenty-five in 1971.[82] A more reliable set of statistics on torture in Brazil shows that between 1969 and 1974, 1,558 Brazilians were tortured by police or by the military during interrogation.[83]

When asked in 1971 by the Senate Subcommittee on Western Hemisphere Affairs what he knew about torture and police repression in Brazil, Brown responded that he had "read newspaper items on the subject." Pressed by Senator Frank Church for his reaction to such information, this senior public safety adviser for Brazil explained that it was not his "right to judge the Brazilian people or the police."[84]

Another charge leveled against AID's public safety program was that the United States had used its police assistance to destabilize regimes of which it disapproved. The data for Brazil lend strong support to such a charge. Between 1962 and 1963, the number of Brazilian police trained in the United States rose from twenty-six to sixty-two. Of the 1963 trainees, 67 percent came from states whose governors were conspiring with the United States against Brazilian President João Goulart. Furthermore, of the $10 million in police training grants and aid given by the United States to Brazil between 1957 and 1971, the largest single allocation occurred in 1964, the year of the U.S.-backed coup.[85] The Brazilian coup of 1964 and the subsequent military dictatorship received ample U.S. support, in part through its police and internal security training operations.

CONCLUSIONS

The brief review of U.S. training of Latin American police suggests elements common to the past and the present: The threads of Iran/Contragate stretch back into the long history of U.S. police training abroad. But the relationship of recent scandals and the present course of U.S. foreign policy to earlier policies has not been recognized by the public or the media. Yet the events of Iran/Contragate are a continuation of U.S. policies that pursue almost any activity which furthers perceived U.S. interests and destroys their enemies.

In the first place, the diversion of profits from illegal arms sales to Iranian "moderates" to the U.S.-trained Contras, who attempted the overthrow of an elected government of Nicaragua, continues a long history of U.S. violations of domestic and international law. In 1954, the United States violated international treaties and Latin American agreements with the CIA-orchestrated overthrow of the democratically elected Guatemalan government of President Jacobo Arbenz; it continued such violations of international law in Latin America again in 1973, when it engineered the demise of Chile's democratic government and its president, Salvador Allende. U.S. government assistance to the police of Guatemala and Chile before and after these coups helped ensure that the internal security and political climate of those countries would be receptive to U.S. manipulation of the internal balance of power.

The United States has also demonstrated a willingness historically to use third countries and private citizens to carry out illegal training or to support covert operations with foreign governments (or political factions) when such support could not be given through official U.S. government channels. As far back as 1923, when the United States found it legally complicated and politically difficult directly to establish a U.S.-officered constabulary in Nicaragua, it arranged for a private citizen, retired U.S. Army Colonel Calvin Boone Carter, to do so: Carter helped topple the president of Nicaragua. Our research has uncovered at least one more recent U.S. attempt at covert engineering of internal political conditions in Latin America: In 1961, after the U.S. had suspended diplomatic relations with the Dominican Republic at the end of the Trujillo dictatorship, Secretary of State Dean Rusk arranged for retired officers of the Chilean Carabineros to work with the Dominican police to break the grip of Rafael Trujillo, Jr., the dictator's son, over the Dominican Republic's police and security forces.[86]

More recently, the Israelis are said, during the late 1970s, to have provided arms, presumably without U.S. disapproval, to military regimes in Guatemala with whom the United States had officially broken relations over widespread human rights violations. Until the collapse of the military regime in Argentina, that country was training the anti-Sandinista Contras with U.S. encouragement; allegations have surfaced that Israel, too, was involved in that training, as well as in supplying arms to the Contras.[87]

We do know that between 1984 and 1986, the Reagan administration used Lt. Col. Oliver North to facilitate the transfer of arms to the Contras. Such aid was in contravention of the Boland Amendment and other congressional prohibitions against the U.S. government's giving military aid to groups attempting to overthrow the government of Nicaragua. Congress was also ignored, in January 1986, when President Reagan issued a secret "finding" authorizing a covert CIA program to provide "intelligence, training, guidance and communications" to Iran.[88]

History has demonstrated the willingness of U.S. presidential administrations to work with repressive, authoritarian governments so long as such governments have demonstrated a pro-U.S. orientation. This was starkly articulated in the early 1950s by former Secretary of the Treasury George Humphrey, who thought that the United States was "much too idealistic" in its relations with other nations. Humphrey declared that the United States "should . . . stop talking so much about democracy, and make it clear that we are quite willing to support dictatorships of the right if their policies are pro-American."[89]

Such thinking has been, and remains, the basis for U.S. foreign policy. Moreover, it exposes the real motives for the establishment by the United States of the legislated material and personnel infrastructure, in the form of overseas internal security programs, that facilitates the institutionalization of state terror in Latin America. The United States has no moral basis for accusing its opponents of "terrorism" so long as it creates and supports such terror among its friends and utilizes it against its "enemies."

NOTES

This chapter originally appeared as an article in *Crime and Social Justice*, nos. 27–28 (1987), pp. 149–71. Reprinted by permission.

1. *New York Times* (1986), 1/16, Sec. 4; *COHA* (Council on Hemispheric Affairs) *Bulletin*, 10/30/85, p. 3.

2. *New York Times* (1985), 9/16, p. A2.

3. *New York Times* (1986), 10/27.

4. *New York Times* (1988), 7/18.

5. *New York Times* (1989) 8/27, p. 14.

6. *New York Times* (1988), 1/22.

7. M. K. Huggins, (1986) *Los Angeles Times*, pt. II, 3/25.

8. M. Curti and K. Birr (1954), *Prelude to Point Four: American Technical Missions Overseas, 1838–1938* (Madison: University of Wisconsin Press), p. 93.

9. Ibid.

10. M. Goldwert, (1962), *The Constabulary in the Dominican Republic and Nicaragua*, Latin America Monographs No. 17 (Gainesville: University of Florida Press), p. 26.

11. H. R. Fernandes (1974), *Política e segurança: Força pública do Estado de São Paulo: Fundamentos histórico-sociais* (São Paulo: Alfa-Omega), pp. 157, 165.

12. Ibid. p. 165.

13. G–2 (1936), G–2 Report, Military Intelligence Number 2257-E–65 (December 2) (Washington, D.C.: National Archives, Records and Administration, Old Military Branch).

14. W. Dawson (1936), Legation of the U.S.A., Bogotá, Colombia, to Sumner Welles, Under Secretary of State, Memorandum Number 614 (February 24) (Washington, D.C.: National Archives, Records and Administration, Old State Department Branch).

15. U.S. Department of State (1945), Memorandum of conversation (MEMCON), U.S. Department of State (September 11) (Hyde Park, N.Y.: Franklin D. Roosevelt Library), p. 1.

16. Ibid., p. 2.

17. H. Gibson (1936), U.S. Ambassador to Brazil, Rio de Janeiro, to Secretary of State (January 23), 832,105/9 L/Ho (Washington, D.C.: National Archives, Records and Administration, Old State Department Branch).

18. H. Gibson (1936), U.S. Ambassador to Brazil, Rio de Janeiro, to Lawrence Duggan (January 30), 832,105/16 (Washington, D.C.: National Archives, Records and Administration, Old State Department Branch).

19. Gibson to Secretary of State.

20. Gibson to Duggan.

21. R. Scotten (1938), U.S. Ambassador to Brazil, Rio de Janeiro, to Sumner Welles, Under Secretary of State (November 4), 832.105 (Washington, D.C.: National Archives, Records and Administration, Old State Department Branch).

22. R. M. Levine (1970), *The Vargas Regime: The Critical Years, 1934–1938* (New York: Columbia University Press), p. 56.

23. E. O. Briggs (1938), U.S. Department of State, to American Embassy, Rio (November 4), 832.105 (Washington, D.C.: National Archives, Records and Administration, Old State Department Branch).

24. S. Braden (1939), U.S. Ambassador, Bogotá, Colombia, to Secretary of State, (March 4), 821.105 (Washington, D.C.: National Archives, Records and Administration, Old State Department Branch).

25. S. Welles (1939), to Franklin D. Roosevelt (May 5), 821.105 (Washington,

D.C.: National Archives, Records and Administration, Old State Department Branch).

26. L. Rout and J. Bratzel (1986), *The Shadow of War: German Espionage and U.S. Counter Espionage in Latin America During World War II* (Washington, D.C.: University Publications of America), p. 37.

27. Ibid. pp. 37, 45.

28. Ibid., p. 40.

29. U.S. Department of State (1939), Memorandum of conversation (MEMCON), U.S. Department of State to the FBI, "Loan of a Special Agent of the FBI to Assist the Colombian Government" (August 16) (Washington, D.C.: National Archives, Records and Administration, Old State Department Branch).

30. Rout and Bratzel, *The Shadow of War*, p. 42.

31. Federal Bureau of Investigation (1940), FEB Report on Rolf Larson, File Number 67–759 (August 31) (Washington, D.C.: FBI), p. 1.

32. R. Larson (1941), Rio de Janeiro, to FBI, Washington, D.C., FBI Com. No. 2A (November 18) (Washington, D.C.: FBI).

33. U.S. Consul, Natal, Brazil (1942), [Consul in Natal] to the Secretary of State (January 14), 800.20232/118 (Washington, D.C.: National Archives, Records and Administration, Old State Department Branch).

34. Ibid.

35. Rout and Bratzel, *The Shadow of War*, p. 192.

36. Ibid., p. 193–94.

37. R. Divine (1975), *Since 1945: Politics and Diplomacy in Recent American History* (New York: John Wiley), p. 56.

38. Institute for Defense Analysis (1959), "Studies for the President's Committee to Study the U.S. Military Assistance Program" (March 31) (Abilene Kans.: Dwight D. Eisenhower Library), Draper Commission, Box 11, pp. 4–5.

39. Operations Control Board (1955), Report to the National Security Council (November 23) (Abilene, Kans.: Dwight D. Eisenhower Library).

40. Operations Control Board (1955), Minutes (June 6) (Abilene, Kans.: Dwight D. Eisenhower Library), White House Office, NSC Staff, OCB Secretariat, Box 12.

41. Operations Control Board (1958). Report in National Security Council, "U.S. Policies Toward Latin America" (November 26) (Abilene, Kans.: Dwight D. Eisenhower Library), p. 24.

42. National Security Council (1955), National Security Council Policy Report (February 3) (Abilene, Kans.: Dwight D. Eisenhower Library), NSCPP, OSANSA, Box 13.

43. Ibid., p. 21.

44. Operations Control Board (1957), "U.S. Policies in Mainland Southeast Asia" (March 14) (Abilene, Kans.: Dwight D. Eisenhower Library).

45. Operations Control Board, Minutes (June 6, 1955), p. 2.

46. International Cooperation Administration (1956), International Cooperation Administration Report to National Security Council, "Status of Mutual Security Programs. Defense-Supporting Programs and Other Non-Military Programs, Part II" (September 17) (Abilene, Kans.: Dwight D. Eisenhower Library).

47. E. Arnold II (1958), DD/S, to J. H. Smith, Jr., D/ICA, "World-wide Review

of Public Safety Programs (FY 59/60)" (November 12) (Abilene, Kans.: Dwight D. Eisenhower Library), Records of the Agency for International Development, p. 4.

48. Operations Control Board (1957), "U.S. Policy Toward Latin America" (September 11) (Abilene, Kans.: Dwight D. Eisenhower Library), NSC Policy Papers, Box 18, pp. 2–3.

49. P. Agee (1975), *Inside the Company: CIA Diary* (New York: Stonehill Publications), p. 611.

50. R. Amory (1966), oral history, interview by J. E. O'Connor (February 17) (Cambridge, Mass.: John F. Kennedy Library).

51. Operations Control Board, "U.S. Policy," p. 3.

52. Memorandum from R. P. Crenshaw, Jr., to Mr. Dearborn (n.d.; ca. 1955), "U.S. Internal Security Activities in Honduras and El Salvador" (Abilene, Kans.: Dwight D. Eisenhower Library), OCB, subseries OSANSA, Box 3.

53. Operations Control Board, "U.S. Policy," p. 24.

54. Operations Control Board (1958), Report to National Security Council, "Status of Mutual Security Programs as of 6/30/58" (September 15) (Abilene, Kans.: Dwight D. Eisenhower Library), p. 7.

55. W. W. Rostow (1964), oral history, interview by R. Neustadt (April 4) (Cambridge, Mass.: John F. Kennedy Library), p. 124.

56. Ibid.

57. U. A. Johnson (1984), *The Right Hand of Power* (Englewood Cliffs, N.J.: Prentice-Hall), p. 329.

58. Ibid, p. 338.

59. Agency for International Development (1962). AID memorandum pursuant to previous AID memorandum of November 2, "Measures to Strengthen AID's Police Assistance Program" (Cambridge, Mass.: John F. Kennedy Library), National Security Files, 335.

60. Agency for International Development (1962). AID memorandum of November 1 (Cambridge, Mass.: John F. Kennedy Library), National Security Files, 335.

61. Amory, oral history, p. 102.

62. Committee on Foreign Affairs, U.S. House of Representatives (1964), *Hearings on Foreign Assistance Appropriation, HR 118:2* (Washington, D.C.: U.S. Government Printing Office).

63. F. Coffin (1962), Memorandum for the Special Group (CI), "AID-Supported Counterinsurgency Activities" (July 18) (Cambridge, Mass.: John F. Kennedy Library), Agency for International Development documents.

64. Agee, *Inside the Company*, p. 262.

65. Ibid, p. 611.

66. W. Gaud, (1966), oral history, interview by Joseph F. O'Connor (February 16) (Cambridge, Mass.: John F. Kennedy Library), p. 48.

67. General Accounting Office (1976), General Accounting Office report to the Congress by the Comptroller General of the U.S., *Stopping U.S. Assistance to Foreign Police and Prisons* (Washington, D.C.: U.S. Government Printing Office), pp. 15–17; A. J. Langguth (1978), *Hidden Terrors* (New York: Pantheon), pp. 126–31.

68. General Accounting Office, *Stopping U.S. Assistance*, p. 16.

69. Committee on Foreign Affairs, *Hearings on Foreign Assistance*, p. 74.

70. Ibid, p. 76.
71. Ibid.
72. Ibid.
73. Ibid.
74. Ibid, pp. 82–83.
75. *Police Chief* (1955), 22, no. 3 (March), p. 4.
76. Committee on Foreign Affairs, U.S. Senate (1971), Hearings before the Subcommittee on Western Hemisphere Affairs, *United States Policies and Programs in Brazil* (Washington, D.C.: U.S. Government Printing Office), p. 6.
77. *Tribuna da Imprensa* (1985), April 13, p. 12.
78. J. Black (1977), *United States Penetration of Brazil* (Philadelphia: University of Pennsylvania Press), p. 146.
79. Agency for International Development (1971), TOAID, 232, Public Safety Report for March 1971, from Rio de Janeiro to AID, Washington, D.C. (April 7). (Washington, D.C.: Agency for International Development), p. 2.
80. *Vêja* (1984), 11/23.
81. Committee on Foreign Affairs, U.S. Senate (1971b), U.S. Senate staff memorandum for Subcommittee on Western Hemisphere Affairs, "Guatemala and the Dominican Republic" (December 30), p. 312.
82. *Isto É* (1983), "Dossié da Repressão," 11/23.
83. Archdiocese of São Paulo (1986), *Torture in Brazil* (New York: Vintage Books), p. 79.
84. Committee on Foreign Affairs, "Guatemala and the Dominican Republic," p. 18.
85. Black, *United States Penetration*, p. 144.
86. D. Rusk (1961), D. Rusk to John F. Kennedy, Memorandum to the president, "Actions Taken or Underway in the Dominican Republic" (n.d., circa August) (Cambridge, Mass.: John F. Kennedy Library), National Security Council, Country File, Dominican Republic, 65A–66.
87. *New York Times* (1987), 1/12.
88. Ibid.
89. *Foreign Relations of the United States*, 7, no. 1, *1952–1954* (Washington, D.C.: U.S. Government Printing Office), p. 838.

SELECTED BIBLIOGRAPHY

Ackroyd, Carol, et al. *The Technology of Political Control*. London: Pluto, 1980.

Adorno, S. (Coord.), "Justiça criminal e violência urbana." Unpublished research report, Centro de Estudos de Cultura Contemporânea, Universidade de São Paulo, January 1989.

Affonso, A., and H. Souza. *O estado e o desenvolvimento capitalista no Brasil: A crise fiscal*. Rio de Janeiro: Editora Paz e Terra, 1977.

Agosin, Marjorie. "Notes on the Poetics of the Acevedo Movement against Torture." *Human Rights Quarterly* 10 (1988): 339–43.

Ahmad, E. "The New Fascist State: Notes on the Pathology of Power in the Third World." *Arab Studies Quarterly* 3 (1981): 170–80.

Alavi, H. "The State in Post-Colonial Societies: Pakistan and Bangladesh." *New Left Review* 74 (1972): 59–81.

Albuquerque, Klaus de. "A Comparative Analysis of Violent Crime in the Caribbean." *Social and Economic Studies* (University of the West Indies) 33 (1984).

Alves, Maria Helena. *State and Opposition in Military Brazil*. Austin: University of Texas Press, 1985.

Americas Watch. *Derechos humanos en el Perú: Primer año del Presidente García*. Lima, 1986.

———. *Human Rights in Jamaica*. New York, 1986.

———. *Derechos humanos en el Perú: Cierta pasividad frente a los abusos*. Lima, 1987.

———. *Police Abuse in Brazil: Summary of Executions and Torture in São Paulo and Rio de Janeiro*. New York, 1987.

———. *The Killings in Colombia*. New York, 1988.

Amnesty Action. "Children of the Streets: Life and Death Among Brazil's Disposable Youth." (September–October 1990), pp. 1, 3.

Amnesty International. *Report on Torture*. London: Gerald Duckworth, 1973.

———. *Guatemala*. London: Amnesty International Publications, June 1977.

———. *Guatemala: Los derechos humanos en Guatemala*, Published with the democratic Front against Repression, Guatemala, Programa gubernamental de asesinatos políticos, Mexico City, 1981.

———. *Guatemala: Programa gubernamental de asesinatos políticos*. Mexico City, 1981.

———. *Torture in the Eighties*. London: International Secretariat, 1984.

———. *Guatemala*. London: Amnesty International Publications, December 1987.

———. *Perú: La matanza de Cayara*. London: Amnesty International Secretariat, 1989.

Arango, M., and J. Child. *Los condenados de la coca: El manejo politico de la droga*. Medellín, Colombia: J. I. Arango, 1985.

Archdiocese of São Paulo. *Torture in Brazil*. New York: Vintage Books, 1986.

Arendt, Hannah. *Eichmann in Jerusalem: A Report on the Banality of Evil*. Harmondsworth, U.K.: Penguin, 1963; rev. and enl. ed., 1965.

———. *The Origins of Totalitarianism*. New ed. Harcourt, Brace and World, 1966.

———. *On Violence*. New York: Harcourt, Brace and World, 1969.

"Argentina: The Human Rights Record. Comments on the Government of Argentina's Official Report to the Human Rights Committee." New York: International League for Human Rights, 1990.

Austin, Diane. *Urban Life in Kingston, Jamaica*. London: Gordon & Breach, 1984.

Barber, James David. "Rationalizing Torture: The Dance of the Intellectual Apologists." *The Washington Monthly* 17, 11 (1985): 17–18.

Benevides, Maria-Victoria. "Linchamentos: Violência e justiça popular." In Roberto da Matta et al., *Violência brasilera*. São Paulo: Brasiliense, 1982.

———, and Rosa-Maria Fischer Ferreira. "Respostas populares e violência urbana: O caso de linchamento no Brasil (1979–1982)." In Paulo Sérgio Pinheiro, ed., *Crime, violência e poder*. São Paulo: Brasiliense, 1983.

Black, J. *United States Penetration of Brazil*. Philadelphia: University of Pennsylvania Press, 1977.

Bodenheimer, Susan Jones. *Guatemala: Plan piloto para el continente*. San José, Costa Rica: EDUCA, 1981.

Brown, Richard Maxwell. *The Strain of Violence*. New York: Oxford University Press, 1975.

Casement, Roger. "Putumayo Report and the Explanation of Torture." *Contemporary Studies in Society and History* 26 (1984).

Castro, Myriam Publiese de. "State and Society: A Violation of the Right to Life." Unpublished research monograph. 1990.

Castro Escudero, Teresa. "Movimiento popular y democracia en Chile." *Revista mexicana de sociología* 48, no. 3 (1986): 51–73.

Centro de Estudios Legales y Sociales (CELS). "Muertos por violência policial." Unpublished report. Buenos Aires, 1987.

Centro de Estudios y Promoción del Desarrollo (DESCO). *Violencia política en el Perú: 1980–1988*. Lima; 1989.

Chaui, M. *Conformismo e resistencia: Aspectos da cultura popular no Brasil*. São Paulo: Brasiliense, 1987.

Chomsky, Noam. "Our Little Region over Here." *The National Reporter* (Fall 1987).

———, and Edward S. Herman. *The Political Economy of Human Rights. Vol. I,*

The Washington Connection and Third World Fascism. Montreal: Black Rose Books, 1979.

CINEP (Centro de Investigación y Educación Popular, a Jesuit Research and Grass-roots Educational Center). *Documentos: Conflicto social y violencia*. Bogotá, 1988–1989.

Collier, David. *The New Authoritarianism in Latin America*. Princeton, N.J.: Princeton University Press, 1979.

Comisión Andina de Juristas. "Military Tribunals and the Law of Repentance." *Andean Newsletter* (Lima) nos. 35–36 (November 9, 1989).

Comisión de Estudios sobre Violencia. *Colombia: Violencia y democracia*. Bogotá: Universidad Nacional de Colombia, 1987.

Corradi, Juan. *The Fitful Republic*. Boulder, Colo.: Westview Press, 1985.

———. "A Difficult Transition to Democracy." *Telos* no. 75 (Summer 1988): 141–47.

Díaz, E. *El clientelismo en Colombia: Un estudio exploratorio*. Bogotá: El Ancora, 1986.

Duff, Ernest, and John McCamant. *Violence and Repression in Latin America*. New York: Free Press, 1976.

Fernandes, Heloísa Rodrigues. *política e segurança: Força pública do Estado de São Paulo: Fundamentos historico-sociais*. São Paulo: Alfa-Omega, 1974.

Frank, A. G. *Lumpenbourgeoisie, Lumpendevelopment*. New York: Monthly Review Press, 1972.

Gallon, G. *Quince años de estado de sitio en Colombia, 1958–1978*. Bogotá: América Latina, 1979.

Halliday, Fred. *Iran: Dictatorship and Development*. Harmondsworth, U.K.: Penguin, 1979.

Hardinghaus, N. "Droga y crecimiento econónuci: El narcotráfico en las cuentas nacionales." *Nueva sociedad* no. 102 (1989).

Hein, W., and K. Stenzel. "The Capitalist State and Underdevelopment in Latin America—The Case of Venezuela." *Kapitalistate* 2, (1973): 31–48.

Herman, Edward S. *The Real Terror Network*. Boston: South End Press, 1982.

Huggins, Martha K. "Political Policing: Eighty Years of United States Training of Latin American Police." (Forthcoming.)

Hughes, Thomas L. "Guatemala: A Country Running Wild." Intelligence note, U.S. Department of State, Intelligence and Research Memorandum, October 23, 1967. Austin Tex.: Lyndon Baines Johnson Library. NSF, Guat. V.II.

Hutchful, Eboe. "The Modern State and Violence: The Peripheral Situation." *International Journal of Sociology and Law* 14 (1986): 153–78.

Ignatieff, Michael. "Torture's Dead Simplicity." *New Statesman*, September 20, 1985, pp. 24–26.

Jacques, Hylah M. "Spain: Systematic Torture in a Democratic State." *Monthly Review* 37 (November 1985): 57–62.

King, R. *The State in Modern Society: New Directions in Political Sociology*. Chatham, N.J.: Chatham House, 1986.

Klare, Michael, and Cynthia Arnson, with Delia Miller and Daniel Volman. *Supplying Repression*. Washington, D.C.: Institute for Policy Studies, 1977.

Kowarick, L., and C. Ant. "Reflexos sobre a banalidade do cotidiano em São

Paulo." In R. Boschi, ed., *Violência e cidade*. Rio de Janeiro: Zahar Editores, 1981.

Langbein, John H. *Torture and the Law of Proof: Europe and England in the Ancien Regime*. Chicago: University of Chicago Press, 1976.

Langguth, A. J. *Hidden Terrors*. New York: Pantheon, 1978.

Leal, F. *Estado y política en Colombia*. Bogotá: Siglo XXI- Cerec, 1984.

LeMoyne, J. "Testifying to Torture." *The New York Times Magazine*, June 5, 1988, pp. 45–66.

Lewin, A. "Social Control in Jamaica." Ph. D. diss., City University of New York, 1977.

Maestre, Juan. *Guatemala: Violencia y subdesarrollo*. Madrid: IEPALA, 1969.

Mason, David T., and Dale A. Krane. "The Political Economy of Death Squads: Toward a Theory of the Impact of State-Sanctioned Terror." *International Studies Quarterly* 33 (1989): 175–98.

Mathebula, J. "Vigilantes: An Arm of State Terrorism." *Sechaba*, December 1987, pp. 19–29.

Matta, Roberto da. *Carnavais, malandros e herois*. 4th ed. Rio de Janeiro: Zahar Editores, 1979.

Mercado, René Zavaleta. *La nacional popular en Bolivia*. Mexico City: Siglo XXI Editores, 1986.

Moncayo, V., F. Rojas, and G. Palacio. "Tendencias reorgánicas del estado colombiano contemporáneo." In *Democratización, modernización y actores socio-políticos*. Buenos Aires: CLACSO, 1989.

Murillo, G. "Hacia la democracia participativa en Colombia: Restos y posibilidades." In *Pensamiento iberoamericano* no. 13. Madrid: 1988.

Nairn, Allan. "An Exclusive Report on the U.S. Role in El Salvador's Official Terror." *The Progressive*, May 1984.

———. "Senate Report Says CIA Created Ties to Salvadoran Death Squad Figures." *Philadelphia Inquirer*, September 1984.

National Reporter. "Vigilante Terror: A Report on CIA- Inspired Death Squads in the Philippines." Fall 1987.

Navarro, Marysa. "The Personal Is Political: Las Madres de Plaza de Mayo." In Susan Eckstein, ed., *Power and Popular Protest*. Berkeley and Los Angeles: University of California Press, 1989.

Núcleo de Estudos da Violência. *Violência do estado e militarização: Mortes em conflitos policiais em São Paulo nos años 1980*. São Paulo: Núcleo de Estudos da Violência, Universidade de São Paulo, 1989.

Nunca Más, the Report of the Argentinian Commission on the Disappeared. New York: Farrar, Straus and Giroux, 1986.

O'Donnell, G. *Transições do regime autoritario: Primeiras conclusões*. São Paulo: Vertice, 1988.

Oliveira, A., and Sofia Tiscornia. "Extra-Legal Executions Among Popular Sectors in Argentina, 1982–1989." Buenos Aires: CELS, 1990. Unpublished report, Spanish version: "Ejecuciones extralegales sobre sectores populares en la Argentina: 1982–89." Buenos Aires: CELS, 1989.

Olmo, R. del. *La cara oculta de la droga*. Bogotá: Editora Temis, 1987.

Paixão, Antonio Luiz, "Crimes e criminosos em Belo Horizonte: Uma exploração inicial das estatísticas officiais de criminalidade." Belo Horizonte: João Pinheiro Foundation, 1981. Unpublished internal paper.

———. "Crimes e criminosos em Belo Horizonte." In Paulo Sérgio Pinheiro, ed., *Crime, violência e Poder*. São Paulo: Brasiliense, 1983.

Palacio, G. "Democracia y crisis de la justicia en Colombia." In Pedro Medellín, ed., *La reforma del estado en América Latina*. Bogotá: Fescol, 1988.

———. "El descurso sobre la violencia: Hacia la reconstrucción de la neutralidad del estado." Paper presented at Seminario Crisis Institucional y Violencia, Bogotá, 1989.

Peters, Edward. *Torture*. New York: Basil Blackwell, 1985.

Petras, J., and M. Morley. "Supporting Repression: U.S. Policy and the Demise of Human Rights in El Salvador, 1970–1981." In *The Socialist Register*, 47–71. London: Merlin Press, 1981.

———. *U.S. Hegemony under Siege*. London and New York: Verso, 1990.

Pinheiro, Paulo Sérgio, "Violência e cultura." In B. Lamounier, F. C. Weffort, and Maria-Victoria Benevides, eds., *Direito, cidania e participação*. São Paulo: T. A. Queiroz, 1981.

———. "Policia e crise política." In Maria Célia Paoli, Maria-Victoria Benevides, Paulo Sérgio Pinheiro, and Roberto da Matta, eds., *A violência brasileira*. São Paulo: Brasiliense, 1982.

———. *Escritos indignados: Policia, prisões e política*. São Paulo: Brasiliense, 1984.

———. "O controle da polícia no processo de transição democrática no Brasil." *Temas Imesc* 2, 1985.

Pion-Berlin, David. "Political Repression and Economic Doctrines: The Case of Argentina." *Comparative Political Studies* 16, no. 1 (April 1983):37–66.

Pizarro, E. "100 años de la constitución: Reforma política o catástrofe." *Revista foro* 1 (1986).

———. "Democracia restringida y desinstitucionalización política." In Pedro Medellín, ed., *La reforma del estado en América Latina*. Bogotá: Fescol, 1988.

Restrepo, D. "Política económica neoliberal y descentralización." In Pedro Medellín, ed., *La reforma del estado en América Latina*. Bogotá: Fescol, 1988.

Reyes, A. "Conflictos agrarios y luchas armadas en la Colombia contemporánea: Una visión geográfica." *Análisis político*, no. 5 (1988).

Rojas, F. "El estado en los ochenta: Hacia un régimen político." *Controversia*, no. 5 (1980).

Rosenbaum, H. Jon, and Peter Sederberg. *Vigilante Politics*. Philadelphia: University of Pennsylvania Press, 1976.

Rouquie, Alain. "Demilitarization and the Institutionalization of Military-Dominated Politics in Latin America." In Guillermo O'Donnell et al., eds., *Transitions from Authoritarian Rule*. Baltimore: Johns Hopkins University Press, 1986.

Rubin, Barry. *Paved with Good Intentions: The American Experience in Iran*. Harmondsworth, U.K.: Penguin, 1981.

Rubinstein, Richard. "The Bureaucratization of Torture." *Journal of Social Philosphy* 13 (1982):31–51.

Russell, D. *Rebellion, Revolution and Armed Force*. New York: Academic Press, 1974.

Schirmer, Daniel B. *Republic or Empire: American Resistance to the Philippine War*. Cambridge, Mass.: Schenkman, 1972.

Schoultz, Lars. *Human Rights and United States Policy Towards Latin America*. Princeton, N.J.: Princeton University Press, 1981.

Senkiewicz, Robert M., S.J. *Vigilantes in Gold Rush San Francisco*. Stanford, Calif.: Stanford University Press, 1985.

Sexton, William Thaddeus. *Soldiers in the Sun: An Adventure in Imperialism*. Freeport, N.Y.: Libraries Press, 1939.

Souza, Percival de. *A maior violência do mundo*. São Paulo: Editora Traco, 1980.

Stepan, Alfred. "The New Professionalism of Internal Warfare and Military Role Expansion." In Abraham F. Lowenthal, ed., *Armies and Politics in Latin America*. New York: Holmes and Meier, 1976.

———. *Democratizing Brazil: Problems of Transition and Consolidation*. London and New York: Oxford University Press, 1989.

Stohl, Michael, and George A. Lopez, eds. *The State as Terrorist*. Westport, Conn.: Greenwood Press, 1984.

Stone, Carl, and Aggrey Brown. *Essays on Power and Change in Jamaica*. Kingston: Jamaica Printing House, 1977.

Taussig, Michael. "Terror as Usual." Paper delivered at the Conference "Talking Terrorism: Ideologies and Paradigms in a Postmodern World." Stanford University, February 4–6, 1988.

Tilly, Charles. "Does Modernization Breed Revolution?" *Comparative Politics* 5, no. 3 (April 1973): 425–48.

———. "War Making and State Making as Organized Crime." In Peter Evans et al., eds., *Bringing the State Back In*. Cambridge: Cambridge University Press, 1985.

———. *Coercion, Capital and European States*. Cambridge, Mass.: Basil Blackwell, 1990.

Vargas, A. "Guerrilla y régimen político in Colombia." Paper presented at Seminario Crisis Institucional y Violência (ILSA), Bogotá, 1989.

Visconte, Tomas Amadeo. "Argentina e Brasil: Perspectivas de dos transiciones democráticas." *Revista mexicana de sociología* 48, no. 3 (1986): 31–43.

Ward, Michael. *Political Economy of Distribution*. New York: Elsevier, 1978.

Welch, Richard E., Jr. *Response to Imperialism: The United States and the Philippine–American War 1899–1902*. Chapel Hill: University of North Carolina Press, 1979.

Wolfgang, M., and F. Ferracuti. *The Subculture of Violence*. London: Tavistock, 1967.

Wolpin, Miles. *Militarization, Internal Repression and Social Welfare in the Third World*. London: Croom Helm, 1986.

Zaffaroni, Raúl. *Política criminal latinoamericana*. Buenos Aires: Hamurabi, 1982.

Zaluar, Alba. "Condominio do diablo: As classes populares urbanas e a logica do ferro e do fumo." In Paulo Sérgio Pinherio, ed., *Crime, violência e poder*. São Paulo: Brasiliense, 1983.

———. *A máquina e a revolta*. São Paulo: Brasiliense, 1985.

INDEX

ABOUT THE EDITOR AND CONTRIBUTORS

Maria-Victoria Benevides is Professor of Sociology, Universidade de São Paulo, São Paulo, Brazil.

Paul G. Chevigny is Professor of Law, New York University School of Law, New York.

Heloísa Rodrigues Fernandes is Professor of Sociology, Universidade de São Paulo, São Paulo, Brazil.

Rosa-Maria Fischer Ferreira is Professor of Sociology, School of Economics and Administration, Universidade de São Paulo, and Counselor and Supervisor of Pesquisas do CEDEC, São Paulo, Brazil.

Tosca Hernández is Professor of Criminology, Instituto de Ciencias Penales y Criminológicas, Universidad Central de Venezuela, Caracas.

Martha K. Huggins is Roger Thayer Stone Professor of Sociology and Anthropology, and Professor of Sociology, Union College, Schenectady, New York.

Carlos Figueroa Ibarra is Coordinator of Latin American Political Studies, Centro de Ciencia Política, Universidad Autónoma de Puebla, Puebla, Mexico.

Laura Kalmanowiecki is a Ph.D. candidate, Department of Sociology, New School for Social Research, New York.

Elena S. Manitzas is a Researcher, Instituto Latinoamericano de Servicios Legales Alternativos (ILSA), Bogotá, Colombia, formerly of Comisión Andina de Juristas, Lima, Peru.

José de Souza Martins is Professor of Sociology, Universidade de São Paulo, São Paulo, Brazil.

Germán Alfonso Palacio Castanêda is Professor of Law, Universidad Nacional de Bogotá, and Researcher, Instituto Latinoamericano de Servicios Legales Alternativos (ILSA), Bogotá, Colombia.

Paulo Sérgio Pinheiro is Associate Professor of Political Science, and Director, Núcleo de Estudos da Violência, Universidade de São Paulo, São Paulo, Brazil.

Darius Rejali is Assistant Professor of Political Science, Reed College, Portland, Oregon.

Alfonso Reyes Echandía was President of the Supreme Court, Bogotá, Colombia, killed in the retaking of the Supreme Court building from guerrillas by the military.